Moonshadows

Moonshadows

Conventional Truth in Buddhist Philosophy

THE COWHERDS

OXFORD
UNIVERSITY PRESS
2011

OXFORD
UNIVERSITY PRESS

Oxford University Press, Inc., publishes works that further
Oxford University's objective of excellence
in research, scholarship, and education.

Oxford New York
Auckland Cape Town Dar es Salaam Hong Kong Karachi
Kuala Lumpur Madrid Melbourne Mexico City Nairobi
New Delhi Shanghai Taipei Toronto

With offices in
Argentina Austria Brazil Chile Czech Republic France Greece
Guatemala Hungary Italy Japan Poland Portugal Singapore
South Korea Switzerland Thailand Turkey Ukraine Vietnam

Published by Oxford University Press, Inc.
198 Madison Avenue, New York, NY 10016

www.oup.com

Library of Congress Cataloging-in-Publication Data
Cowherds (Authors)
Moonshadows : conventional truth in Buddhist philosophy / the Cowherds.
p. cm.
Includes bibliographical references and index.
ISBN 978-0-19-975142-6; ISBN 978-0-19-975143-3 (pbk.)
1. Truth—Religious aspects—Buddhism. 2. Buddhist philosophy.
I. Title.
BQ4255.C69 2011
121.088'2943—dc22 2009050158

Printed in the United States of America
on acid-free paper

Preface

This is an unusual volume. It is neither an anthology nor a monograph. We prefer to think of it as a *polygraph*—a collectively written volume reflecting the varying views of a large collection of authors. Many chapters are written by single authors. Some are written by teams. But every chapter is informed by extensive discussion among us, both of general philosophical and exegetical issues and of the chapters themselves. So, in an important sense, no matter whose name appears at the head of each chapter, the chapter is the fruit of extensive collaboration. This is so despite the fact that we recognize substantial differences among us regarding interpretation and philosophy. We believe that those differences, as much as the agreements that have emerged from our collective effort, as well as the connections between these essays, which have been forged in argument, add to the richness of this treatment.

The volume is written by the Cowherds. First a comment is in order about the name. Those familiar with Madhyamaka literature will recognize the reference to Candrakīrti's phrase, "what even people like cowherds and women recognize" (*gopālāṅganājanaprasiddha*).[1] We are bothered by the sexism of the reference to women, an attitude taken for granted in Candrakīrti's cultural milieu but no

1. See Candrakīrti (1970b), 260, line 14. See also the use of the phrase *gnag rdzi yan chad la grags pa* ("acknowledged/recognized by everyone from cowherds on up") in Kamalāśīla's *Sarvadharmaniḥsvabhāvasiddhi* (chapter 9, n5).

longer acceptable. There is a whiff of classism in the use of "cowherds" (*gopāla, gopa, gopī;* Tibetan *glang rdzi, gnag rdzi*) as well. But we hope that the irony in our use of this term to refer to ourselves is apparent. We hope that we can appropriate "cowherds" as a synonym for "the man on the street," to indicate the ordinary working person. What cowherds know, in this sense, is what you need to know to do whatever you do, whether it be dairy farming or philosophy. To paraphrase JFK, we are all cowherds! Of course, what it is that we each, or we all, need to know, is not clear. Hence this book—an exploration of conventional truth and what is true about it.

Caveat lector! We should be clear that, while this book is about conventional truth and while it is firmly anchored in Madhyamaka ideas about conventional truth (*saṃvṛtisatya, vyavahārasatya*), it is *not* a history of the concept of conventional truth in Buddhist philosophy; it is not a philological study of Buddhists texts or doctrines on conventional truth; it is not an attempt to present a "fair and balanced" representation of Buddhist accounts of conventional truth. Instead, it is an exploration, by a diverse group of philosophers with a set of related interests, of a set of questions about conventional truth that arise from the way the idea of conventional truth is deployed in certain corners of Buddhist philosophy.

In particular, we are animated by four principal questions that arise primarily from a consideration of Candrakīrti's treatment of this topic and the way his treatment is taken up by subsequent Buddhist scholars, prominently including Tibetan commentators:

1. What *is* conventional truth?
2. What is *true* about conventional truth?
3. How *flexible* is conventional truth? How much can it be revised?
4. What are the implications of all of this for how we live our lives?

The first question forces us to start textually and doctrinally, to figure out what Candrakīrti, those with whom he was in dialogue, and those who read and commented on him understood by *saṃvṛtisatya* or *vyavahārasatya*. The second, third, and fourth, though, take us well beyond exegesis and into philosophical puzzles, albeit puzzles anchored in and arising from the Buddhist tradition. In what sense is something true that in another is characterized as entirely false, misleading, to be taken seriously only by fools and cowherds? How fixed is it? If it is determined by conventions, and if conventions are malleable, is conventional truth similarly malleable? And what is its import for ethics, for science, for epistemology?

In addressing these questions we may do philosophy *with* Candrakīrti, but we are beholden neither to him nor to anyone else in the Buddhist tradition when we answer those questions. We are after truth, or at least insight, not just understanding of antique positions. For this reason, many of the essays in this volume are not textual at all but are systematic philosophical explorations of questions raised, but not answered, by classical Buddhist texts. We are, after all, contemporary philosophers with contemporary concerns and a conviction that we can address those concerns in part by attention to Buddhist thought.

This commitment to philosophy of course raises interesting methodological questions about Buddhist studies. Are we doing real Buddhist studies when we deploy ideas and techniques from contemporary analytic philosophy to address questions arising from seventh-century Indian debates as adumbrated in fifteenth-century Tibet? We think so. And we think that Buddhist philosophy has much to contribute to twenty-first-century Western philosophy. We also think that contemporary philosophy has much to contribute to Buddhist thought. We hence hope that our explorations will be of interest both to those who care deeply about what *some* scholars in the tradition thought about conventional truth and to those who just care about conventional truth and are open to learning from Buddhist philosophy.

The Cowherds are Georges Dreyfus (Williams College), Bronwyn Finnigan (University of Auckland), Jay L. Garfield (Smith College, the University of Melbourne, and the Central University of Tibetan Studies), Guy Newland (Central Michigan University), Graham Priest (University of Melbourne, St. Andrews University, City University of New York), Mark Siderits (Seoul National University), Koji Tanaka (University of Auckland), Sonam Thakchöe (University of Tasmania), Tom Tillemans (University of Lausanne), and Jan Westerhoff (Durham University).

Acknowledgments

We gratefully acknowledge the generous support of the Elisabeth de Boer Fund of the University of Lausanne for making this project possible. Thanks also go to the Department of Philosophy of the University of Melbourne and the Center for Buddhist Studies of the University of Kathmandu for hosting meetings of the Cowherds. We thank Dr. Andreas Doctor in particular for arranging a colloquium in Kathmandu and for encouraging student participation during that visit, and we thank the many students and scholars who contributed to that discussion. Thanks also go to Constance Kassor for logistical help during our conclave in Atlanta during the 2007 conference of the International Association of Buddhist Studies. We are grateful to Caroline Moore for creating and maintaining the website that enabled cowherds in North America, Europe, Asia, and Australasia to collaborate effectively between conclaves, and to Ms. Adina Bianchi and Ms Margaret Dodge for helping with the index. We appreciate the assistance of Elizabeth Wallett in resolving issues with cross-platform diacritic fonts. Bronwyn Finnigan and Koji Tanaka thank the University of Auckland for travel and research support. An earlier version of Chapter 2 appeared in *Philosophy East and West* 60:3 (2010), pp 341–354.

Contents

1. An Introduction to Conventional Truth, 3
Guy Newland and Tom J. F. Tillemans

2. Taking Conventional Truth Seriously: Authority regarding Deceptive Reality, 23
Jay L. Garfield

3. Prāsaṅgika Epistemology in Context, 39
Sonam Thakchöe

4. Weighing the Butter, Levels of Explanation, and Falsification: Models of the Conventional in Tsongkhapa's Account of Madhyamaka, 57
Guy Martin Newland

5. Identifying the Object of Negation and the Status of Conventional Truth: Why the *dGag Bya* Matters So Much to Tibetan Mādhyamikas, 73
Jay L. Garfield and Sonam Thakchöe

6. Can a Mādhyamika Be a Skeptic? The Case of Patsab Nyimadrak, 89
Georges Dreyfus

7. Madhyamaka and Classical Greek Skepticism, 115
Georges Dreyfus and Jay L. Garfield

8. The (Two) Truths about Truth, 131
Graham Priest, Mark Siderits, and Tom J. F. Tillemans

9. How Far Can a Mādhyamika Buddhist Reform Conventional Truth? Dismal Relativism, Fictionalism, Easy-Easy Truth, and the Alternatives, 151
Tom J. F. Tillemans

10. Is Everything Connected to Everything Else? What the Gopīs Know, 167
Mark Siderits

11. Carnap's Pragmatism and the Two Truths, 181
Bronwyn Finnigan and Koji Tanaka

12. The Merely Conventional Existence of the World, 189
Jan Westerhoff

13. Two Truths: Two Models, 213
Graham Priest

14. Ethics for Mādhyamikas, 221
Bronwyn Finnigan and Koji Tanaka

References and Abbreviations, 233

Index, 245

Moonshadows

I

An Introduction to Conventional Truth

Guy Newland and Tom J. F. Tillemans

> *dve satye samupāśritya buddhānāṃ dharmadeśanā /*
> *loksaṃvṛtisatyaṃ ca satyaṃ ca paramārthataḥ //*

> The various buddhas' teaching of the Dharma relies upon two truths: the conventional truth of the world (*lokasaṃvṛtisatya*) and what is true from the ultimate perspective (*paramārthataḥ*). (MMK XXIV.8)

This famous verse was composed by the second-to-third-century CE South Indian thinker Nāgārjuna. It is the clearest statement of the two truths anywhere in Nāgārjuna's corpus and is often cited in the literature of the Madhyamaka, or "Middle Way," school of Buddhist philosophy.[1]

This book is a journey through some of the epistemological, metaphysical, and ethical byways that lead from this distinction between the two truths, especially those on the conventional side. The thinker we meet most frequently along these roads is Candrakīrti, an enigmatic sixth-to-seventh-century scholar of Nālandā monastery, whose interpretation of Nāgārjuna remained on the

1. There is an enormous and burgeoning secondary literature on Madhyamaka that we cannot detail here. For an excellent introduction to Madhyamaka, see Arnold (2005b). On the history, philosophy, and literature of the Indian Madhyamaka school, see Seyfort Ruegg (1981), May (1979). On the Svātantrika-Prāsaṅgika distinction in Madhyamaka, see Dreyfus and McClintock (2003), Seyfort Ruegg (2006); on the two truths in Tibetan Ge-luk Madhyamaka, see Tauscher (1995), Newland (1992), Hopkins (1983).

margins in India but took center stage in Tibet. Mādhyamikas such as Bhā(va)-viveka, Kamalaśīla, Tsongkhapa, Patsab, and Gorampa are among the others we encounter.[2] We invite you to join us in this hermeneutical and philosophical journey of rationally warranted reconstruction governed by the principle of charity and a concern to discover what is of value to us in this ancient tradition. Our exploration will be guided by the following considerations.

What Is Truth?

We begin with a vexing problem for philosophically savvy translators. Introductions to Buddhism routinely tell us that Buddhist philosophers have long distinguished two truths: conventional and ultimate. Buddhist texts sometimes characterize these truths as *statements* (very roughly, those that are just taken to be true and those that are actually true) and other times as *states of affairs* or *sorts of things* (those generally taken to be real and those that are fully real). Now, it would seem on a little analysis that we cannot call both statements and things "truths." Is "truth" then just a misnomer or sloppy translation? Could we do better with some other rendering?

"Truth" here translates the Sanskrit *satya*, the Tibetan *bden pa*, and the Chinese *di* 諦, and it certainly is neither a wrong nor a sloppy translation. Nonetheless, it is problematic. The problem is that rendering *satya*, or its Tibetan, Pali, and Chinese equivalents, as "truth" naturally suggests that conventional and ultimate truths are all *truthbearers*, that is, statements, propositions, or, if we take a larger perspective, beliefs, ideas, and theories—in short, the sort of things to which we can properly attribute truth and falsity. As we shall see, the Buddhists did often use *satya* as pertaining to statements. This seems to be the initial way the two truths were formulated. However, *satya* pertains not only to such truthbearers; things like pots and atoms can just as well be *satya*, and it is at least anomalous to ascribe truth to them.

In short, because *satya* means "truth" but also can mean "real" and "what is existent," translational problems are unavoidable. There is no English term that is equivalent in all contexts. The problems can however be significantly

2. In the present book we follow the modern convention of using "Madhyamaka" for the philosophy or school and "Mādhyamika" for the thinkers who profess this philosophy. This modern convention was promoted by P. L. Vaidya and others, who were inspired by the clear distinction between the Tibetan terms *dbu ma* and *dbu ma pa*. On the rather shaky Indian basis for this Tibetan-inspired hypercorrection, see May (1979, 472) (*Hōbōgirin* s.v. *chūgan*). Akira Saitō in a forthcoming paper ("On the Meaning and Beginning of the Madhyamaka/Mādhyamika School") finds some evidence for taking "Madhyamaka" as referring (on the balance) to the thought and "Mādhyamika" (on the balance) to the thinkers.

attenuated if we are conscious of the differing semantic ranges of "truth" and *satya* and if we adjust our translation when needed. The Cowherds have therefore agreed to use "truth" as our default translation of *satya* but to use "reality" or "existence" when the context demands. We have sought to minimize confusion by avoiding gratuitous use of the word "truth" as a translation for *satya* in the many cases where the term refers to an object rather than to a semantic notion. The relationship between the two senses of *satya* will be taken up in more detail later.[3] But for the moment, let us ask: How did the doctrine of two truths develop?

The Two Truths

The Buddhist notion of two truths (*satyadvaya*), conventional and ultimate, was initially a construct for reconciling apparently contradictory statements in scripture based on their pedagogical intent. It developed in connection with another pair of terms that was also used in sorting out conflicts between scriptural passages, that is, the distinction between statements whose meaning is definitive (Pali *nītattha* = Skt. *nītārtha*) and those whose meaning requires interpretation (Pali *neyyattha* = Skt. *neyārtha*); the *Aṅguttaranikāya* commentary (*Aṭṭhakathā*) attributed to Buddhaghosa and other texts make this linkage explicit.[4] Indeed, the use of a double truth as a way of sorting out apparently conflicting statements in the Buddhist teaching is what we see in the passage from Nāgārjuna's *Mūlamadhyamakākarikā*, with which we began this introduction; it also seems to lie behind a famous passage in the commentary to the *Kathāvatthu* of the *Abhidhammapiṭaka:*

3. See introduction, pp. 8–10, and especially chapter 8.

4. References in Karunadasa (1996, 25–26 and n. 139); see also Karunadasa (2006). These two valuable articles have been heavily relied upon in connection with *Nikāya* and *Aṭṭhakathā* passages. On *nītattha* and *neyyattha* see, for example, *Aṅguttaranikāya* II, p. 60 (Pali Text Society, ed.= PTS): *Dve 'me bhikkhave Tathāgataṃ nābbhācikkhanti. Katame dve? Yo ca neyyatthaṃ suttantaṃ neyyattho suttanto ti dīpito: yo ca nītatthaṃ suttantaṃ nītattho suttanto ti dīpeti. Ime kho bhikkhave Tathāgataṃ nābbhācikkhanti.* "These two, O Monks, do not misrepresent the Tathāgatha (Buddha). Which two? He who proclaims that a discourse whose meaning requires interpretation is one whose meaning requires interpretation and he who proclaims that a discourse of definitive meaning is a discourse of definitive meaning: these two, O Monks, do not misrepresent the Tathāgatha." Note that not just Buddhaghosa but also later Mahāyāna authors make the connection with the two truths. Certain controversial statements whose meaning requires interpretation (*neyārtha*) are classified as conventional (*saṃvṛti*) and not ultimate (*paramārtha*). *Bodhicaryāvatārapañjikā* (ed. Vaidya 233, 5–7), in discussing the *Dhammapada*'s seeming acceptance of the self (*ātman*), states: *tad api cātmadṛṣṭyabhiniviṣṭānām anyatrātmagrāhaparikalpavicchedārthaṃ neyārthatayā saṃvṛtyā cittam ātmeti prakāśitaṃ na tu paramārthataḥ* "This too [i.e., the fact that mind is said to be the controller (*damana*) is said] so that those who are attached to the view of self will on another occasion eliminate their imaginary grasping at self; from the point of view of interpretive meaning, that is, conventionally, the mind is taught to be the self, but not ultimately."

> The Enlightened One, the best of all teachers, propounded two truths, conventional and ultimate; we do not see a third. A statement governed [purely] by agreement is true because of the world's conventions, and an ultimate statement is true in that it characterizes things as they are.[5]

Both Nāgārjuna and the commentator to the *Kathāvatthu* thus claim that the origins of the two truths go back to the Buddha or even the buddhas. It is impossible to determine whether this is historically accurate. In any case, seeking to construct integrated systems from the many discourses the Buddha gave to diverse audiences, early Buddhist scholars relied upon the two truths as a hermeneutic device. Only passages taken to be pointing to the final nature of reality were read as ultimate truth, while conventional truth was found in passages taken to rely upon, rather than to reject, more superficial constructs.

For example, the Buddha famously teaches that the person is a mere nominal designation based upon an ever-changing flux of mental states and physical elements. The person is utterly empty of intrinsic nature; the notion of an intrinsically real person or self is a delusion. In the *Saṃyuttanikāya*, the Buddha explains how ultimate awakening involves recognition of this process of conventional designation and consequent understanding of the person's lack of intrinsic nature:

> Those who go by names, who go by concepts . . . are subject to the reign of death; he who has discerned the naming-process does not suppose that *one who names* exists. No such case exists for him in truth, whereby one could say: "He's this or that."[6]

Nonetheless, in the *Aṅguttaranikāya* we read that there was indeed "a *person*" who "was born out of compassion for the world" and that this person was a fully enlightened one, a buddha.[7] The two truths were deployed to reconcile such affirmative statements about, and distinctions with regard to, persons, ethics, and spiritual attainment with the notion that there is *ultimately* no way to say that the Buddha—or any person—is this or that.

5. *Kathāvatthuppakaraṇaṭṭhakathā*, p. 34; *Aṅguttaranikāya Aṭṭhakathā Manorathapūraṇī* I, p. 54:

duve saccāni akkhāsi saṃbuddho vadataṃ varo /
sammutiṃ paramatthañ ca tatiyaṃ nūpalabbhati //
saṃketavacanaṃ saccaṃ lokasammutikāraṇam /
paramatthavacanaṃ saccaṃ dhammānaṃ tathalakkhaṇam //

6. *Saṃyuttanikāya* 1.20, trans. Maurice Walshe in *Samyutta Nikāya: An Anthology* (Kandy, Sri Lanka: Buddhist Publication Society, 1985).

7. See *Aṅguttaranikāya*, trans. Woodward and Hare (1965–1973), vol. 1, pp. 14–15. Other examples would be frequent statements in the Jātaka tales such as "I was that swan."

On what basis might an enlightened person be justified or even *truthful* in thus speaking in a manner contrary to her or his ultimate understanding? The *Saṃyuttanikāya* tells us that such a person would, for example, use personal pronouns in reference to (empty) persons because "well aware of common worldly speech, he would speak conforming to such use."[8]

Buddhapālita—an early commentator on Nāgārjuna's classic presentation of the emptiness (*śūnyatā*) of all phenomena in the *Mūlamadhayamakakārikā*—gives us a vivid story on conventional truth as a property of speech conforming to the world's perspective:

> As two villagers were passing through a city on business, they entered a temple to take in the sights. As they began examining the paintings, one remarked, "The one holding the trident is Narāyāna; the one with the discus is Maheśvara." The other answered, "You have it wrong. Mhaeś-vara holds the trident and Narāyāna has the discus." As they argued, they came upon a nearby wandering sage. They paid their respects and each explained his opinion. To one of them the sage replied, "What you say is true," and to the other he said, "What you say is not true."[9]

The sage knows that neither god is present; these are just paintings on the wall. Yet he is not lying when he answers the villagers because what he says is "true through the force of worldly convention." The story concludes by stating that, like the sage, the Buddha employs distinctions between right and wrong, true and false, real and unreal, within a conventional framework quite different from his own deep understanding of emptiness.

How are sources like these to be interpreted? Afamiliar formula has it that conventional truths are somehow considered truths for strategic reasons, with understanding the ultimate as the goal.[10] Indeed conforming to the world's language is often presented as skillful method (*upāyakauśalya*) to lead *beyond* the conventional. Nāgārjuna's *Mūlamadhyamakārikā* states:

> The ultimate is not taught without depending upon the conventional;
> one will not attain *nirvāṇa* without having understood the ultimate.[11]

8. *Saṃyuttanikāya* 1.25, in *Saṃyutta Nikaya*.

9. Translation based on edition of chapter 18 of the *Buddhapālitamūlamadhyamakavṛtti* in Lindtner (1981, 197–198).

10. See, for example, Mav VI.80: *tha snyad bden pa thabs su gyur pa dang / don dam bden pa thabs byung gyur pa ste* "Conventional truth is the means/approach and ultimate truth is the goal." See Tauscher (1995, 3–4). Cf. *Bodhicaryāvatārapañjikā* (ed. Vaidya 236, 4): *tatra ca upeyabhūtaḥ paramārthādhigama eva / tasyāpy upāyabhūtaṃ saṃvṛtisatyam* / "Now in this context it is just the mastery of the ultimate that is the goal; for that too the understanding of the conventional is the means (*upāya*)."

11. MMK XXIV.10: *vyavahāram anāśritya paramārtho na deśyate / paramārtham anāgamya nirvāṇaṃ nādhigamyate* //. Sanskrit in Louis de la Vallée Poussin's edition of PP, p. 494. French translation, May 1959, 229.

Such passages then tempt the interpretation that conventional truth is not indeed truth *at all* but just a set of worldly beliefs and language usage that are *pedagogically* necessary in order for one to be taught how to replace them or go beyond them to the actual truth. Nāgārjuna's disciple Āryadeva seems to lean toward this interpretation when he writes:

> Just as one cannot make a barbarian understand by any language other [than his own], so too ordinary persons cannot be made to understand without [using] what is mundane.[12]

Yet from the outset, exegetical and pedagogical conceptions of the two truths were mixed with more deeply philosophical considerations that, in some circles, gradually came to the fore. When Ābhidharmika scholars indicate that a statement is an "ultimate truth," this is on account of its main referent's location within the class of ultimate realities, existents discerned under the deepest analysis of appearances. *Mutatis mutandis*, for conventional truth. We thus have in Abhidharma two sorts of *existent things*—that is, conventional existents (*saṃvṛtisat*) and ultimate existents (*paramārthasat*)—that are described by the two sorts of *true statements*. Laying out the Abhidharma's understanding of *saṃvṛtisat* and *saṃvṛtisatya* (not to be confused with that of Madhyamaka!), Vasubandhu states in the *Abhidharmakośabhāṣya:*

> Suppose that when a thing is broken up into parts the idea of it then will no longer occur. That thing is conventionally existent (*saṃvṛtisat*), as for example, a pot. . . . But people have applied a conventional term [like "pot" or "water"] to just those [constitutive elements], and thus because of that convention they say "Pots and water exist." So they say that this [statement] is true and not false. Thus it is a conventional truth.[13]

The two truths thus involve a conception of *standpoints* ("ultimately" = *paramārthatas* or "conventionally" = *saṃvṛtitas*) from which (1) certain types of objects exist and (2) certain types of statements are true. These ultimate and conventional standpoints are often linked to the distinction between analytical knowledge (*paricchede ñāña*) and knowledge of linguistic conventions (*sammutiñāna*), which is found in the *Saṅgītisutta* of the *Dīghanikāya* and also many Mahāyāna texts.[14]

12. Āryadeva's *Catuḥśatakaśāstrakārikā* as cited in PP, ed. L. de la Vallée Poussin 370: *nānyabhāṣayā mlecchaḥ śakyo grāhayituṃ yathā // na laukikaṃ ṛte lokaḥ śakyo grāhayituṃ tathā //.*

13. Vasubandhu (1967, 334): *yasminn avayavaśo bhinne na tadbuddhir bhavati tat saṃvṛtisat / tadyathā ghaṭaḥ / . . . teṣv eva tu saṃvṛtisamjñā kṛteti saṃvṛtivaśāt ghaṭaś cāmbu cāstīti bruvantaḥ satyam evāhur na mṛṣety etat saṃvṛtisatyam /.*

14. *Dīghanikāya*, PTS, vol. III, p. 226.

From this basis the two truths came to be understood most often as the *two classes of things* that those two standpoints present to view. Indeed, many texts emphasize the position of the two truths as objects (*viṣaya*), explaining them as two sorts of things to be known (*jñeya*) by two radically different types of mind, that is, those of ordinary beings, who understand wrongly, and those of the spiritually realized "noble ones" (*ārya*), who understand rightly. The *Pitṛputrasamāgamasūtra* states that "objects of knowledge are exhausted within the two, conventional realities and ultimate realities."[15] And Candrakīrti's *Madhyamakāvatāra* states:

> All things bear two natures constituted through correct and false views. The object (*viṣaya*) of those who see correctly is said to be "reality" (*tattva*) and the object of those who see falsely is said to be "conventional existence" (*saṃvṛtisatya*).[16]

Historically, thus, there seems to have been a move from statements to objects, but, philosophically speaking, how could this happen? At this point we must return to the disconcerting fact that the very term we generally render as "truth" (*satya*) is extensively used for existent realities (*satya*) rather than the veracity of statements or ideas. It might be facilely answered that this is not a problem, for we do on occasion apply "true" to people and things. That is, we can say of the forty-third U.S. president that he was a true fool, or we may characterize a pond in the desert as a true oasis when we had earlier suspected that it was only a mirage. Yet the quandary remains, for true fools are just very misguided people, and true oases are just real ones. Neither example suggests that people or ponds are somehow *truthbearers* in anything like the way statements, ideas, etc. are. This oft-heard answer thus does not work. Is there then a type of core element in the meaning of *satya* that would enable us to see why the term might have the broad semantic range it does and why it is not just simply equivocal?

15. Cited in Śāntideva's *Śikṣasamuccaya* dbu ma vol.16 in D. (Tokyo ed.), 142b.

16. Mav VI.23, cited in *Bodhicaryāvatārapañjikā* 361:

samyagmṛṣādarśanalabdhabhāvam /
rūpadvayaṃ bibhrati sarvabhāvāḥ //
samyagdṛśāṃ yo viṣayaḥ sa tattvam /
mṛṣādṛśāṃ saṃvṛtisatyam uktam //

See also Newland (1992, 40ff). We have translated *labdhabhāvam* as "constituted," literally "whose being is gained." This is in keeping with Louis de la Vallée Poussin's French translation: "les choses portent une double nature qui est constituée par la vue exacte et par la vue erronée." The Tibetan *rnyed pa* (=*labdha*), if taken as "[whose being] is found," could (if taken literally) yield an interpretation of the verse as meaning that the two natures are in some sense there and then found by two types of perceptions. Note that Graham Priest's interpretation of this verse as showing two aspects stemming from two perspectives on one thing (chapter 13) can be seen as in keeping with "constituted." Garfield (chapter 2) clearly opts for "found," as does Tsongkhapa.

For such a charitable reading of *satya*, we could begin with the widely held intuition, East and West, that a statement, a mental state or any other truthbearer presents a certain picture of how things are. Tibetan Madhyamaka commentaries regularly emphasize that if there is some particular sense (conventional or ultimate) in which this picture (*snang tshul*, literally "mode of appearance") accords (*mthun pa*) with how things are (*gnas tshul*), literally "mode of existence," then we may be disposed to consider that the statement or mental state is true in that particular sense (conventional/ultimate).[17] What we see in Tibetan commentaries is that this same distinction—between a mode of appearance and a mode of existence—is also used to apply to objects. Accord or discord is used to explain how those objects are *satya/bden pa* (true, real) or *mṛṣā/rdzun pa, slu ba* (false, deceptive).[18] The term *satya* (truth/reality) thus often came to signify existent things—the referents of such statements or the objects of mental states—while the criteria for applying the term, that is, accord/discord, nonetheless remained the same.

What is needed to more fully understand this transition—and cannot be undertaken here—is a detailed analysis of the Buddhist notion of an object (*viṣaya, yul*) whether in Madhyamaka philosophy or in the epistemology of Dignāga and Dharmakīrti. It may well be that objects in many of these contexts have to be seen as not simply garden-variety things but as *intentional* objects, what thought and language are directly *about*.[19] Intentional objects could match or fail to match ordinary things—when we think of, say, the political situation in Nepal, the object that directly appears to our thought (given a limited understanding of complex Nepalese politics) may bear only a very partial accord with what is actually going on there.

Finally, some may wonder: Why should one care much about what conventional truth is and is not? How important can conventional truth be if, in any case, it is not the ultimate? Each Buddhist school has its view of this matter, but a strong theme (especially in Mahāyāna philosophies) is that the conventional is not just pedagogically necessary but is the *only actual basis* for the ultimate. The ultimate (i.e., emptiness) captures the deepest/final way in which the conventional exists. For example, the *Bodhicittavivaraṇa*—a text traditionally attributed to Nāgārjuna—says:

17. To make a long story short, this can best be seen as a weak sense of "accord"/"correspondence," one that should not be thought to require the full-blown correspondence theory of truth. See chapter 8 on truth and truth theories for a more detailed discussion.

18. The term frequently used in Indian Madhyamaka texts is *mṛṣā moṣadharmaka = brdzun pa slu ba'i chos can* "something false and deceptive"; see Candrakīrti's *Catuḥśatakaṭīkā* ad v. 324 (Tillemans 1990, 198). See also chapter 3, sections 2–4.

19. On such objects, see Crane (2001). Tillemans (1986) took up some of these themes, notably referential opacity in Buddhist philosophy of language. On opacity and the Buddhist epistemological school's idea of an object, see also Stoltz (2006).

> Just as sweetness is the nature of sugar and hotness the nature of fire, so we assert that the nature of things is emptiness . . . Reality is not to be seen as something different from conventionalities. Conventionalities are described as emptiness and just emptiness is the conventional because neither occurs without the other.[20]

Along these lines, some Tibetan philosophers see the conventional as that which is empty (or the basis of emptiness) (*stong gzhi*) and the ultimate as the quality of being empty (*stong chos*). There is on this reading no possibility or even desirability that conventional truth be *replaced* by the ultimate. Indeed, the conventional becomes exactly what it is important to get right, and the ultimate, emptiness, is vital precisely because it strips away false superimpositions so as to allow right understanding of the conventional.

In the present book we take this sort of philosophical reading of the two truths rather than a pedagogical reading as our point of departure. Our priority here is *to take the conventional seriously*, seeing it as interesting and important.

Three Senses of *Saṃvṛti*

Both traditional exegetes and their modern interpreters and translators find many levels of meaning in the term *saṃvṛtisatya*, usually translated as "conventional truth." We can begin by asking, "What is *conventional* about *saṃvṛtisatya*?"

First of all, "conventional" (i.e., *saṃvṛti* and the equivalent term *vyavahāra*) would prima facie suggest that we are dealing with some type of agreement between members of a community on an essentially arbitrary matter, such as devising rules of the road and other regulations (where general consensus promotes welfare) or choosing proper names (where again general acceptance of the name is vital to its practical success). Buddhists, of course, maintain that many things are conventional in the banal sense that rules of the road are: proper names, Sanskrit idiomatic expressions like calling the moon "that which has a rabbit" (*śaśin*), and so on, proceed purely by common acknowledgment (*pratīti*). Beyond that, however, *any* connection (*sambandha*) between words and their referents is conventional and purely arbitrary (*yādṛcchika*). Buddhists, contrary to the Mīmāṃsā (one of the main Brahmanical schools), took pains to deny that there was any objective constraint or appropriateness (*yogyatā*) behind any of our linguistic usage. Interestingly enough, on an ethical-political level,

20. *Bodhicittavivaraṇa* v. 57 and 67cd–68. See Hopkins (2008, 107); Lindtner (1986, 54); and Newland (1992, 73).

caste rules too were taken by Buddhists as being purely conventional in just this way.[21]

One can also very plausibly say that many ideas and ways of thinking or behavior are governed purely by convention. Saying that *entities* are conventional, however, might seem to some harder to accept. That said, certainly some objects are linked to or result from agreements and practices: Stock markets, borders, and castes are created by agreements and rule-guided behavior, as are arguably numbers (for those who are not realists about mathematics). While it is not obvious to most of us that trees and mountains are also conventional in that way, the prospects for seeing physical objects as very heavily dependent on agreement and transactions is not hopeless. After all, the thrust of Madhyamaka philosophy is that entities are not reducible to their components but always depend on a mind that organizes and creates wholes in keeping with interests. Which wholes are created and focused upon and which are not is largely a matter of tacit common agreements about what is useful to the human form of life.

But do traditional textual sources actually confirm that the term *saṃvṛti*—be it used to designate linguistic usage, ideas, or objects—does indeed mean what we understand by "conventional," i.e., "agreement governed"? It is not immediately obvious that they do. Part of the reason for this lack of clarity seems to be a vacillation between two etymological derivations. The evidence is somewhat complex. As Edgerton had suggested and Karunadasa seconds, what the Pali renders as "consensus" or "agreement" (*sammuti*), based on √*MAN* "to think," is unexpectedly rendered in Sanskrit by *saṃvṛti*, which comes from the Sanskrit √VṚ *vṛṇoti*, "to cover, conceal."[22] It is plausible then to think, with Edgerton, that what should have led to a Sanskrit term like *saṃmati* (consensus, agreement) in fact ended up mistakenly as *saṃvṛti*. Although *sammuti/saṃmati* would have clearly indicated that conventional agreements are involved, Indian and Tibetan commentators instead had to deal with an etymology leading to the root *VṚ* "to cover, conceal."

Candrakīrti's three usages of the term *saṃvṛti* are instructive regarding the formidable task facing the commentator who wishes to account both for the use of this term and its Sanskrit etymology. In his *Prasannapadā* he tells us that one usage of *saṃvṛti* is to refer to *ignorance*, whereby one takes as true what is

21. On the Buddhist logicians' ideas of "purely arbitrary words" (*yadṛcchāśabda / yādṛcchikaśabda*), see Tillemans (2000, 186, 214–216). On the technical term "fitness" (*yogyatā*) in Dharmakīrti's philosophy of language, see Tillemans (2000, 155ff., 219–228). On Buddhist logicians on caste, see Eltschinger (2000).

22. Edgerton (1977 s.v. *saṃvṛti*). See also Karunadasa (1996, 25). Cf. the *Ratnakūṭa* passage cited at the beginning of chapter 9, which clearly shows conventional truth explained as what is agreed upon (*saṃmata*) rather than what is concealed.

not, thus concealing the actual way things are.[23] Another usage is as dependent arising (*pratītyasamutpāda*), more exactly as "mutual dependence" (*parasparasaṃbhavana*), and hence means things that lack intrinsic nature (*svabhāva*). The third usage is to mean agreements governing the use of signs, that is, *saṃketa*, as well as the various worldly practices, or more accurately, worldly *transactions* (*lokavyavahāra*). Included here are both agreed-upon linguistic expressions (*abhidhāna*) and objects of expressions (*abhidheya*), as well as cognitions (*jñāna*) and their objects (*jñeya*).

The first usage of *saṃvṛti* clearly relies on an etymological understanding in terms of the Sanskrit √VṚ *vṛṇoti*, "to cover, conceal," resulting in *saṃvṛtisatya* having the sense "true-for-the-ignorant," "true-for-the-obscured," or "true-for-the-benighted." This *saṃvṛti* has only a remote connection, if any, with what we understand as "convention" in the sense of rules and rule-guided activities, ways of thinking, and so on. It does, however, capture the aspect of the English term "conventional" when it is used to say that something is *superficial*, shallow to the point of being misleading, and thus deceptive.

As for *saṃvṛti* meaning mutual dependence, this *saṃvṛti* includes all that exists—everything lacks intrinsic natures and exists through causal dependence, mereological dependence, and/or dependence upon a cognizing mind. When the term is used in this way, its extension includes too much for it to coincide with that of *saṃvṛtisatya*, for even an ultimate reality, like emptiness, fits this bill.[24]

The third use of *saṃvṛti*, however, does recognizably involve conventions in a fairly standard sense of the word. *Saṃketa* ("convention-governed symbols," "agreed-upon usage") is, for example, at the heart of the word-world relation in Buddhist philosophies of language. In short, we see that *saṃvṛtisatya* used in this way is indeed understandable as "conventional truth."

The temptation might then be to simply dismiss the first sense because it might seem to rest on a dubious choice of √*VṚ* rather than √*MAN* as the basis for constructing the Sanskrit term. In fact, such a dismissal would be a mistake. Important thinking in Indo-Tibetan traditions often proceeds on the basis

23. Commenting on MMK XXIV.8, PP (ed. LVP) 492.10 states: *samantād varaṇaṃ saṃvṛtiḥ / ajñānaṃ hi samantāt sarvapadārthatattvāvacchādanāt saṃvṛtir ity ucyate / parasparasaṃbhavanaṃ vā saṃvṛtir anyonyasamāśrayeṇety arthaḥ / atha vā saṃvṛtiḥ saṃketo lokavyavahāra ity arthaḥ / sa cābhidhānābhidheyajñānajñeyādilakṣaṇam //* "It is *saṃvṛti* in being completely an obstruction. Indeed, ignorance, because it masks completely the nature of all entities, is said to be *saṃvṛti*. Alternatively, the meaning is that what arises in mutual dependence is *saṃvṛti* because of one thing being dependent on another. Or again *saṃvṛti* means agreed upon usage (*saṃketa*) or worldly transactions (*lokavyavahāra*). This is characterized as expressions, what is expressed, cognitions and what is cognized and so on and so forth."

24. It appears that here the term may quite possibly be understood as derived from the root √VṚT *vartate*, "turn," "go on," "take place," "exist," with *saṃvṛtti* (with two *ts*) meaning "being," "becoming," "happening."

of contestable etymological derivations, and the commentarial elaborations upon "truth for the ignorant" that one finds in writers like Longchen Rabjampa (*klong chen rab 'byams pa*), Tsongkhapa Lozang drakpa (*tsong kha pa blo bzang grags pa*), and others are good examples of that phenomenon. A more sober perspective would be to say that whatever the interest in taking *saṃvṛtisatya* etymologically as "what is true for the ignorant," it is Candrakīrti's explanation of the third use of *saṃvṛti* that works best to capture the fundamental philosophical idea and the long-standing Buddhist usage of the term.

The emphasis we place on one or more of these three senses of *saṃvṛti* is closely correlated with our interpretation of Madhyamaka. The first sense is what many interpreters have conveyed in translating *saṃvṛtisatya* as *"vérité d'enveloppement,"* "obscurational truth," "truth for a concealer," and so on. Some Tibetan schools, such as the Jonangpa (and no doubt a number of modern interpreters, too) do not take this as simply an etymological understanding based on the root *VṚ* "to cover." Instead, they take the first sense as also conveying the core philosophical point of what *saṃvṛti is*. Thus, for example, for Jonangpas *saṃvṛti* means what is "existent [only] for mistaken understandings" (*blo 'khrul ba'i ngor yod pa*).

Interestingly, Tsongkhapa also attaches importance to the first interpretation in his etymological explanation of *saṃvṛtisatya*. However, he differentiates *saṃvṛtisatya* and "conventional existence" (*saṃvṛtisat*); in this latter case he opted for the second and third senses and thus maintained that when Mādhyamikas say that all things exist conventionally, they do *not* mean that things exist only from the point of view of obscured minds but rather intend that they exist as dependent arisings and worldly conventions.[25] Those modern writers who translate *saṃvṛtisatya* as "relative truth" (Stcherbatsky), "everyday truth" (Sprung), or "conventional truth" (the majority, including the Cowherds herein) are, in effect, choosing to downplay or even disregard the first sense in favor of the second or third.

In India and Tibet there has often been strong emphasis on *saṃvṛtisatya* as "truth for the benighted." Nonetheless, there are also good philosophical grounds to question the interpretation that *saṃvṛtisatya* is epistemological fool's gold. The obvious danger is that if *saṃvṛtisatya* is not true at all but only mistakenly thought to be true, then it carries no normative force, collapsing the important distinction between what is true and what is merely thought to be true. There would then be little of interest to say about such "truth" beyond simply describing what people believe. Some might indeed accept this view, construing it as exactly what Madhyamaka quietism is all about—but those

25. See Newland (1992, 83).

who rather see Madhyamaka as allowing constructive philosophy will differ. The question of the normative versus merely descriptive status of conventional truth constitutes a major theme in this book.

Four Questions

Four questions animate and structure this project:

1. What is conventional truth?
2. What kind of truth is it, and what sort of truth theory would best fit it?
3. How and how much can such truths be criticized and improved?
4. How should one act in a world of conventional truth?

These philosophical questions arise naturally as one puts analytic pressure on Buddhist ideas of conventional truth. Not only do they arise now in a contemporary context, but they also arose in the past on several occasions within the tradition. For example, from the ancient *Mahāvibhāṣa* to sixth-century Yogācāras such as Dharmapāla, we find critics interrogating the very notion of such a truth: Isn't "conventional truth" just a euphemism for "false"? Isn't the ultimate the only actual truth?[26] The question as to whether significant reforms and philosophical improvements can and should be made to the world's truths is also amply treated in scholastic treatises: Candrakīrti's famous debate with the Svātantrikas in *Madhyamakāvatāra* turns in part on this matter.[27] Finally, on the fourth point, Buddhists are of course very concerned with the ethical implications of conventional truth, maintaining that understanding this matter rightly preserves the law of karma and the goal of liberation, whereas misunderstanding opens the door to nihilism.

Although the four questions are interrelated, the chapters vary in their focus upon them. Chapters 2–8 focus mainly on the first two questions. Chapters 9–12 shift the emphasis to the third question, that is, how and how much can conventional truth be critiqued and improved? Chapter 13 introduces two models for the truths and for enlightenment, the second construing buddhahood primarily in terms of enlightened action and hence in terms of ethics. Chapter 14 continues this thread by concentrating on the fourth question, that

26. *Mahāvibhāṣa*, Taishō (1545, 400a4–24). Dharmapāla, cited in Śāntarakṣita's *Satyadvayavibhaṅgapañjikā* 27b3. Both texts quoted in Lindtner (1981, 162–163, 199).

27. See the initial section of Mav VI, where Candrakīrti argues at length against the Svātantrika idea of production from causes that are distinct from their effects (*gzhan las skye ba*). Candrakīrti rejects this philosophical sophistication about causality and prefers to stick simply with the linguistic usage of ordinary people. See chapter 9 on Candrakīrti's acceptance of the ordinary in this and other debates.

is, the ethical importance of Madhyamaka's two truths. With these four questions before us, we now summarize how the details play out in the individual chapters of the book.

Chapters 2, 3, and 4 examine how conventional truth is *truth* in Candrakīrti's and Tsongkhapa's Madhyamaka philosophies. Jay Garfield, in "Taking Conventional Truth Seriously: Authority regarding Deceptive Reality," argues that Mādhyamikas acknowledge a very significant role for truth in conventional truth, all the while insisting that the world is thoroughly mistaken. Roughly, although people may see such and such a thing wrongly, it is in fact conventionally true both that they are seeing it and that they see it wrongly. Garfield subscribes to Tsongkhapa's interpretation of Candrakīrti's *Madhyamakāvatāra* VI.23 and other such passages, according to which entities have two distinct natures (*ngo bo* = *rūpa*) that are found (*rnyed pa* = *labdha*) in objects.[28] Thus, the conventional and the ultimate are not simply ways of apprehending one object but are themselves two different aspects of the object. When mundane cognition apprehends one aspect and the awakened person's insight apprehends the other, both are right.

In chapter 3, Sonam Thakchöe's "Prāsaṅgika Epistemology in Context," we ask whether there are reliable epistemic instruments (*tshad ma* = *pramāṇa*) that can get conventional truth right. Many Indian and Tibetan commentators insisted unequivocally that Candrakīrti did not accept reliable epistemic instruments, arguing that since conventional existents are deceptive (*slu ba*), cognitions of them must also be deceptive. Thakchöe defends Tsongkhapa's interpretation of Madhyamaka, in which reliable epistemic instruments are clearly accepted. Thakchöe argues that a Prāsaṅgika endorses epistemology but that—contrary to logicians like Dignāga and Dharmakīrti—he does not subscribe to foundationalism.

Chapter 4 looks at another epistemological issue: the Madhyamaka's use and acceptance of analysis.[29] Although emptiness is understood via analysis that asks how things ultimately exist, it is often thought that the conventional is completely nonanalytical. Guy Newland, in "Weighing the Butter," argues that this is not Tsongkhapa's position at all; conventional analysis is not only possible, but is indeed critical to the project of ethics and liberation. Knowledge gained from this analysis is not contradicted or superseded by ultimate realization of emptiness—a fact Newland illustrates via analogy with academic

28. See n. 16 for more on the question of how to interpret *labdha* = *rnyed pa*.

29. Cf., for example, PP 67.7 (ed. LVP): *naitad evaṃ / laukike vyavahāra ithaṃvicārāpravṛtter avicārataś ca laukikapadārthānām astitvāt*. "No, it's not so, for in the world this type of analysis does not operate with regard to the conventional, and entities for the world exist [only] from a non-analytic point of view."

disciplines, each with its own standpoints and concerns. Emptiness entails that things exist as mere "imputations," allowing diverse living beings—humans, gods, animals, etc.—to have contradictory but conventionally correct perspectives.

Any discussion of truth and epistemology in Candrakīrti and Tsongkhapa's Madhyamaka will invariably lead to the idea of "identifying the object of negation" (*dgag bya ngos 'dzin*). This is taken up in chapter 5 by Garfield and Thakchöe. Many Tibetan scholars maintain that since emptiness in Madhyamaka is a negation (*dgag pa*), it can be understood only by first understanding what object is targeted by this negation (*dgag bya*). For Tsongkhapa all things, conventional and ultimate, are empty of intrinsic natures; thus, *intrinsic nature* is the object to be negated. For the fifteenth-century Sakyapa scholar Gorampa Sonam Senge (*go rams pa bsod nams seng ge*), however, things are empty of existence *tout court*, and the object to be negated must be taken accordingly. The degree to which conventional truth is true depends directly on what is identified as the object negated by emptiness. For Tsongkhapa, the conventional stripped of the object of negation is something existent; for Gorampa it is not.

Whereas chapters 2–5 advance considerable optimism about the possibility of constructive philosophy and epistemology concerning conventional truth, the tone changes radically in chapters 6 and 7. In "Can a Mādhyamika Be a Skeptic?" Georges Dreyfus considers a simple and jarring response to the question of what is true about conventional truth: Nothing—or at least nothing whatsoever of any interest to philosophers or anyone else who seeks truths. Dreyfus bases his explanation on a newly discovered manuscript of the twelfth-century Tibetan Prāsaṅgika, Patsab Nyimadrak (*pa tshab nyi ma grags*). This philosopher adopts the Madhyamaka's suspension of philosophical theses (*phyogs = pakṣa; dam bca' = pratijñā*) but radicalizes it; the goal is not to reject views and theses as false but to overcome all attempts to make truth claims, whether they are assertions or negations. This leaves a purely skeptical acceptance of the conventional as only a description of how we live and the opinions people hold to further their practical ends. Patsab, like Sextus Empiricus (the second-century CE Greek skeptic), seems to offer a type of purgative therapy: We abandon the mind-set and activity of making truth claims and thus attain peace. Conventional truth is just a name for the human practices that are left.

It may, however, be possible to take a less radical approach, allowing a limited scope for constructive philosophy within skepticism. In chapter 7, Dreyfus and Garfield ("Madhyamaka and Classical Greek Skepticism") broaden the debate to include Academic and Pyrrhonian varieties of skepticism along with the Buddhist Madhyamaka variety. Could a Prāsaṅgika skeptic or Pyrrhonist, who do not regard skepticism as exempt from its own critique, accommodate some form of constructive philosophy without making assertions about what is and is not so in reality? Dreyfus and Garfield argue that they *could*—on the condition that seeming assertions are not taken as representations, but rather as skeptical assertions, that is, mere moves within a set of rule-guided practices. Such a skeptic could practice the art of philosophy, obey the rules of logic, and so on in order to dissuade others from claims about what is really so—without claiming an alternative account of reality.

Chapter 8 closes the section on truth and epistemology by returning to the second question ("What kind of truth is conventional truth, and what sort of truth theory would best fit it?"), isolating the semantic notion of truth implicit in *satya*. In "The (Two) Truths about Truth," Graham Priest, Mark Siderits, and Tom Tillemans ask whether correspondence, coherentism, pragmatism, or deflationism would be appropriate theories for us to account for statements being conventionally or ultimately true. Is there a notion of truth common to both types of statements? And what is specific to each? Is the feature common to both an acceptance of the T-schema, that is, that a statement *p* is true if and only if *p* is the case? Examining both Abhidharma and Madhyamaka versions of the two truths in this light, they sketch a deflationist Madhyamaka theory that can capture an ordinary account of truth while avoiding ontological commitment to real entities as truthmakers.

Chapters 9–12 bring the third question ("Can conventional truth be criticized and improved?") to the forefront. One way to look at the Prāsaṅgika-Svātantrika debate within Indo-Tibetan Madhyamaka[30] is in terms of allegiance to or rejection of the unschooled world's opinions on conventional matters. Some Prāsaṅgikas, styling themselves as "Mādhyamikas who accept [as conventionally true just] what the world acknowledges [to be true]" (*'jig rten grags sde pa'i dbu ma pa*), seem to advocate a kind of extremely pure conventionalism in which a Buddhist should just read off the surface and acquiesce in the world's opinions and epistemic practices as they are. The rationale they invoke is as follows: That all things are empty of intrinsic nature implies that there simply *can* be no more sophisticated or defendable truths than what the world offers us. If such deeper truths were possible—so the argument goes—they would have to be grounded in real facts, and real facts are precisely what Mādhyamikas' philosophy of emptiness must rule out.

As Tom Tillemans brings out in chapter 9 ("How Far Can a Mādhyamika Buddhist Reform Conventional Truth?"), Svātantrikas, like the eighth-century Indian thinker Kamalaśīla, strongly argue against this deliberate adoption of the world's stance. Their argument is essentially that when truth loses normative

30. See Dreyfus and McClintock (2003) and Seyfort Ruegg (2006).

force and collapses into simply what is widely accepted, criticism and growth of knowledge become impossible—a dismal consequence indeed and one that Svātantrikas rightly perceive to be unacceptable. The Cowherds agree that merely "reading off the surface" to find truth is unacceptable; where they differ is on how a Mādhyamika can espouse emptiness and yet avoid having to accept extreme conventionalism.

Tillemans argues that that dismal consequence may be unavoidable for what he calls "typical Prāsaṅgikas." These are Mādhyamikas who take emptiness as leading to fictionalism about the conventional; they hold that whatever the world maintains to be true is actually completely false for a spiritually realized person but fictionally true when that person adopts the pretense-perspective of the world's story. Such a Mādhyamika fictionalist might tinker with the story here and there to make it more internally coherent, but there could be no basis for wide-ranging or global upgrades. Emptiness does not, however, have this same consequence for certain *atypical* Prāsaṅgikas, who are not fictionalists but are more like deflationists about truth (see chapter 8). For them, the world and spiritually realized beings share truths in common; there can be a normative conception of conventional truth without the metaphysical baggage of intrinsic natures.

Chapter 10 offers an escape from extreme conventionalism. Mark Siderits, in "Is Everything Connected to Everything Else? What the Gopīs Know," seeks to show that Mādhyamikas can allow for improvement in our epistemic practices, providing they can make room for reductionism. Like all who promote the growth of knowledge, a Mādhyamika has to allow that certain ordinary phenomena can be better explained in terms of deeper, underlying entities (e.g., pharmaceutical effects are explained by microbiology). The price for accepting such reductionism, however, is that a Mādhyamika will have to allow at least a provisional place for intrinsic natures (*svabhāva*) as conventionally existent and should lean toward an epistemology like that of Dignāga and Dharmakīrti. Intrinsic natures will be only provisionally accepted in that every such nature, if in turn examined with the Madhyamaka dialectic, will turn out to be mind dependent and empty. The chapter defends a Svātantrika-style program having as its elements Abhidharma-style reductionism, the epistemology of Dignāga and Dharmakīrti, and an acceptance of conventionally established intrinsic natures. Siderits argues that this combination better allows the growth of knowledge about conventional truth than the Nyāya-oriented positions of Candrakīrti.

Chapter 11 offers another escape route—without embracing Svātantrika or intrinsic natures. In "Carnap's Pragmatism and the Two Truths," Bronwyn Finnigan and Koji Tanaka challenge the notion that all things being empty of intrinsic natures makes criticism of the world's conventional truths impossible. Finnigan and Tanaka see this principle as a holdover from semantic realism;

the realist demands that there be real truthmakers if we are to ground amendments to the world's views. They argue instead that a Mādhyamika could reject the metaphysical realists' demand that statements be somehow *about* real entities but still allow for criticism and growth of knowledge by relying on purely practical considerations. Rudolph Carnap's distinction between internal and external existence questions can be invoked to preserve serious debate and the normative value of truth. An internal question about whether entities of such and such a sort exist is not a question *about* entities in the real world. It is a question as to whether the operating linguistic framework allows for statements formulated in a certain way. Frameworks give rules for testing and accepting or rejecting statements, and frameworks themselves may be accepted or rejected for practical reasons of efficiency, fruitfulness, and simplicity—but not because of any metaphysical considerations involving *aboutness*.

Can one account for criticism and growth of knowledge, all the while taking quite literally the claim that all is conventional construction? Chapter 12 addresses this question. Jan Westerhoff, in "The Merely Conventional Existence of the World," offers a rational reconstruction of the Madhyamaka idea that everything is mind dependent and conceptually constructed. He seeks to avoid three pitfalls: (1) that truth becomes subjective when nothing objectively/really exists; (2) that construction must rest on a foundation of something real; (3) that, without an objective world, constructions are unlimited and can be any way people think they are or wish them to be. Westerhoff relies on David Lewis's account of the conventional nature of linguistic signs whose reference is fixed without reliance on previously existing language. He extends this idea to include objects that are constructed at the same time as the conventional word-world linkage. Successful interactions determine how words are used correctly and also bring objects into existence. That some actions are successful and others are not is not due to properties of real entities but is itself a constructed fact brought into existence at the time of the creation of the conventional objects; thus, success is not arbitrary, purely subjective, or unrestricted. The result is that there is no "world that is there anyway," but neither have we unlimited freedom to make up our world as we wish.

Previous chapters brought out complex epistemic issues implicit in traditional and modern approaches to the two truths. A common thread in the discussions of Candrakīrti's and Tsongkhapa's positions was that the conventional and the ultimate were defined as objects of two different sorts of understanding—hence, the focus was often on subjects and the possibility of their being reliable epistemic instruments (*pramāṇa*). In chapter 13 ("Two Truths: Two Models"), Graham Priest sees this subject-oriented model (that is, model A) as one that accounts for much of Indian Madhyamaka; it takes the conventional and the ultimate as two natures or aspects that are due to or constituted by two perspectives on one thing.[31] By contrast, model B, which is predominant in Buddha-nature theories and Chinese Avataṃsaka schools inter alia and may owe much to Daoism, construes conventional existents as manifestations of what is ultimate (e.g., phenomena are manifestations of mind, buddha nature, or the principle [Chinese *li* 理] and are thus not subjective in that they do not depend on differing apprehensions for their being). While model A takes awakening as involving a new perspective, for model B the buddha nature/principle is already present and is not newly acquired. Awakening is thus better seen in ethical rather than epistemic terms; it is the actualization of an innate nature in actions that spontaneously manifest it.

Chapter 14 pursues the implications of these analyses for the possibility of a Madhyamaka ethics based on conventional truth. If the conventional and the ultimate are to be seen in purely epistemic terms—one being wholly erroneous, one being accurate—it would seem to be very difficult to imagine how a Mādhyamika could rationally *justify* ethical claims by relying on conventional truths. Such is the problem taken up by Bronwyn Finnigan and Koji Tanaka in "Ethics for Mādhyamikas." In short, how could a Mādhyamika bodhisattva, like Śāntideva or others, ever use theoretical arguments to persuade an unbeliever that the bodhisattva path is the one that is ethically justified? Finnigan and Tanaka's answer is a radical one: Mādhyamikas do not primarily seek to justify behavior codes by appealing to ethical theory. Madhyamaka ethics is instead concerned with showing fulfillment of the bodhisattva precepts in practical situations. The discussion is thus reoriented from justificatory issues to those of moral phenomenology.

Concluding Reflections

This book is not a general collection of disparate articles but a polygraph authored by a collective of people who have worked closely together over several years. We have learned much from one another, and this volume reflects that mutual influence. Nonetheless, it offers no unanimous answer to any of the four questions animating it. *Moonshadows* is not a manifesto. It is rather a collaborative effort to do philosophy *ensemble*, each Cowherd bringing his or her positions, methods, training, and talents, along with an openness to one another and to the texts we address. To detractors who argue on methodological grounds that this cannot be done: *solvitur ambulando*.[32]

31. See n. 16 for the issue of "constituted" versus "found."

32. "It is solved by walking." This Latin phrase originally described the refutation by Diogenes of Sinope to the Eleatic arguments showing that motion is impossible: He simply got up and walked.

What, then, do we offer our reader? Our work is informed by history but is not itself a historical study; it is based on extensive use of original Sanskrit and Tibetan sources—even some previously unknown manuscripts—but it is not typical philology. Instead, we ask hard conceptual questions and pursue them in depth, looking for ways to avoid the usual formulations, which are often too close to clichés and hand waving. The works of Candrakīrti and the other great Mādhyamikas merit nothing less than serious philosophical analysis. We find our way in their long shadows.

2

Taking Conventional Truth Seriously: Authority regarding Deceptive Reality

Jay L. Garfield

The Problem

Tsongkhapa, following Candrakīrti closely, writes that "'Convention'[1] refers to a lack of understanding or ignorance; that is, that which obscures or conceals the way things really are [*Ocean* 479–480]."[2] Candrakīrti himself puts the point this way in the *Madhyamakāvatārabhāṣya:*

> Obscurational truth[3] is posited due to the force of afflictive ignorance, which constitutes the limbs of cyclic existence. The śrāvakas, pratyekabuddhas and bodhisattvas, who have abandoned afflictive ignorance, see compounded phenomena to be like reflections, to have the nature of being created; but these are not truths for them because they are not fixated on things as true. Fools are deceived, but for

1. There is a translational problem posed throughout this chapter by the terms *vyavahāra* and *saṃvṛti* in Sanskrit and *tha snyad* and *kun rdzob* in Tibetan. In this chapter we use "convention" to translate the first members of these pairs and frequently "obscuration" to translate the second. The only time that this difference is important is where they are glossed. Both Candrakīrti and Tsongkhapa regard them as absolutely coextensive. See "Three Senses of Saṃvṛti" in chapter 1.

2. Quotations are from *Ocean* (= Tsongkhapa 2006), the sDe dge edition of the Tibetan canon, from Candrakīrti (2003) and from the edition of VV in Yonezawa (2008).

3. Here we use the term *obscurational truth* instead of the normal *conventional truth* to reflect the gloss Candrakīrti is developing for the Sanskrit *saṃvṛti*. In general, in this chapter, as we will be occasionally refer to his and Tsongkhapa's gloss of this term, we will require this alternative translation to make sense of what they are doing.

> those others—just like an illusion—in virtue of being dependently originated, they are merely obscurational.[4]

So it might seem that for Candrakīrti and Tsongkhapa conventional truth (understood here as *obscurational truth*) is merely illusion, wholly false, accepted only by the fools it deceives.

But, of course, for several reasons that can't be the whole story. First of all, both Candrakīrti and Tsongkhapa refer to conventional truth as a *truth*. Indeed, in *Madhyamakāvatāra* VI.24 and its commentary, Candrakīrti explicitly argues that there is a big difference between conventional truth and conventional falsehood. Second, they also indicate that the term *convention*, though it can mean *concealing* (PP 439), can also refer to *mutual dependence* and to *signifiers* (*Ocean* 480, MavBh 252b, PP 439–440). In *Prasannapadā*, Candrakīrti emphasizes the presence of these more positive meanings asserting that "positing the person as a dependent designation based upon the aggregates" is an example of mundane convention (PP 439), that *mutual dependence* is a meaning of "conventional," and that, therefore, "term and referent; consciousness and object of knowledge, *and all such conventions without exception are called 'mundane conventional truth' (lokasaṃvṛtisatya)*."[5]

Third, Candrakīrti also asserts that "It has been shown that each phenomenon has its own two natures—a conventional and an ultimate nature."[6] The fact that these are natures of phenomena means that they are in some sense both *existent*. In fact, the very fact that Candrakīrti refers to these as *natures* of objects indicates that he does *not* reduce the sense of "conventional" (*saṃvṛti, vyavahāra*) to *illusory*. Fourth, Nāgārjuna asserts quite plainly, in the verse to which all of the passages to which I have just adverted are commentaries, that "the Buddha's teaching is based on two truths: a truth of worldly convention and an ultimate truth" (MMK XXIV.8, *Ocean* 479). Finally, given the doctrine of the identity of the two truths (MMK XXIV. 18–19), a doctrine of which both Tsongkhapa and Candrakīrti approve, if the

4. *dBu ma 'a* 255a, *Ocean* 481–482: *de ltar na re zhig srid pa'i yang lag gis yongs su bsdus pa nyon mongs pa can gyi ma rig pa'i dbang gis kun rdzob kyi bden pa rnam par gzhag go//de la nyan thos dang rang sangs rgyas dang byang chub sems dpa' nyon mongs ba can gyis gzigs pa spangs pa/'du byed gzugs brnyan la sogs pa'i yod pa nyid dang 'dra bar gzigs pa rnams la ni bcos ma'i rang bzhin gyi bden pa ma yin te/bden par mgnon par rlom pa med pa'i phyir ro//byis pa rnams la ni slu bar byed pa yin la/de las gzhan pa rnams la ni sgyu ma la sogs pa ltar rten cing 'brel par 'byung ba nyid kyis kun rdzob tsam du 'gyur ro//.*

5. Candrakīrti (2003, 440): *brjod bya dang/rjod byed dang/shes pa dang/shes bya la sogs pa'i tha snyad ma lus pa 'di dag thams cad ni/'jig rten gyi kun rdzob kyi bden pa zhes bya'o//.* Skt. ed. LVP 493.5–6. See also "Three Senses of Saṃvṛti," n. 23, in chapter 1.

6. MavBh 253a: *dngos po thams cad kyi rang gi ngo bo rnam pa gnyis nye bar bstan te/'di lta ste/ kun rdzob dang don dam pa'o//. Ocean* 483.

ultimate truth is a truth, a conventional truth that is identical with it just has to be true in some sense.

Here we explore specifically how Candrakīrti and Tsongkhapa understand the idea of conventional truth, most specifically, the sense in which and the reasons for which they regard conventional truth as *true*. We must therefore reconcile the claims that conventional truth is *concealing, deceptive, truth only for fools* with its *identity* with ultimate truth and its being one of the two *natures* of any object. We thus must also explain the sense in which conventional truth is distinct from and the sense in which it is identical to ultimate truth and why these two claims are mutually consistent.

We are interested in the work of Candrakīrti because it appears that he, more than any other Indian Mādhyamika, worries about how to interpret this doctrine and thinks it through with more clarity than any other Indian commentator on Nāgārjuna. We are interested in the work of Tsongkhapa because he, more than any other commentator on Indian Madhyamaka, understood and appreciated the force of Candrakīrti's analysis and took seriously the implications of taking conventional truth seriously for Buddhist epistemology and practice. If we can make sense of the doctrine of the two truths and of the reality of the conventional despite its implication with primal ignorance at all, we can make sense of it in the context of the work of these two philosophical giants.

Two Reasons That Conventional Truth Is a Truth (Preliminaries)

We begin by noting two prima facie reasons for treating conventional truth as a truth both in the work of Candrakīrti and in that of Tsongkhapa.[7] First, there is a very important sense in which the conventional truth is the only truth that there is. There are two ways of making this point. First, as we noted earlier, the two truths are in *some* sense identical. If that is true, then even ultimate truth is only conventional. The second way to make this point is this, though: The ultimate truth is emptiness, the absence of true, or intrinsic, existence in things. The ultimate truth is thus the fact that they are merely conventionally

7. It is important to bear in mind that Candrakīrti and Tsongkhapa are different philosophers, with different projects and different views. This is particularly important as often, when we quote or refer to views of Tsongkhapa, those views are articulated by him in the course of commenting on Candrakīrti. So, sometimes we will talk directly about Candrakīrti, sometimes about Tsongkhapa's own reading of Candrakīrti, sometimes about Tsongkhapa's own view, and sometimes we talk about our own views influenced by both of theirs.

existent. Neither Tsongkhapa nor Candrakīrti would put the point this way. Instead, Tsongkhapa argues, following Candrakīrti very closely, that the ultimate truth—emptiness—is an external negation, a mere elimination of any intrinsic existence in things and of any conceptualization (*Ocean* 51–54). But this in the end amounts to the same thing since to be merely existent is to lack any intrinsic identity. The ultimate truth is hence, even for Tsongkhapa, that the conventional truth is all that there is. We return to this consideration at the end of this chapter.

A second reason for treating conventional truth as truth will occupy more of our analytic attention in what follows. Tsongkhapa and Candrakīrti each emphasize that conventional truth is the domain of conventional authoritative cognition and hence that conventional truth is a domain about which there is a difference between getting it wrong and getting it right and that one can be *correct* about conventional truth in two different but equally important senses. First, ordinary people can be right about the fact there is a rope on the ground, wrong about the fact that there is a snake there. The fact that there is a rope, not a snake, is hence in some sense *true*. Second, as we have seen, āryas can know the conventional nature of conventional reality in a way that ordinary fools cannot. What is deceptive to fools is not deceptive to āryas, although it is merely conventional. In that sense, too, convention can be seen *truly*.

The important point here, and the principal topic of this chapter, is that, for both Candrakīrti and Tsongkhapa, it is the fact of epistemic authority that guarantees truth in convention and the reality of the conventional. When we ask why conventional truth is a *truth*, the answer will turn on the fact that there is a difference to be drawn *within* the conventional between truth and falsehood, as well as a truth *about* the conventional. There is something that counts as getting it right about conventional reality.

Interlude: Epistemic Authority for Mādhyamikas

Inasmuch as the role of the authority of epistemic instruments (*tshad ma* = *pramāṇa*) in Madhyamaka metaphysics will play a significant role in the following discussion, a few remarks on Nāgārjuna's and Candrakīrti's attitudes toward these instruments and their authority are necessary. It is often urged that Nāgārjuna, in *Vigrahavyāvartanī*, rejects the authority of any epistemic instruments. This is incorrect. Nāgārjuna, in that text, takes on a Nyāya account of epistemic instruments and their authority according to which the *instruments* are taken to be *foundational* to all knowledge. He does so because this kind of foundationalism[8] would require their intrinsic identity and authority as instruments and so would undermine his account of emptiness.

The Nyāya interlocutor in *Vigrahavyāvartanī* argues that Nāgārjuna himself cannot argue cogently for his own position, as that would presuppose that it is delivered and so justified by an epistemic instrument; that, in turn, the interlocutor argues, requires that the instruments be self-verifying and hence nonempty. Hence, he argues, Nāgārjuna must presuppose nonempty epistemic categories in order to argue for the emptiness of everything and so is self-refuting:

> V. Suppose one were to deny the things
> One apprehended through perception.
> That by which one apprehended things—
> Perception itself—would be nonexistent![9]

That is, as the autocommentary makes clear, the opponent is arguing that any argument for the emptiness of the objects of knowledge is an equally good argument for the emptiness of the instruments of knowledge. But if the instruments are empty, they cannot serve as foundations for knowledge, and so in the absence of such foundations, there would be no reason to believe even the Mādhyamika's claims.[10]

8. A note about the use of the word "foundationalism" in this chapter is in order here. The term often is used only to denote an epistemological position according to which certain sentences or cognitive episodes are taken to be self-warranting and to stand as the foundation for all other knowledge. That is a foundationalism of *content*. But there is also a foundationalism of *method*, according to which certain faculties or methods of knowing are taken to be self-warranting and foundational. Descartes' use of clear and distinct perception in the *Meditations* is a good example of this kind of foundationalism. It is this latter kind of foundationalism that Nāgārjuna is here concerned to refute. See also the section in chapter 3 on "Antifoundationalism" and n. 8, where a distinction is made between epistemic and ontological foundationalisms.

9. Yonezawa (2008, 229.5–230.3): *re zhig dngos rnams mngon sum gyis/ dmigs nas zlog par byed yin na/ gang gis dngos rnams dmigs 'gyur ba/ mngon sum de ni med pa yin//.*

10. See VV to v. 5, Yonezawa (2008, 229): *gal te khyod kyis dngos po thams cad mngon sum gyis dmigs nas dngos po thams cad ni stong pa'o zhes zlog par byed na ni mi rung ngo // de yang 'thad pa ma yin te/ ci'i phyir zhe na/ dngos po thams cad kyi nang du mngon sum gyi tshad ma yang 'dus pa'i phyir stong pa yin la/ dngos po la dmigs par byed pa gang yin pa de yang stong pa yin no// de'i phyir mngon sum gyi tshad mas dmigs pa med do// mi dmigs pa 'gog pa yang mi 'thad pas de la dngos po thams cad ni stong pa'o zhes smras pa gang yin pa de 'thad pa ma yin no// 'on te khyod kyi blo la rjes su dpag pa dang lung dang dpes 'jal bas dmigs nas dngos po 'di thams cad zlog par byed do snyam du sems na 'dir smra bar bya ste/* "Suppose you were to say, after having apprehended everything by means of perception, that everything is empty. This rejection [of things] would make no sense! Why is that? Because, since perception—an epistemic instrument—must be included among everything, it would also be empty! And even the apprehender of these things would be empty! Thus there would be no such thing as apprehension through the epistemic instrument of perception. And since it makes no sense to reject that which is not even apprehended, the assertion that everything is empty wouldn't make any sense at all. Maybe you think that by using inference, scripture or analogy you can reject everything that you have apprehended. We reply as follows." See also Bhattacharya (1986, 99).

Nāgārjuna replies not by denying the utility of the epistemic instruments, but rather by arguing, in what must be the first explicit defense of epistemological coherentism[11] in the history of world philosophy, that these instruments are themselves useful and authoritative precisely because they are dependent. They are dependent upon their epistemic objects (*prameya*), the objects of knowledge:

> 40: If epistemic instruments were self-established,
> Then an epistemic instrument would be established for you
> Independently of epistemic objects.
> Indeed, what is self-established depends on nothing else.
>
> 41: If, as you would have it, the epistemic instruments
> Are established independently of their objects, the epistemic objects
> Then these epistemic instruments
> Would pertain to nothing at all.[12]
>
> . . .
>
> 46: Suppose that by establishing the epistemic instruments
> The epistemic objects are thereby established for you
> And that by establishing the objects the instruments are established,
> Then, for you, neither [the instruments nor the objects] can be established.[13]

Foundationalism, even of this methodological kind, according to Nāgārjuna, makes no sense. Neither instrument nor object of knowledge can serve as a foundation. We are entitled to rely on epistemic instruments, that is, just because they deliver epistemic objects; we are entitled in turn to confidence in our judgments about our epistemic objects just because they are delivered by these epistemic instruments. You are entitled to believe that your vision is good just because it delivers visible objects to you; you are entitled to believe that those objects are present just because your vision is good.

11. Once again, a terminological clarification is needed. The kind of coherentism Nāgārjuna is defending is not one in which all *beliefs* are mutually supportive but rather one according to which the warrant of mechanisms of attaining knowledge and the warrant of the beliefs they deliver are mutually supportive.

12. Yonezawa (2008, 287): *gal te rang las tshad ma grub/gzhal bya rnams la ma ltos par/ khyod kyi tshad ma 'grub 'gyur 'dir/ gzhan las mi ltos rang 'grub 'gyur// gal te gzhal bya'i don rnams la/ ma ltos khyod kyi tshad ma grub/ tshad ma 'di rnams kho na ni/ gang gi'ang yin par mi 'gyur ro//*. Cf. translation in Bhattacharya (1986, 120).

13. Yonezawa (2008, 293): *'on te khyod kyis tshad grub pas/gzhal bar bya ba 'grub 'gyur la/ gzhal bya grub pas tshad grub na/ khyod kyis gnyis ga'ang 'grub mi 'gyur//*. See Bhattacharya (1986, 122).

Candrakīrti, in *Prasannapadā*, is even more explicit in his endorsement of the Nyāya set of epistemic instruments (perception, inference, analogy, and scriptural authority). He enumerates them specifically but argues that they have only a dependent, conventional validity, concluding, "Thus, in this way it is established that mundane objects are known by the means of the fourfold epistemic instruments."[14] And of course, Tsongkhapa makes explicit use of this theory of epistemic instruments and objects, using this theory as an account of authority or warrant throughout his corpus. It is therefore a serious mistake to think that Madhyamaka, at least as articulated by Nāgārjuna, Candrakīrti, and Tsongkhapa, eschews reliance on or an account of epistemic authority.

Mirages for Mādhyamikas

Among the many similes for conventional truth that litter Madhyamaka texts, the most fruitful is that of the mirage. Conventional truth is false, Candrakīrti tells us, because it is deceptive (*Yuktiṣaṣṭikāvṛtti dBu ma ya* 7b). Candrakīrti spells this out in terms of a mirage. A mirage appears to be water but is in fact empty of water—it is deceptive and, in that sense, a false appearance. On the other hand, a mirage is not *nothing:* It is an *actual* mirage, just not actual water.

The analogy must be spelled out with care to avoid the extreme of nihilism. A mirage appears to be water but is only a mirage; the inexperienced highway traveler mistakes it for water, and for him it is deceptive, a false appearance of water; the experienced traveler sees it for what it is—a real mirage, empty of water. Just so, conventional phenomena appear to ordinary, deluded beings to be intrinsically existent, whereas in fact they are merely conventionally real, empty of that intrinsic existence; to the āryas, on the other hand, they appear to be merely conventionally true and hence to be empty. For us, they are deceptive, false appearances; for them, they are simply actual conventional existents.

We can update the analogy to make the point more plainly. Imagine three travelers along a hot desert highway. Alice is an experienced desert traveler; Bill is a neophyte; Charlie is wearing polarizing sunglasses. Bill points to a mirage up ahead and warns against a puddle on the road; Alice sees the mirage as a mirage and assures him that there is no danger. Charlie sees nothing at all and wonders what they are talking about. If the mirage were entirely false—if there were no truth about it at all, Charlie would be the most authoritative of the

14. Candrakīrti (2003, 55): *de'i phyir de ltar tshad ma bzhi las 'jig rten gyi don rtogs par rnam par 'jog pa yin no//.* Skt. ed. LVP 75.9.

three (and Buddhas would know nothing of the real world). But that is wrong. Just as Bill is deceived in believing that there is water on the road, Charlie is incapable of seeing the mirage at all and so fails to know what Alice knows—that there is an actual mirage on the road, which appears to some to be water, but which is not. There is a truth about the mirage despite the fact that it is deceptive, and Alice is authoritative with respect to it precisely because she sees it as it is, not as it appears to the uninitiated.

A Message from Our Sponsors: Candrakīrti and Tsongkhapa

Let's now consider a few crucial passages from the relevant texts to get a better sense of the constraints that an account of Madhyamaka theory of conventional truth must satisfy. Tsongkhapa, in his discussion of the status of arising and ceasing and so forth in the context of the negations presented in the Homage verses for the *Mūlamadhyamakakārikā*, remarks:

> [I]f there were no place for conventional phenomena, the existence of which is established by the epistemic instruments, these phenomena would be like the snake—that is, the rope grasped as a snake—of which no cause or effect is possible . . .
>
> [I]f one were forced to maintain that there is no place for bondage, liberation, etc in the meaning of "conventional existence," and that these must be placed only in the erroneous perspective, that would be a great philosophical error . . .
>
> Even worse, as long as convention is conceived as entirely nonexistent, since there would be no role for the epistemic instruments, neither the proposition maintained nor the person who maintains it nor the proof—including scriptural sources and reasoning—could be established by epistemic instruments. So it would be ridiculous to maintain that there are no genuine phenomena delivered by the epistemic instruments.[15]

Tsongkhapa makes it plain here that conventional phenomena, unlike the snake thought to be perceived when one sees a rope, have causes and effects and are actual. Moreover, he argues that the repudiation of the reality of the conventional would undermine the possibility of epistemic authority, undermining even the ability to argue cogently that the conventional does not

15. *Ocean* 30–31. Note slight changes in the translation to conform to the conventions of this volume.

exist. Such a position would be self-refuting. Returning to the discussion of MMK XXIV.8, Tsongkhapa, citing Candrakīrti, emphasizes the deceptive side of the conventional:

> Suppose someone asks, "what is conventional and what is truth?" The convention from the perspective of which such things as form are posited as true is the ignorance which fabricates the intrinsic existence of phenomena which do not intrinsically exist . . . Thus *Madhyamakāvatāra* VI.28 says:
>
> > Since the nature of confusion is to veil, it is obscurational.
> > That which is created by it appears to be truly existent.
> > The sage has said that it is the obscurational truth.
> > Created phenomena are obscurational.[16]

Here the *Madhyamakāvatārabhāṣya* says:

> Obscurational truth is posited due to the force of afflictive ignorance, which constitutes the limbs of cyclic existence. The śrāvakas, pratyekabuddhas and bodhisattvas, who have abandoned afflictive ignorance, see compounded phenomena to be like reflections, to have the nature of being created; but these are not truths for them because they are not fixated on things as true. Fools are deceived, but for those others—just like an illusion—in virtue of being dependently originated, they are merely obscurational. (MavBh 255a, *Ocean* 481–482)

There are subtle philosophical distinctions to be drawn here. On the one hand, conventional truth is obscurational, confusing, and veiling. The reason for that is that conventional reality appears to most of us as though it is truly (intrinsically) existent—as more than merely conventional. Those who have transcended afflictive ignorance, Candrakīrti emphasizes, in fact do see the compounded phenomena comprised by conventional reality but see them as miragelike, as actual, but deceptive.

Tsongkhapa comments that this means that ignorance is not a necessary condition of positing conventional truth but that ignorance is instead the source of the superimposition of intrinsic existence on that which is conventionally existent:

16. *gti mug rang bzhin sgrib phyir kun rdzob ste/ des gang bcos ma bden par snang de ni/ kun rdzob bden zhes thub pa des gsungs te/ bcos mar gyur pa'i dngos ni kun rdzob tu'o//.* Once again, note the use of "obscurational," which is needed to render *kun rdzob/saṃvṛti* in order to make sense of the gloss, instead of the standard "conventional." Cf. chapter 1, n. 23, for a similar etymological interpretation in *Prasannapadā.*

> This does not demonstrate that those who posit the existence of conventional truth posit through ignorance, nor that from the perspective of the śrāvakas, pratyekabuddhas and bodhisattvas . . . it is not posited as conventional truth. . . . Since it is through afflictive ignorance that one grasps things as truly existent, the object that is thereby grasped cannot exist even conventionally, and whatever is an obscurational truth must exist conventionally.
>
> . . . When it is said that compounded phenomena are "merely conventional" from their perspective, the word "mere" excludes *truth*, but in no way excludes *conventional truth*. . . . Thus, the sense in which the conventional truth is true is that it is true merely from the perspective of ignorance—that is, obscuration.
>
> [When] Candrakīrti . . . says, "since it is obscurationally true, it is obscurational truth" (MavBh 254b), [he] means that conventional truth is that which is true from the perspective of ignorance—obscuration—but not that it is truly existent from the standpoint of nominal convention. (*Ocean* 482)[17]

Tsongkhapa next turns to the question of whether the distinction between conventional and ultimate truth is drawn on the basis of two distinct perspectives on the same reality or on the basis of two distinct natures of that reality. Following Candrakīrti, he adopts the latter position, arguing that when we distinguish conventional from ultimate truth we are distinguishing between two aspects of the object, not between two ways of apprehending the object, despite the fact that we indeed apprehend these aspects by using different faculties:

> Each of the internal and external phenomena has two natures: an ultimate and a conventional nature. The sprout, for instance, has a nature that is found by a rational cognitive process, which sees the real nature of the phenomenon as it is, and a nature that is found by a conventional cognitive process, which perceives deceptive or unreal objects. The former nature is the ultimate truth of the sprout; the latter nature is the conventional truth of the sprout.
>
> [Candrakīrti's assertion that] "It has been shown that each phenomenon has two natures—a conventional and an ultimate nature"

17. Again, note slight translational differences to conform to the standards of this volume.

> (MavBh 253a) does *not* show that a *single* nature is in fact two truths in virtue of the two *perspectives* of the former and latter cognitive process.

The distinction between the two natures or two truths about a phenomenon is drawn, on the other hand, according to both Tsongkhapa and Candrakīrti, on the basis of the kind of epistemic instrument appropriate to each, and it is important that there is a kind of epistemic instrument that is authoritative with respect to each. To be empty and to be deceptive are different. It is one thing for a mirage to be *empty of water*; it is another thing for it to be a *deceptive appearance*. These are two natures of the mirage, and the distinction between them is the difference not between two perspectives on the mirage but between two objects of knowledge, which in turn are apprehended through different cognitive processes.

When one perceives the emptiness of a phenomenon, one perceives a nature that that phenomenon has, regardless of one's perspective on it, and the kind of cognitive process that perceives that emptiness is one that is authoritative with respect to ultimate truth; when one perceives the conventional character of a phenomenon, one perceives its deceptive nature, both the way it appears and the fact that it does not exist in that way, and the kind of cognitive process that perceives that is one that is authoritative with respect to the conventional. On the other hand, to perceive a conventional phenomenon as intrinsically existent is not even to be authoritative with respect to the conventional:

> In order to ascertain a pot for instance, as a deceptive or unreal object, it is necessary to develop the view that refutes . . . the object of fixation that is the object grasped as truly existent. This is because without having rationally refuted its true existence, its unreality is not established by epistemic instruments. So, for the mind to establish anything as an object of conventional truth, it must depend on the refutation of its ultimate existence. (*Ocean* 483)
>
> . . .
>
> Ordinary beings grasp such things as pots as truly existent, and grasp them as ultimately existent as well. Therefore, from the perspective of their minds, such things as pots are ultimately existent, but they are not conventional objects. The things, such as pots, which are ultimately existent from their perspective, are conventional objects from the perspective of the āryas, to whom they appear as illusionlike. Since they cannot be posited as truly existent as they are

apprehended by an āryan consciousness, they are referred to as merely conventional. (*Ocean* 484)

. . .

That which is perceived by ordinary people
By being grasped through any of the six unimpaired sense faculties
Is regarded by ordinary people as real.
All the rest is said to be unreal. (Mav VI.25)[18]

Finally, there is a standard of correctness for conventional truth. Truth, for Candrakīrti and for Tsongkhapa, must contrast with falsehood. And the standard for the truth of a judgment regarding conventional truth is that it is vouchsafed by the authority of conventional epistemic instruments and cannot be undermined by those instruments, just as the standard of truth of a judgment regarding the ultimate is that it is vouchsafed by the authority of ultimate epistemic instruments and not undermined by cognition of that kind. This in turn requires a distinction between sound and impaired conventional faculties:

The internal impairments of the sense faculties are such things as cataracts, jaundice, and such things as hallucinogenic drugs one has consumed. The external impairments of the sense faculties are such things as mirrors, the echoing of sounds in a cave, and the rays of the autumn sun falling on such things as white sand. Even without the internal impairments, these can become the causes of grasping of such things as mirages, reflections and echoes as water, etc . . .

The impairments of the mental faculty are . . . such things as erroneous philosophical views, fallacious arguments and sleep. . . .

Taking conventional objects grasped by such unimpaired and impaired cognitive faculties to be real or unreal, respectively, merely conforms to ordinary cognitive practice. This is because they actually exist as they appear or do not, according to whether or not they are undermined by ordinary cognition. This distinction is not drawn from the perspective of the āryas. This is because just as such things as reflections do not exist as they appear, such things as blue, that appear to exist through their own characteristics to those who are afflicted by ignorance do not actually exist as they appear. Therefore there is no distinction between those two kinds of cognitive faculties in terms of whether or not they are erroneous. (*Ocean* 485)

18. *gnod pa med pa'i dbang po drug rnams kyis/ gzung ba gang zhig 'jig rten gyis rtogs te/ 'jig rten nyid las bden yin lhag ma ni/ 'jig rten nyid las log par rnam par gzhag//.*

Note the emphasis on ordinary cognitive practice. Conventional truth, according to Tsongkhapa, is that which is delivered by unimpaired cognitive faculties when they are used properly. This is not an accidental generalization; instead, it is *constitutive* of conventional truth. It entails that any judgment about truth is in principle revisable but that, *to be true* is to endure through revision. But the distinction between the conventionally true and the conventionally false has nothing to do with ultimate truth. Conventional existents and conventional nonexistents are all ultimately deceptive, all false from the ultimate perspective. Those who are taken in by the conventional fail to understand its deceptive character and so fail to understand the two truths.

The Centrality of Epistemic Authority

The authority of the epistemic instruments is hence central to the story that Candrakīrti tells on Tsongkhapa's interpretation, and that is so in two respects. First, conventional truth is conventionally *true* precisely because it is that which is delivered by conventional epistemic instruments and not undermined by it. Without an antecedent account of these instruments and their authority, there is no way to distinguish conventional truth from conventional falsity. On the one hand, without such an account, we might take only the ultimate epistemic instruments to be authoritative. But then, since all phenomena are ultimately unreal, reliance on these instruments would deliver only the verdict that everything is false, and we would have no domain of truth whatsoever. On the other hand, in the absence of such an account, we might take the object of *any* cognition to be conventionally existent. But that would make a hash of all inquiry, as there is always somebody crazy or deluded enough to believe, or to believe *in*, anything. It is therefore the fact of conventional authority and of the robustness of ordinary epistemic standards that allows us to distinguish truth from falsity and to engage in inquiry in the first place.

Second, the genuine actuality of conventional truth, as opposed to a status simply as an object of deluded thought, is a consequence of the fact that the epistemic instruments of āryas—of those who have transcended the primal ignorance that fabricates intrinsic existence—deliver conventional phenomena as *actual*, although deceptive, phenomena. Once again, the authority of their epistemic instruments doesn't so much *reflect* the fact that it is true that conventional phenomena are existent but *constitutes* their existence, as it constitutes a standard by means of which we can distinguish the true from the false.[19]

19. See chapters 11 and 12 for interesting explorations of how this constitution might be modeled.

Truth for Candrakīrti and Tsongkhapa is always that which is delivered by authoritative epistemic instruments. But what makes these instruments authoritative? Here is where the epistemic rubber hits the soteriological *mārga* and where the term *conventional* (*vyavahāra, tha snyad*) gets its punch. An ultimate epistemic instrument is simply defined as one that is authoritative with respect to ultimate truth. It is hence the kind of cognition finally necessary to attain awakening and to engage in the world informed by awakened consciousness. A conventional epistemic instrument, much more straightforwardly, is just one that is authoritative with regard to what we conventionally accept. As we have seen, Nāgārjuna argues persuasively in *Vigrahavyāvartanī*, this is not a static set—epistemic instruments depend for their authority on their epistemic objects, and the objects, in turn, depend for their actuality on the instruments in a coherentist spiral that defies grounding but characterizes epistemic practice in the only way we could ever hope to do so. Candrakīrti follows Nāgārjuna in accepting the authority of conventional epistemic instruments in the conventional domain.

Seeing Mirages Correctly

We can now see why it is so important to see mirages and to see *that* mirages *are* mirages. Mirages are genuine parts of our world, and they cause real problems. If one were to spend one's life in polarizing sunglasses, one would never know this, and one would be less useful to everyone else. (Of course, if we evolved with polarizing eyes, like some birds, there would be no mirages.) To see a mirage as water is not to see conventional truth but conventional falsehood, for conventional epistemic instruments undermine the assertion that there is water on the road. But conventional epistemic instruments vindicate the claim that there is a mirage that appears to be water. That is why it is conventionally existent.

There are two levels of apprehension of mirages, though. There is a difference between the *novice* desert driver, who *sees* the mirage *as water* but then *infers* its mirage status, and the *experienced* driver, who sees it *as a mirage*. They each apprehend conventional existence, but the first does so as do most of us ordinary but sophisticated Mādhyamikas—inferentially. The latter sees conventional existence as an arhat—immediately, perceptually, noninferentially. *We* see it as deceptive because we are, at least in the first moment of perceptual consciousness, deceived. *The experienced desert driver, or the arhat,* sees the mirage, or reality, as deceptive because she knows what it is like to be us. The transcendence of ignorance is hence not the transcendence of the *apprehension* of the conventional but the transcendence of *deception* by it.

Buddhism is about solving a problem—the problem of the omnipresence of suffering—and the central intuition of Buddhism is that the solution to that problem is the extirpation of ignorance. Epistemology is located at the foundation of morality and gets its point just from that location. The mechanism of the extirpation of ignorance is the competent use of our authoritative epistemic instruments. What that use delivers is hence, at least indirectly, always of soteriological significance—always instrumental to liberation. Inasmuch as that is the central moral virtue, and inasmuch as epistemology is so tightly bound to the soteriological project, it is also the central epistemic virtue, and what we call the goal of epistemic activity is *truth*. Conventional truth is hence not to truth as blunderbusses are to buses or as fake guns are to real guns but rather is simply one kind of *truth*.

The Identity and Difference of the Two Truths

One of the Buddha's deepest insights was that there are two truths and that they are very different from one another. They are the objects of different kinds of cognition, and they reflect different aspects of reality. They are apprehended at different stages of practice. Despite the importance of the apprehension of ultimate truth, one can't skip the conventional. Despite the soteriological efficacy of ultimate truth, even after Buddhahood, omniscience and compassion require the apprehension of the conventional.

Nāgārjuna's deepest insight was that, despite the vast difference between the two truths in one sense, they are, in an equally important sense, identical. We can now make better sense of that identity and of why the fact of their identity is the same fact as that of their difference. Ultimate reality is, as we know, emptiness. Emptiness is the emptiness not of *existence* but of *intrinsic existence*. To be empty of intrinsic existence is to exist only conventionally, only as the object of conventional truth. The ultimate truth about any phenomenon, on this analysis, is hence that it is merely a conventional truth. Ontologically, therefore, the two truths are absolutely identical. This is the content of the idea that the two truths have a single basis: That basis is empty phenomena. Their emptiness is their conventional reality; their conventional reality is their emptiness.

Nonetheless, to *know* phenomena conventionally is not to *know* them ultimately. As objects of knowledge—that is, as intentional contents of thought, as opposed to as mere phenomena—they are objects of different kinds of knowledge despite the identity at a deeper level of those objects. Hence the difference. But the respect in which they are different and that in which they are identical are, despite their difference, also identical. A mirage is deceptive because it is a refraction pattern, and it is the nature of a refraction pattern to be visually deceptive. The conventional truth is merely deceptive and conventional because, upon ultimate analysis, it fails to exist as it appears—that is, because it is ultimately empty. It is the nature of the conventional to deceive. Ultimately, since all phenomena, even ultimate truth, exist only conventionally, conventional truth is all the truth there is, and that is an ultimate and therefore a conventional truth. To fail to take conventional truth seriously as truth is therefore not only to deprecate the conventional in *favor* of the ultimate but also to deprecate *truth* per se. That way lies suffering.

An earlier version of this chapter appeared in *Philosophy East and West*. I (Garfield) thank two anonymous referees for valuable critique of an earlier draft of this paper.

3

Prāsaṅgika Epistemology in Context

Sonam Thakchöe

Some argue that a Prāsaṅgika Mādhyamika is committed to rejecting all epistemic instruments (*pramāṇa*) because they reject intrinsic natures (*svabhāva*) and intrinsic characteristics (*svalakṣaṇa*). This chapter takes a different perspective, arguing that Candrakīrti accepts both conventional and rationally warranted epistemic instruments and develops a cogent account of their respective roles in our cognitive lives. To be sure, any Mādhyamika rejects intrinsic nature, but Candrakīrti shows that epistemic instruments give us access to epistemic objects (*prameya*) precisely because they lack such nature and that each has its appropriate sphere of use simply because, relative to the standards appropriate to those spheres, each apprehends its respective object.

Setting Up the Problem

In the *Madhyamakāvatāra* VI.30, Candrakīrti writes:

> If ordinary cognitions were epistemic instruments (*tshad ma = pramāṇa*), then the mundane cognitions would see the reality as it is.

> Then what necessity would there be for those other noble beings (*āryas*)? What purpose would the noble path serve? It makes no sense that fools are epistemic instruments.[1]

The *Samādhirājasūtra* reads as follows:

> The eye, ear and nose are not epistemic instruments.
> The tongue, body and mind are also not epistemic instruments.
> If these sensory faculties were epistemic instruments,
> Of what purpose would the noble path serve to anyone?[2]

Citing these two sources, Tibetan Mādhyamikas Gorampa (*go rams pa bsod nams seng ge* 1429–1489),[3] Taktsang Lotsawa (*stag tsang lo tsā ba* 1405–?),[4] and Gendün Chöpel (*dge 'dun chos 'phel* 1903–1951)[5] argue that for the Prāsaṅgika Mādhyamika there can be no epistemic instruments at all. These two passages, they argue, leave no doubt that Candrakīrti *unequivocally* rejects conventional cognitions as epistemic instruments. Three key arguments are used to support their position: First, what is ontologically unreal and deceptive must also be epistemically flawed. Since all conventional cognitions are ontologically deceptive and illusory in virtue of being causally conditioned, they must be epistemically flawed. Thus, the so-called conventionally reliable cognition must be rejected unequivocally. Second, mundane cognitions (conventional consciousnesses) all reify their objects under the influence of primal ignorance. Thus, they are all flawed and epistemically unreliable. Third, since no conventional cognitions enable one to perceive ultimate reality directly, they are hence unreliable.

We will, however, argue that Candrakīrti's Prāsaṅgika Madhyamaka does indeed incorporate its own system of śūnyavādin epistemology. Given the scope of this chapter, we will set aside detail and specific issues surrounding

1. *dBu ma* 'a 205b; Candrakīrti (1996b, 156): *gal te 'jig rten tshad ma yin na ni/ 'jig rten de nyid mthong bas 'phags gzhan gyis/ ci dgos 'phags pa'i lam gyis ci zhig bya/ blun po tshad mar rigs pa'ang ma yin no//.*

2. *mDo sde* da, 20b: *mig dang rna ba sna yang tshad ma min/ lce dang lus dang yid kyang tshad ma min/ gal te dbang po 'di dag tshad yin na/ 'phags pa'i lam gyis su la ci zhig bya//.*

3. Gorampa (1969) 375, 382: *'on na kun rdzob 'jal ba'i tshad ma med par 'gyur zhing/ de'ang 'dod na tshig gsal las/ de'i de ltar tshad ma bzhi las 'jig rten gyi don rtogs par rnam par 'jog pa yin no/ zhes gsungs pa dang 'gal lo zhe na/ de ni 'jig rten la ltos nas tshad ma yin pa'i don yin gyi dbu ma pa rang gi bden pa gnyis su phyi ba'i tshe tshad ma min te/ yul brdzun pa mthong ba dang/ yul can tshad ma yin pa 'gal ba'i phyir ro/.*

4. Taktsang (2001, 156–158): *yul kun rdzun dang yul can bslu med 'gal/ yul der 'khrul dang de la tshad ma 'gal/.* In glossing this verse, he writes: *thal 'gyur rang lugs la kun rdzob rdzun par rtogs bzhin pas kun rdzob kyi yul kun rdzob zhing bslu bar 'dod pa dang de'i yul can gyi blo bslu med kyi tshad mar 'dod pa 'gal te/ yul de bslu chos yin na blo de tshad mar song ma srid pa'i phyir/ dper na skra shad snang pa'i blo bzhin no/.*

5. Gedün Chöpel (1990, 161): *yod med blo yis bzhag pa'i shes bya dang/ bden rdzun yul la ltos pa'i tshad ma gnyis/ gcig gi rdzun khungs gcig la gtad mthong nas/ tha snyad tshad grub 'jog la blo ma bde// ma brtag ma dpyad 'jig rten rnam gzhag dang/ brtags shing dpyad pa'i grub mtha'i gzhung lugs gnyis/ gcig gi rtsa ba gcig la thug mthong na/ tha snyad tshad grub 'jog la blo ma bde//.*

Candrakīrti's conception of perceptual cognition (*pratyakṣa*) and inferential cognition (*anumāna*) and focus on Candrakīrti's general conception of the reliability of cognition as it is presented in his major works on the Madhyamaka—*Prasannapadā*, *Madhyamakāvatāra*, *Madhyamakāvatārabhāṣya*, and *Catuḥśatakaṭīkā* (*CST*). Section 1 addresses Candrakīrti's definition of a mundane epistemic instrument and argues that Prāsaṅgika Mādhyamikas (the cowherds on up, including *arhats, āryas, bodhisattvas, buddhas*, deluded ordinary beings) are, for Candrakīrti, "mundane cognitive agents." All persons are equipped with reliable, conventionally nondeceptive epistemic instruments that enable them to create and participate in the mundane epistemic convention with which the Prāsaṅgika is in agreement.

Section 2 addresses Candrakīrti's explanation of how Prāsaṅgikas accept epistemic instruments within the conventional context. I argue that, for Candrakīrti, being an epistemic instrument is a status that is conditioned and acquired and therefore lacks real foundations. Conventional epistemic instruments (*tha snyad pa'i tshad ma*) meet only the standards of the Prāsaṅgikas' conventional epistemic practices, whereas rationally warranted epistemic instruments (*rigs shes kyi tshad ma*) fulfill the standard of the Prāsaṅgikas' ultimate, or critical, epistemic practices.[6] Sections 3, 4, and 5 explore Candrakīrti's arguments in support of this account of two sorts of epistemic instruments and argue that, on Candrakīrti's account, ontologically deceptive, empty, false, and illusion-like epistemic instruments are nonetheless epistemically efficient and reliable; this is because, although they are empty of any given intrinsic natures (*svabhāva, svalakṣaṇa*), they are nonetheless epistemic instruments in relation to their principle epistemic objects (*prameya*).

Epistemic Instruments in the Mundane Context

We begin with Candrakīrti's definition. In the *Catuḥśatakaṭīkā* he says, "[N]ondeceptive cognition is regarded as an epistemic instrument in the world."[7] There are two key issues raised in Candrakīrti's definition of epistemic

6. The term *rigs shes*, which we are translating as "rationally warranted cognition," means a cognition that engages with its object analytically (in contrast to mundane cognitions, which engage with their objects nonanalytically). Rationally warranted cognition, however, is itself not intrinsically established and, therefore, just like any other object, does not withstand analysis by reason (*rigs pas dpyad mi bzod pa*). It is thus the type of critical cognition that enables āryas to understand that the ultimate status of things is that nothing is established through an intrinsic nature. It is of course not simply any understanding that proceeds through reasoning and is not to be confused with simple "inference" (*anumāna*). The term is purely Tibetan in origin and has no Sanskrit equivalent.

7. *dBu ma* ya 197b, Candrakīrti (1996a, 334): *mi slu ba'i shes pa ni 'jig rten na tshad ma nyid du mthong na //*.

instrument: (1) the defining criterion of a reliable epistemic instrument and (2) the context within which it is defined. On the first point, Candrakīrti clearly admits the nondeceptiveness of a cognition as the defining criterion for it to be an epistemic instrument. The nondeceptiveness at issue here is only conditional in that it is what is acceptable in mundane practice. In the analysis of the compound *lokasaṃvṛtisatya* (mundane conventional truth/reality) in *Prasannapadā* XXIV, Candrakīrti shows the nondeceptive character of mundane epistemic conventions:

> On the other hand, the "non-mundane" (*aloka*) are those [people] who live seeing erroneously due to their sense organs being damaged by opthalmia, cataracts, jaundice and the like. A convention (*saṃvṛti*) that such [people] might have is not [regarded as] a mundane convention (*alokasaṃvṛti*). Thus (*ato*) one specifies (*viśeṣyate*) "real according to mundane conventions" (*lokasaṃvṛtisatya*).[8]

Candrakīrti's argument hinges on an important distinction he draws between two mundane epistemic practices: One he calls "mundane convention" (*lokasaṃvṛti*), and the other "not [even] mundane convention" (*alokasaṃvṛti*). He regards the former as a mundane epistemic instrument, as it is conventionally authoritative and reliable; the latter he denies to be a mundane epistemic instrument since it is not reliable even conventionally. He thus regards it as conventionally *deceptive* by the mundane standards. Since mundane cognitions of ordinary beings—and arguably those of *arhats, āryas,* and *buddhas* as well—satisfy the epistemic standards of mundane conventions, they are, unlike defective cognitions, conventional epistemic instruments; they are thus part of the process that constitutes conventional truth, contrary to cognitions of "that which is not [even] mundane convention" (*alokasaṃvṛti*), such as hairs falling from the sky or yellow snow.

The second point raised in Candrakīrti's definition of epistemic instruments is critical in order to contextualize the definition. Candrakīrti clearly states that the type of nondeceptiveness that is the defining criterion of an epistemic instrument is one that is accepted within the realm of *loka*—the mundane, worldly, or ordinary. This restates the point that the criterion of the Prāsaṅgika's epistemic practice accords with mundane conventions

8. *dBu ma* 'a 163ab; Candrakīrti (2003, 440); Tib. in May (1959, 432); Skt. ed. LVP 493.2–4: *rnam pa gcig tu na / rab rib dang ling thog sngon po dang / mig ser la sogs pas dbang po nyams pas mthong ba phyin ci log la[1] gnas pa de dag ni 'jig rten ma yin te / de dag gi kun rdzob gang yin pa de ni / 'jig rten kun rdzob[2] ma yin pas / 'jig rten kun rdzob bden pa[3] / zhes de las khyad par du byas so //*. [1] Read *la*, following Peking, Narthang, May; [2] Omit *bden pa* following May. *Satya* is absent in Skt.; [3] Omit *dang*, following May and Skt.

(*lokaprasiddha, 'jig rten grags pa*) and that the nondeceptivity in question is only nondeceptivity *within the mundane context.*

The key term in Candrakīrti's definition that positions or contextualizes his definition of epistemic instrument is *loka*. Given that the term *loka* plays a significant role in shaping Candrakīrti's epistemology, it is worth asking, What is *loka?* In *Prasannapadā*, Candrakīrti attributes at least three interconnected criteria for applying the term *loka*. Here are the first two:

> Here the doctrine taught by the illustrious buddhas is based on the exposition of the two truths. What are two truths? They are the truth of mundane convention (*lokasaṃvṛtisatya*) and the ultimate truth (*paramārthasatya*). As it is said: "The *aggregates* themselves are known as *loka*, indeed they are that upon which the *loka* definitively depends" (*Brahmaviśeṣacintāparipṛcchāsūtra, mDo sde* ba 36b). It follows that *loka* is the *person* (*pudgala*) designated dependently upon the aggregates.[9]

For Candrakīrti *loka* is thus (1) the aggregates and (2) the person designated dependently upon the aggregates. Hence, according to commentators such as Tsongkhapa, *loka* applies to all sentient beings that are *persons*. Not only ordinary confused beings but also enlightened beings—*āryas, arhats, bodhisattvas,* and *buddhas* are, on this characterization of *loka*, "mundane," "worldly," or "ordinary."

A third criterion for applying the term *loka* is that its understanding must proceed nonanalytically (*avicāratas*). It is this nonanalytical mode of engagement of mundane cognitions (of all persons) that determines what Candrakīrti calls "mundane convention" (*lokasaṃvṛti*). Candrakīrti hence excludes from mundane epistemic convention, critical rational insight (*rigs shes*) inquiring into the metaphysical character of how things really are, how things are ultimately. Conventional or ordinary epistemic practice, according to Candrakīrti, does not require the analysis of whether things visually seen, sounds heard, aromas smelled, tactile sensations felt, or ideas thought have intrinsic natures or ultimate reality.

The Prāsaṅgikas' account of epistemology is defined within the realm of the mundane practice, and their epistemic practice accords with mundane convention (*lokaprasiddha, 'jig rten grags sde spyod pa*). As far as Candrakīrti is

9. *dBu ma* 'a 163a; Candrakīrti (2003, 339); May (1959, 432): *di na sangs rgyas bcom ldan 'das rnams kyis chos bstan pa ni / bden pa gnyis la brten nas 'jug go / bden pa gnyis gang zhe na / 'jig rten kun rdzob kyi bden pa dang / don dam pa'i bden pa'o// de la / 'jig rten phung por rab grags pa / de la 'jig rten nges par brten / zhes 'byung ba las na phung po la brten nas brtags pa'i gang zag la 'jig rten zhes brjod do //*. Skt ed. LVP 492.6–9.

concerned, all cognitive agents are *mundane beings* to the extent that they all fulfill the triple criteria of *loka:* (1) all have nonanalytical cognitions, (2) all are constituted by the five "aggregates," and (3) all are "persons designated dependently upon the aggregate." So it is nondeceptive and nonanalytical cognition that determines the criterion of mundane convention, sets the standard of conventional epistemic practice, and is therefore regarded as a conventional epistemic instrument. A conventional epistemic instrument is a common epistemic faculty potentially available all across cognitive agents—because everyone has eyes, ears, nose, tongue, body, mind (except for the last, all engage their objects nonanalytically in all persons.)[10] So for Candrakīrti the Prāsaṅgika is a *player* in mundane conventions, not a *silent spectator.* It is in this sense the Prāsaṅgika is said to be epistemically in accord with worldly convention.[11]

Two Epistemic Instruments: Rationally Warranted and Conventional

Candrakīrti applies this account of mundane convention to define *epistemic instruments* in the context of the two truths. In the *Catuḥśatakaṭīkā,* while commenting on verse 280, Candrakīrti recognizes inferential (*anumāna*) and perceptual (*pratyakṣa*) cognitions as epistemic instruments.[12] In the *Madhyamakāvatāra* VI.23, however, he uses two kinds of epistemic instruments—conventional and rationally warranted—to explain the knowledge of conventional and ultimate realities, that is, to define the two as two natures of a single entity ascertained by two forms of nondeceptive cognition. Candrakīrti's definitions of the two truths read as follows:

> All things bear two natures (*rūpa*) found (*labdha*) by correct (*samyag*) and false (*mṛṣā*) views. The object of those who see correctly is said to

10. However, *loka* excludes two types of cognitions: *rigs shes,* that is, reasoning that critically engages and analyzes ultimate truth, and defective sense faculties, which are considered deceptive even by the standard of worldly epistemic practice.

11. If *loka* comprises exclusively naïve ordinary beings (*so skye, pṛthagjana*), as Gorampa claims it is, then the mundane conventions (*lokasaṃvṛti*) to which the Mādhyamika accords (*'jig rten grags sde spyod pa*) will be conventions purely constructed by the deluded ordinary beings. Conventional epistemic standards thus will have nothing whatsoever in common with the Mādhyamika's own account of knowledge. For a partial defense of Gorampa on this point, see chapter 9

12. *dBu ma* ya 186b; Candrakīrti (1996a, 312): *dngos po thams cad mngon sum du shes pas go bar bya ba ni ma yin gyi rjes su dpag pas rtogs par bya ba yang yod do*—"It is not the case that all things are cognizable by means of perceptual consciousness; there are also those cognizable by means of inferences." Manifest objects give rise to perceptually valid cognition, and nonapparent or occult objects give rise to inferentially valid cognition. This follows on Candrakīrti's account since, as we will see later, it is the objects that determine the epistemic status of cognitions.

> be "reality" (*tattva*) and the object of those who see falsely is said to be "conventional existence" (*saṃvṛtisatya*).[13]

So, according to Candrakīrti, just as every conventionally real phenomenon has two natures that correspond to the two truths, all competent cognitive agents have two nondeceptive cognitive capacities enabling them to apprehend the two truths. While rational insight takes *ultimate* truth to be its principal object, a rationally warranted epistemic instrument such as an *ārya*'s wisdom is *not*, in Candrakīrti's view, an *ultimate truth*. Instead, it is a conventional phenomenon and is *unreal, deceptive*, and illusory, just like any other conventional entity. A *conventional* epistemic instrument is, on the other hand, nondeceptive in conventional terms since its principal object of engagement is conventional reality.

Candrakīrti's definition of the two truths/realities in *Madhyamakāvatāra* VI.23 provides us two arguments to support the thesis that the two epistemic instruments deliver their cognitive objects very differently, each making its own contribution to knowledge without undermining the other. First, rational insight is *not* capable of apprehending conventional entities because, while a conventional entity is always posited nonanalytically, rational insight engages with its object analytically. Hence, conventional reality is not regarded as its principal epistemic object, whereas ultimate reality is. It follows that, while Candrakīrti regards rational insight as nondeceptive with respect to the ultimate, he denies the nondeceptive status of rational insight with regard to the conventional. Hence, not even the *ārya*'s transcendent wisdom in meditative equipoise or any form of analytical cognition is considered as a nondeceptive means of knowing the conventional.

Second, no conventional epistemic instrument is capable of apprehending ultimate reality because, while ultimate reality is always posited analytically, conventional cognition engages with its object nonanalytically. Therefore, *no* conventional cognition, in Candrakīrti's view, is authoritative with respect to the ultimate:

> It makes no sense that ordinary understanding would elucidate understanding of reality. For one thing, it is an epistemic instrument only with respect to mundane reality. Its apprehended object is proven to have the property of existing falsely and deceptively (*brdzun pa bslu ba'i chos can*).[14]

13. *dBu ma* 'a 205a; Candrakīrti (1996b, 155): *dngos kun yang dag brdzun pa mthong pa yis/ dngos rnyed ngo bo gnyis ni 'dzin par 'gyur/ yang dag mthong yul gang de de nyid de/ mthong ba brdzun pa kun rdzob bden par gsungs/.*

14. *dbu ma* ya 202b; Candrakīrti (1996a, 343): *'jig rten pa'i mthong bas de kho na nyid mthong ba gsal bar rigs pa yang ma yin te / de ni 'jig rten pa kho na las tshad ma nyid yin pa'i phyir dang / des dmigs pa'i don yang brdzun pa bslu ba'i chos can nyid du bsgrubs pa'i phyir ro //.* Cf. Tillemans (1990, 188, §57).

Therefore, neither form of cognition encroaches upon the epistemic domain of the other. Nevertheless, these two epistemic pathways—analytical and nonanalytical—are jointly necessary to deliver ultimate knowledge. Reflection on the selflessness of the person, for example, requires both nonanalytically seeing the five aggregates using conventional cognition and critically establishing them to be selfless by rational insight. If rational insight is excluded, the nonanalytical perspective on the person would remain, but from this perspective one would not be able to establish the person to be selfless, as this requires critical analysis. Similarly, if the role of conventional cognition is excluded, one would not be able to see the conventionally real person, and without this conventional basis, there would be no basis of the knowledge of the ultimate truth.

Rational insight (*rigs shes*): Ontologically Deceptive, Epistemically Nondeceptive

For Candrakīrti, the two forms of cognition are nondeceptive in delivering conventional and ultimate knowledge, respectively, as they satisfy the criterion for being an authoritative epistemic instrument. They are, at the same time, empty of any intrinsic nature. That is, they are *ontologically* empty, deceptive, false and illusion-like in spite of being *epistemically* nondeceptive. Candrakīrti says in his *Catuḥśatakaṭīkā* commenting on XIII.301:

> Given the world regards non-deceptive (*mi slu ba*) consciousnesses as being epistemic instruments, then the Transcendental Victor said that consciousness too, as it is a conditioned phenomenon (*'dus byas*), is false, deceptive and illusion-like. That which is false, deceptive and illusory-like cannot be non-deceptive because while such an entity exists in one way it appears in another. Thus it makes no sense to say that such an entity is an epistemic instrument, otherwise it would follow absurdly that all consciousnesses would be epistemic instruments.[15]

All epistemic instruments, including rational insight, are empty of intrinsic nature because they are produced phenomena; all cognitions are deceptive because they exist in one way and appear in a different way. While they are

15. *dBu ma* ya 197b; Candrakīrti (1996a, 334): *mi slu ba'i shes pa ni 'jig rten na tshad ma nyid du mthong na / rnam par shes pa yang bcom ldan ldas kyis 'dus byas yin pa'i phyir brdzun pa bslu pa'i chos can dang sgyu ma lta bur gsungs so / /gang zhig brdzun pa bslu ba'i chos can dang sgyu ma lta bu yin pa de ni mi bslu ba ma yin te/ rnam pa gzhan du gnas pa'i dngos po la rnam pa gzhan du snang pa'i phyir ro/ de lta bur gyur pa ni tshad ma nyid du brtag par rigs pa ma yin te/ rnam par shes pa thams cad kyang tshad ma nyid du thal par 'gyur pa'i phyir ro / /*. Cf. also Tillemans (1990, 179, §16).

conditioned phenomena and become what they are in virtue of their epistemic objects (*prameya*) and utterly lack any mode of ontological foundation, cognitions do *appear* to be *intrinsically characterized*, intrinsically given as cognitions.

Therefore, the distinction between what counts and what does not count as an epistemic instrument (both conventional and rationally warranted), in Candrakīrti's view, should not be drawn on the basis on the ontological character of the cognition in question. All cognitions are ontologically deceptive, false, and illusory. Nonetheless, it is not contradictory for cognition to be ontologically false and deceptive and at the same time epistemically nondeceptive and reliable. While rational insight is ontologically unreal, deceptive, and illusory, *epistemically* it effectively apprehends the nature of the principal object it is engaged with: ultimate reality. For this reason rational insight is indicated in *Madhyamakāvatāra* VI.23 by the phrase "correct views" (*samyagdarśana, yang dag mthong ba*); the principal object it apprehends is indicated by the phrase "object of those who see correctly" (*samyagdṛśāṃ yo viṣayaḥ, yang dag mthong yul*). In fact, rational insight is so-called in virtue of the fact that it delivers knowledge of how things really are and in virtue of the fact that there is concordance between how this subject sees the object and how the object really is. Therefore, the two seemingly contradictory properties of rational insight—that it is ontologically deceptive and epistemologically nondeceptive—are not only consistent but in fact complement each other as well.

Conventional Cognition: Epistemically Both Nondeceptive and Deceptive

As we have seen, Candrakīrti views conventional and rationally warranted epistemic instruments as having identical ontological characteristics. Epistemically, however, they are viewed differently. Candrakīrti's account of conventional epistemic instruments must be understood both with reference to conventional reality, ultimate reality, and with respect to the cognitive capacity of the epistemic agent.

Candrakīrti maintains that any conventional epistemic instrument is necessarily *epistemically nondeceptive* with reference to conventional reality. With respect to the ultimate, on the other hand, Candrakīrti maintains that conventional epistemic instruments are *epistemically deceptive* (with the sole exception of a buddha's sensory faculties). There are several reasons for this: (1) The principal object of conventional cognition always appears to its subject *deceptively*, as more than just conventional reality—it appears to the cognizing subject as having *svabhāva, svalakṣaṇa*, that is, intrinsic properties with an objectively given mode of existence independent of the mind's reifying and interpretive functions; (2) conventional cognition, according to Candrakīrti, engages with its principal object nonanalytically. Therefore, it operates on the basis of how things appear to it rather than critically assessing whether the object exists as it appears. Conventional cognition correctly apprehends its principal object and therefore is nondeceptive—its only error is to grasp its principal object as metaphysically founded, as if it possessed *svabhāva;* (3) conventional cognition is also differentiated with reference to the cognitive maturity of the epistemic agent in question. Candrakīrti claims that the conventional cognitions of fully enlightened buddhas are the only ones that are *nondeceptive* with respect to ultimate reality.[16] The conventional cognitions of every other sentient being—arhats, ārya-bodhisattvas, ordinary beings—are all *deceptive* to various degrees with respect to ultimate reality. This error is due to the force of the conditioning ignorance operating within the mental continuum of all nonawakened beings.

Candrakīrti is not claiming that the conventional cognitions of a buddha establish ultimate reality to the extent that a rationally warranted epistemic instrument is said to know ultimate reality. If Candrakīrti were claiming this, he would contradict the following: (1) his definition of the two truths in *Madhyamakāvatāra* VI.23; (2) his definition of epistemic instruments as nondeceptive cognitions in the *Catuḥśatakaṭīkā* (see n. 15) and his ascription of nonanalytical functioning to conventional cognition and analytical functioning to rational insight; and finally (3) his assertion that the Prāsaṅgika accords with the worldly convention.

The first would follow because, by definition, ultimate reality is apprehended by rational insight and conventional reality by conventional cognition. The second would follow because a buddha's conventional perceptual faculties would end up having to analytically engage with their principal objects since, without critical engagement, ultimate reality—that is, emptiness—is not apprehended. Likewise, there would be the absurdity that a buddha's rational insight would have to engage with its principal object nonanalytically, without which the conventional is not apprehended.

The third would follow because, if a buddha's rational insight, with its *analytical* mode of engagement, saw conventional truth, it would undermine mundane convention since Candrakīrti clearly says that the mundane epistemic convention is based on conventional cognition's nonanalytical mode of engagement. If, on the other hand, a buddha's conventional cognition, with its *nonanalytical* mode of engagement, were to see ultimate reality, it would follow that mundane senses could be, after all, authoritative with respect to ultimate

16. *rnam kun mkhyen nyid ye shes ni / mngon sum mtshan nyid can du 'dod / gzhan ni nyi tshe ba nyid kyis / mngon sum zhes byar mi 'dod do /* Mav VI.214.

reality. And this would contradict Candrakīrti's *Madhyamakāvatāra* VI.30 (quoted in the earlier section titled "Setting Up the Problem"). There it was stated that if mundane cognitions saw the reality of things as they are, the noble path leading to the cessation of suffering would become redundant. As everyone would see the reality as it is, they would already be released, and hence there would be no need for the noble path.

So how are we to understand Candrakīrti's claim that a buddha's conventional cognition knows ultimate reality? Tsongkhapa proposes a solution to this problem.[17] In *dBu ma dgongs pa rab gsal* Tsongkhapa defends Candrakīrti's claim that a buddha's conventional cognition is nondeceptive with respect to ultimate truth by stressing the concordance between the buddha's conventional and rational insights. This concordance, on Tsongkhapa's interpretation of Candrakīrti, would allow a buddha to have direct and simultaneous knowledge of the two realities, for "when all traces of misconception have been eradicated, the two sorts of enlightened knowledge (*ye shes*) arise uninterruptedly with one nature (*ngo bo gcig*) in each and every moment of enlightened knowledge."[18] By saying that the two sorts of enlightened knowledge "arise uninterruptedly with one nature (*ngo bo gcig*)," Tsongkhapa stresses that and explains how the cognitive activities of a buddha's conventional and rational insight are intertwined. By knowing the conventional, a buddha knows the ultimate, and by knowing the ultimate, a buddha also knows the conventional. Tsongkhapa argues that the uncritical cognitive engagement of every single conventional cognition of an enlightened person is accompanied by the critical cognitive engagement of a rational insight and vice versa. Therefore, at the level of buddhahood, two cognitions no longer function alternatively or separately; they operate simultaneously.

Tsongkhapa's second argument is drawn from the equal cognitive status of a buddha's meditative equipoise and subsequent attainment.[19] Here it is argued that for a buddha these two cognitive states have the same status on

17. For a detailed discussion of this topic, see Thakchöe (2007, 133–158).

18. Tsongkhapa (1984, 201): *'khrul pa'i bag chags ma lus pa spangs pa na ye shes skad cig ma re re'i steng du yang ye shes gnyis ngo bo gcig tu skye ba rgyun mi 'chad pa . . . //.*

19. The meaning attributed to the term *subsequent attainment* (*rjes thob* = *pṛṣṭhalabdha*) by Tsongkhapa is radically different from that of most non-Gelug scholars. For the latter scholars *rjes thob* means "aftermath of meditative equipoise (*mnyam gzhag*)" and is translated as "postmeditation." For Tsongkhapa *rjes thob* means "subsequent attainment." It does not mean the aftermath of the meditative equipoise in the sense of occurring afterward; rather, it means "an attainment due to the power of meditative equipoise, or what is generated from it." See *dGongs pa rab gsal* (Tsongkhapa 1984, 459): *rjes la thob pa zhes pa'i rjes kyi don ni/ mnyam gzhag las langs pa'i rjes zhes dus snga phyi'i rjes min gyi mnyam gzhag de'i stobs kyis thob pa'am byung ba'i don no//.* This is an important distinction for Tsongkhapa, for it allows him to argue that knowledge of both the "subsequent attainment" and "meditative equipoise" of an enlightened being have an equal status, whereas Gorampa and his counterparts argue that the meditative equipoise is superior to the aftermath.

the grounds that a buddha does not alternate between meditative equipoise (wherein rational insight is seen as playing its dominant role) and subsequent attainment (wherein conventional cognition is seen as playing its dominant role):

> Once all the traces of the conception of true existence have been thoroughly eradicated, one attains buddhahood. Thereafter [a buddha] continuously abides in meditative equipoise, directly knowing ultimate truth. Thus there is no longer any alternation between the meditative equipoise and the subsequent attainment which arises from it.[20]

So for Tsongkhapa, whether a buddha appears to be in meditative equipoise or engaged in mundane activities—walking, sitting, standing, or lying down—the mind of an enlightened being does not deviate from direct knowledge of the ultimate truth. "Because there is no enlightened knowledge consisting in a subsequent attainment cognizing phenomenal objects that is distinct in nature (*ngo bo tha dad*) from the enlightened knowledge of meditative equipoise, it should be accepted," Tsongkhapa argues, "that a single moment of enlightened knowledge knows all cognizable objects comprising the two realities."[21] With the end of the alternation between types of cognition of the two realities, the usual qualitative distinction between the cognitive status of meditative equipoise and that of postmeditation no longer applies.[22]

In Tsongkhapa's view, then, an enlightened being still has two modes of knowing ultimate reality. The first way is to know things as *empty*—knowing "*space-like emptiness* (*nam mkha' lta bu'i stong nyid*)" during meditative equipoise by simply negating all dualities such as production and cessation by means of a buddha's critical, rational insight.[23] The second way is to know things as *dependently arising*—knowing "*illusion-like emptiness* (*sgyu ma lta bu'i stong nyid*)" during the subsequent attainment resulting from a meditative equipoise.[24] Moreover, given the identity of emptiness (ultimate reality) and dependent arising (conventional reality) in Candrakīrti's ontology, knowing emptiness and knowing dependent arising are also identical in epistemic

20. Ibid., 458: *bden 'dzin gyi bag chags ma lus pa zad de sangs rgyas pa nas dus rtag tu don dam bden pa mngon sum du rtogs pa'i mnyam gzhag las bzhugs pas/ de las bzhengs pa'i mnyam rjes res 'jog med pa'i phyir//.*

21. Ibid., 458–459: *mnyam gzhag ye shes de las ngo bo tha dad pa'i ji snyad pa mkhyen pa'i rjes thob kyi ye shes med pa'i phyir na/ ye shes gcig gis bden pa gnyis kyi shes bya thams cad mkhyen par 'dod dgos so//.*

22. Ibid., 201: *dus gcig tu shes bya mngon gsum du 'jal mi 'jal gyi res 'jog mi dgos so//.*

23. Tsongkhapa (1993, 742): *rigs pa'i shes pas chos can snang ba la skye 'gag sogs kyi rang bzhin rnam pa bcad pa tsam gyi stong pa la nam mkha' lta bu'i stong nyid//.*

24. Ibid.: *de nas rang bzhin gyis stong yang rang bzhin du snang ba'i gzugs sogs kyi snang ba 'char ba la sgyu ma lta bu'i stong nyid ces sngon gyi mkhas pa rnams gsungs so//.*

terms. Therefore, a buddha is said to know both realities simultaneously. The upshot is that Candrakīrti's claim that buddha's conventional cognition knows ultimate reality does not amount to a claim that a buddha's conventional cognition *by itself* is authoritative with respect to the ultimate. Similarly, Candrakīrti's claim that a buddha's rational insight knows conventional reality does not amount to a claim that a buddha's rational insight *by itself* knows the conventional. Hence, a buddha's unique cognitive capacity neither makes his or her two cognitions redundant nor threatens the consistency of Candrakīrti's definitions of the two realities.

Antifoundationalism: Empty Cognitions and Empty Objects

According to Candrakīrti, cognitions are epistemically efficient just because they are utterly empty of intrinsic nature (*svabhāva*), even conventionally. As he explains in *Madhyamakāvatāra* VI.37–38ab:

> Empty entities such as reflections, which depend upon collections
> [of causes],
> Are not unacknowledged things.
> Just as consciousness can be seen to arise from an empty reflection,
> Having it as its representational content,
> In the same way entities, although all empty,
> Arise from emptinesses.[25]

The heart of Candrakīrti's epistemology is the claim that only because they are empty can cognitions be epistemically efficient. Therefore, cognition (even so-called transcendent wisdom) must be empty of any intrinsic nature that makes it a knower, and its apprehended objects are empty of any intrinsic nature that makes them determinate, known objects. Only in the context of a categorical rejection of any foundationalism, both ontological and epistemic, can there be epistemic practices rooted in the mutually interdependent character of *cognition* and *object cognized*.[26] This distinctive trademark of

25. *dBu ma* 'a 206a: *dngos po stong pa gzugs brnyan la sogs pa / tshogs la ltos rnams ma grags pa yang min / ji ltar der ni gzugs brnyan sogs stong las / shes pa de yi rnam par skye 'gyur ltar // de bzhin dngos po thams cad stong na yang / stong nyid dag las rab tu skye bar 'gyur /.*

26. For the use of the term *foundationalism* in the epistemological context, see Garfield's remarks in chapter 2, n. 8. We are also speaking of "ontological foundationalism," that is, the typical position in Indian Buddhist philosophy that at least certain things must exist by their intrinsic natures and as fully real if nihilism is to be avoided and purely conventional entities are to be possible at all. Cf. also the use of the term in Arnold (2005) and Tillemans (2003).

Candrakīrti's Prāsaṅgika epistemology is inspired by Nāgārjuna's statement in MMK XXIV.14:

> To whomsoever emptiness makes sense,
> Everything makes sense.
> To whomsoever emptiness makes no sense,
> Nothing makes sense.[27]

Candrakīrti glosses this passage in the *Prasannapadā* as follows:

> To whom the emptiness of [the] intrinsic nature of all things makes sense, all that we have discussed makes sense. Why? Because we maintain emptiness to be dependent arising. Therefore, for whomsoever emptiness makes sense, dependent arising makes sense. For whomsoever dependent arising makes sense, the four noble truths make sense. This is why it makes sense: only the dependently arisen suffers, but not that which is nondependently arisen. Since it has no intrinsic nature, it is empty. Since there is suffering, there is origin of suffering, a cessation of suffering, and meditation on path. Since these exist, *knowledge* of suffering, elimination of origin, cessation of suffering, and attainment of path make sense. When *knowledge* of truth of suffering and the like exists, effects also make sense.[28]

Candrakīrti goes on to argue that all mundane conventions makes sense—that is, the buddha, dharma, saṃgha, mundane, supramundane, the sacred, the profane, and so on all make sense—because of their being empty of intrinsic nature and therefore being dependently arisen. Candrakīrti's exegesis on the Nāgārjuna's MMK XXI. 14 concludes in these words:

> All special *knowledge* of all the mundane and supramundane dharmas makes sense. Dharma, adharma and their fruits, and mundane conventions also make sense. For this reason for

27. *gang la stong pa nyid rung ba / de la thams cad rung bar 'gyur / gang la stong nyid mi rung ba / de la thams cad mi rung 'gyur //.*

28. *dBu ma* 'a 166a; Candrakīrti (2003, 447): *gang la dgnos po thams cad rang bzhin gyis stong pa nyid 'di rung ba de la ji skad smras pa de dag thams cad rung bar 'gyur ro / /ji ltar zhe na / gang gi phyir kho bo cag ni rten cing 'brel par 'byung ba la stong pa nyid ces smra ste / de'i phyir / gang la stong pa nyid 'di rung ba de la rten cing 'brel bar 'byung ba rung la / gang la rten cing 'brel bar 'byung ba rung ba de la 'phags pa'i bden pa bzhi rnams rung bar 'gyur ro / /ji ltar zhe na / gang gi phyir rten cing 'brel bar 'byung ba nyid sdug bsngal du 'gyur gyi / rten cing 'brel bar mi 'byung ba ni ma yin no / de ni rang bzhin med pas stong par 'gyur ro / /sdug bsngal yod na ni sdug bsngal kun 'byung ba dang / sdug bsngal 'gog pa dang / sdug bsngal 'gog par 'gro ba'i lam rung bar 'gyur ro / de'i phyir sdug bsngal yongs su shes pa dang / kung 'byung spang ba dang / 'gog pa mngon du bya ba dang / lam bsgom par yang rung ngo / sdug bsngal la sogs pa'i bden pa yongs su shes pa la sogs pa yod na ni 'bras bu rnams rung bar 'gyur ro / /.* Skt. ed. LVP 500.5–501.1.

whomsoever emptiness makes sense, everything makes sense. For whomsoever emptiness makes no sense, dependent arising would not make sense. Hence nothing would make sense.[29]

In Nāgārjuna's *Vigrahavyāvartanī* the discussion centers on four epistemic instruments (*pramāṇa*): perceptual cognition (*pratyakṣa*), inferential cognition (*anumāna*), verbal testimony (*āgama*), and analogy (*upamāna*).[30] In the opponent's (most likely quite accurate) portrayal of Nāgārjuna's stance, these four epistemic instruments, as well as the objects known by them, are all said to be empty (*śūnya*) because every entity is empty of intrinsic nature.[31] Candrakīrti goes further and admits[32] "that mundane objects are known by the means of

29. *dBu ma* 'a 166b; ibid., 447–448: *'jig rten pa dang 'jig rten las 'das pa'i chos thams ca khyad par du rtogs pa thams cad kyang rung la / chos dang chos ma yin pa dang / de'i 'bras bu dang / 'jig rten pa'i tha snyad dag kyang rung bar 'gyur ro / / de'i phyir de ltar na / gang la stong pa nyid rung ba de la thams cad rung bar 'gyur ro / /gang la stong pa nyid mi rung ba de la rten cing 'brel bar 'byung ba nyid med pas / thams cad mi rung bar 'gyur ro / /*. Skt. ed. LVP 501.4–8.

30. Cf. the opponent's objection in VV 6; Yonezawa (2008, 231): *rjes dpag lung dang dpes 'jal dang // rjes dpag lung gis bsgrub bya dang // dpes bsgrub bya ba'i don gang yin // mngon gsum gyis ni lan btab po //* "Through [our discussion of] perception [in VV 5], we have already replied to (i.e., argued against) inference, testimony, analogy, as well as the objects to be established by inference and testimony and those to be established by analogies." Cf. Bhattacharya (1986, 99).

31. Yonezawa (2008, 231): *'di ltar mngon sum gyi tshad ma ni stong pa yin te / dngos po tham cad stong pa nyid yin pa'i phyir ro / de bzhin du rjes su dpag pa dang / dpes 'jal ba dang / lung yang stong pa yin te / dngos po thams cad stong pa nyid yin pa'i phyir ro / rjes su dpag pas bsgrub par bya ba'i don dang / dpes bsgrub par bya ba gang yin pa de dag kyang stong pa yin te / dngos po thams cad stong pa nyid yin pa'i phyir ro / rjes su dpag pa dang lung dang dpes 'jal ba dag gis dngos po rnams la dmigs par byed pa gang yin pa de yang stong pa nyid yin te / de'i phyir dngos po rnams dmigs pa med do / mi dmigs pa'i rang bzhin 'gog pa mi thad pas de la dngos po thams cad ni stong pa'o zhes smras pa gang yin pa de mi rung ngo //*. For translation see Bhattacharya (1986, 99–100).

32. In his "Madhyamaka Critique of Epistemology" Mark Siderits claims the fact that Candrakīrti has the list of four epistemic instruments is an indication that the Prāsaṅgika endorses the Nyāya theory of knowledge. In Siderits's words, "It is clear that he takes their account of the four *pramāṇas* as a model description of our epistemic practices" (Siderits 1981, 157). In the current volume Siderits claims that Candrakīrti endorses Nyāya epistemology rather than Dignāga's because Nyāya epistemology is less open to the reductionist project than is Yogācāra-Sautrāntika epistemology. I agree that there exist some similarities between Candrakīrti's epistemology and the Naiyāyikas' in that the number of epistemic instruments accepted is the same. Unlike the Dignāga-Dharmakīrti tradition, both Candrakīrti and Naiyāyika propose the intermingling role of the perceptual and inferential cognitions in that they can share a common epistemic object and that the perceptual judgement must entail a determinate cognition rather than a purely indeterminate one as suggested by Dignāga. Do these similarlies justify the claim that Candrakīrti endorses the Nyāya theory of epistemology? The evidence is less than convincing. Of course, Candrakīrti's and the Naiyāyikas' epistemology have some shared features at least on the face of it. This is not suprising as these two traditions flourished side by side in India. The real question, though, is how far these similarities can take us. Take the case of perception, for instance. For the Naiyāyikas the definition of perception involves the senses (*indriya*), their objects (*artha*), and the contact of the senses with their objects (*sannikarṣa*); consciousness (*jñāna*) is produced by this contact, the contact of the self and mind (*manas*), and the contact of mind (*manas*) and the senses. On the Naiyāyikas' account of perception, all other conditions may be satisfied, but if the self is not present, perception would be impossible. See Radhakrishnan (1998, 147–148) on perception. Therefore, NS 2.21 rules out the possibility of perception without *ātman*—"Perception cannot arise unless there is conjunction of *ātman* with mind" (Agrawal 2001, 16). Candrakīrti must be seen as endorsing the Nyāyas' metaphysical self if we are to claim that Candrakīrti accepts the Nyāyas' epistemology.

the fourfold epistemic instruments."[33] Candrakīrti then provides us with the following antifoundationalist characterization of the instruments and their objects:

> *Thus, in this way it is established that mundane objects are known by the means of the fourfold epistemic instruments.* Now, these are themselves established through the force of mutual interdependence—by virtue of the presence of epistemic instruments (*pramāṇa*) there come to be epistemic objects (*prameya*), and by virtue of the presence of epistemic objects there come to be epistemic instruments. But there is no intrinsic establishment (*svābhāvikī siddhi*) of either the epistemic instruments or the epistemic objects.[34]

Candrakīrti, in this passage, offers us two key arguments in the defense of his antifoundationalism:

1. The four epistemic instruments exist because of their mutual interdependence and are thus dependently arisen.
2. Epistemic instruments and epistemic objects have no intrinsic natures and are thus empty.

The argument from dependent arising—*pratītyasamutpāda*—acknowledges the dependent existence of epistemic instruments as a conventional reality but denies them any intrinsic epistemic authority on the conventional level. The argument from emptiness also acknowledges the existence of epistemic instruments as a conventional reality since being empty allows for dependently arisen cognitive function, but it denies the existence of ultimately real or intrinsic authority. Central to these arguments is the recognition that cognition (*'jal byed*) lacks any intrinsically given cognitive identity—that is to say that no cognition is authoritative by virtue of itself, that is, intrinsically. Cognition literally becomes what it is in virtue of the objects it apprehends (*'jal yul*).

Both arguments defend the mutual interdependence of epistemic instruments and epistemic objects. As the passage from *Prasannapadā* quoted earlier makes clear, the two, in Candrakīrti's epistemology, literally become what they are through the force of each other's presence. The upshot is that, for Candrakīrti, any systematic account of knowledge must thus

33. *dBu ma* 'a 25b; Candrakīrti 2003, 55: *de'i phyir de ltar tshad ma bzhi las 'jig rten gyi don rtogs par rnam par 'jog pa yin no //*. Skt. ed. LVP 75.9.

34. Ibid.: *de'i phyir de ltar tshad ma bzhi las 'jig rten gyi don rtogs par rnam par 'jog pa yin no/ de dag kyang phan tshun ltos pas 'grub par 'gyur te/ tshad ma dag yod na gzhal bya'i don dag tu 'gyur la/ gzhal bya'i don dag yod na tshad ma dag tu 'gyur gyi/ tshad ma dang gzhal bya gnyis ngo bo nyid kyis grub pa ni yod pa ma yin no/*. Skt. ed. LVP 75.9–11.

reject *all* metaphysical and epistemological foundationalisms, even conventionally. It does not, however, follow from this that the Prāsaṅgika *has no epistemology*, as some would seem to suggest.[35] On the contrary, Candrakīrti is convinced that the Prāsaṅgika alone can come up with a successful epistemological account, a *śūnyavādin* version of epistemic instruments that presupposes empty metaphysics and the mutual interdependence of *pramāṇa and prameya.*

35. See Siderits (1980, 1981). On the question as to whether or not the Prāsaṅgika uses reasons and arguments to establish positions, see Huntington (2007) and Garfield (2008).

4

Weighing the Butter, Levels of Explanation, and Falsification: Models of the Conventional in Tsongkhapa's Account of Madhyamaka

Guy Martin Newland

As to the question of what is true about conventional truth, the first thing to say is that for Tsongkhapa (1357–1419) conventional truths (*tha snyad bden pa*) are true in the sense that they *exist* (*yod pa*). Contrary to established usage in Western philosophy, Tsongkhapa here deploys the term *truth* (*bden pa*) not in a propositional sense but rather to refer to the very existence (*yod pa*) of things. Tsongkhapa (GRS 195.2–3) says, "There are many different claims about the basis of division of the two truths, but here we take it to be objects of knowledge (*shes bya*)."[1] The class of objects of knowledge is coterminous with the class of existents. Thus, as Tsongkhapa chose to use the term, conventional truths are not just propositions or facts about tables, chairs, and so on; they are also those things themselves. Tables, chairs, paths, persons, suffering, and spiritual paths are all conventional truths. As such, they do exist.

Yet we need to make this much clearer because there is existence as in the manner of Captain Ahab or Hamlet, and then there is

1. Tsongkhapa cites a sūtra passage in support: "The Tathāgatas thoroughly understand conventionalities and ultimates. Objects of knowledge comprise these two: conventional truths and ultimate truths." This is found in the *Pitṛputrasamāgamasūtra* as cited in *Śikṣāsamuccaya*, vol. 16, *dbu ma* in *sDe dge Tibetan Tripiṭaka* (Tokyo: 1977-1984), 142b.

existence. When we say that these truths are *conventional,* do we mean that they are useful and widely known fictions?[2] Or are they actualities? Which is meant? For Tsongkhapa, it is not that conventional truths sort of exist. They are not to be understood as confabulations or useful fictions. Their existence is an established fact. If we use the word *real* simply to mean that which *does* exist—and to exclude that which only seems to exist—then in just this sense conventional truths *are* real.

Here, we explore Tsongkhapa's reading of the conventional in Prāsaṅgika Madhyamaka. First, we will consider how it can be that conventional things exist even when they are never found at all by the Madhyamaka analysis that reveals emptiness. Then we will examine what it means to say that conventional things, being empty, exist as mere conceptual imputations (*rtog pas btags tsam*). Finally, we will consider how, when all things are equally and utterly empty of intrinsic nature (*rang bzhin = svabhāva*), we can still make the reliable distinctions we need to function in the world and on the Buddhist path.

Levels of Explanation: Why Emptiness Does Not Contradict Conventional Existence

Tsongkhapa, reflecting ideas derived from Indian Buddhists such as Candrakīrti, stresses that conventional things are illusory, false, and deceptive. But, he argues, none of this means that they do not exist. It means that they deceptively appear as though they were self-existent, that is, existing by way of intrinsic nature, when in fact they are utterly devoid of any shred of self-existence. Like a magician's illusion, an echo, or a mirage, they do seem to be something that they are not, but it is not that they seem to exist while in fact not existing at all. It is rather that they seem to exist intrinsically, established by their own intrinsic power, when in fact they do not exist in that particular manner.

For convenience here again is Candrakīrti's *Madhyamakāvatāra* VI.23:

> All things bear two natures (*ngo bo = rūpa*) found (*rnyed pa = labdha*) by correct (*yang dag =samyag*) and false (*brdzun pa = mṛṣā*) views. The object of those who see correctly is said to be "reality (*de nyid = tattva*)," and the object of those who see falsely is said to be "conventional existence/truth (*kun rdzob bden pa = saṃvṛtisatya*)."[3]

2. See discussion of Steven Yablo's fictionalism in chapter 9 of this volume.

3. For the Sanskrit and Tibetan of this verse, see chapter 1, n. 16, and chapter 3, n. 13. See also the problem of interpreting *rnyed pa = labdha* discussed in chapter 1, n. 16.

Tsongkhapa (GRS: 195.1) takes this to mean that there are two authoritative ways to see things—two modes of reliable cognition. There is one way to look at the world in which one sees conventional phenomena—things that are real in the sense of existing but nonetheless false—that is, deceptive—insofar as they do not *ultimately* exist despite seeming to do so. And then there is another way to look at the world, in which one sees the profound truth, the ultimate nature of things, which is sheer emptiness. Corresponding to each of these ways of seeing the world, there are existing objects of knowledge—but they are different objects of knowledge.

Tsongkhapa's account of the truth of the conventional world hence distinguishes different *levels of explanation*.[4] To take a parallel, many disciplines are represented in a college: humanities, psychology, sociology, biology, chemistry, and physics. Each of these may be broadly conceived as addressing an explanatory level (or a set of closely related levels) at which certain phenomena appear and can be discussed, while other phenomena simply are not observed. We do not find human meaning, emotion, social structure, or stock market crashes at the explanatory level of subatomic physics, yet this is not taken by any sane person to entail the utter nonexistence of meaning and so forth. Likewise, a failure to observe Saturn through the lens of a high-powered microscope does not refute Saturn's existence. Each discipline provides a lens, a point of view, an analytical perspective that allows us to get quite clear about some things *while perforce remaining in the dark about others.* As Tsongkhapa (LRC 607) puts it: "We do not see sounds no matter how carefully we look."

According to Tsongkhapa's articulation of Madhyamaka philosophy, nothing exists ultimately; all existents exist only conventionally. At the same time, however, in regard to these conventionally existent things, there are two levels of explanation or analysis. There is *ultimate* analysis, analysis that interrogates the ultimate conditions of being but does not seem to be of any immediate practical use in getting things done. And there is another kind of analysis, conventional analysis, which ignores ontological inquiry but permits us to draw all manner of pragmatic distinctions and to function in the everyday world of mundane transactions. The ultimate and the conventional are the *existents* that, respectively, show up in the perspectives of these analytic modes and are thereby established as the distinct objects of knowledge of these two perspectives. Both perspectives are reliable means of knowledge, epistemic instruments (*tshad ma = prāmaṇa*), and neither discredits the other even though what they see—in the same place and the same time—is completely different. Conventional analysis allows us to distinguish suffering from happiness, persons

4. On levels of explanation, cf. Owens (1989).

from rocks, virtue from nonvirtue; ultimate analysis shows that all of these phenomena are equally and utterly devoid of any intrinsic nature.

The conventional is often represented as being *nonanalytical*, in contrast to the penetrating analysis of the ultimate perspective.[5] Nonetheless, Tsongkhapa is at great pains to point out that the conventional perspective is not always *utterly* nonanalytical (e.g., LRC 627–628):

> In a sense, conventional consciousness operates in a non-inquisitive manner. It operates within the context of how a given phenomenon appears to it without asking, "Is this how the object actually exists, or does it just appear that way to my mind?" It is thus called non-analytical, but it is not the case that it is utterly non-inquisitive.

For if conventional minds were *completely* nonanalytical, how would one distinguish virtue from nonvirtue? The ultimate perspective tells us only that these are equally empty. If we had only the ultimate perspective to rely upon, there would be no way to cultivate virtue and thus no way to become enlightened and thus no Buddhism. For Tsongkhapa, it is clear that the actual practice of Buddhism *must* somehow entail—even among Buddhists who claim otherwise—reliability in conventional analysis of many matters, such as how least to harm and how best to help living beings. Tsongkhapa holds that the profound emptiness must be understood as complementing and fulfilling, rather than canceling, principles of moral action (e.g., LRC: 582–584). To make cogent the compatibility of emptiness and ethics, Tsongkhapa has to show that the two truths do not contradict, undermine, or supersede one another.

In order to consider more fully how Tsongkhapa does this, let us first describe the perspective of ultimate analysis. All Mādhyamikas agree that there is nothing that exists ultimately. This means that when one uses reason to analyze exactly how it is that a person or a car exists, just what its final ontological status is, one does not arrive at or find any definitive basis or ground upon which to establish it. The intrinsic identity of any object we choose to examine dissolves under analytic ontological scrutiny. The mind seeking to know "what the car ultimately is" does not arrive at an intrinsic car nature. If the mind did find such an identity, then we would say that a car can *withstand ultimate analysis* and that it *exists ultimately*. Instead, the mind analyzing the car arrives at last at the emptiness of the car, that is, the car's utter lack of any intrinsic nature. All Mādhyamikas agree that nothing can withstand ultimate analysis, by which they mean that there is nothing anywhere that exists ultimately, including of

5. David Eckel (Dreyfus and McClintock 2003, 188–196) has fruitfully explored Tsongkhapa's development of the recurrent Madhyamaka theme that conventional things "give satisfaction without analysis."

course the Buddha and the teachings of Buddhism. Even emptiness is itself empty; that is, when one searches for the intrinsic nature of emptiness, it is unfindable, and one finds instead its own emptiness and so on, all the way down.

Following Candrakīrti's interpretations of Nāgārjuna, Tsongkhapa (LRC 606–607) argues that if things had any sort of essence or intrinsic nature of their own, this nature would have to be located under ultimate analysis. Therefore, the fact that things are not found under ultimate analysis means that they utterly lack intrinsic nature *(not* that they are nonexistent). Things lack the sort of existence that would be found, were it there, through ultimate analysis. For Tsongkhapa, not existing under ultimate analysis, not existing ultimately, and not existing intrinsically or essentially are three ways of saying the same thing. The knowledge that things lack essential reality is a liberating insight into emptiness, the absence of intrinsic existence.[6]

Thus, the deeper and ultimate "level of explanation/analysis" in Madhyamaka is in fact that level upon which we see the utter lack or absence of any core or pith to which all matters can be reduced. This very lack, emptiness, is all that is ever discerned at that level. It is the entirety of what can be observed *from that perspective*—but is certainly not on that account the only thing that exists. Still, it must give us pause to consider that ultimate analysis—the mind that knows the final nature of things—does not *at all* find persons or cars. When persons and cars cannot withstand such rational analysis, when their vivid and seemingly solid presence recedes and finally evaporates as they are scrutinized, then does this not suggest that scrupulous investigation has at last refuted them? And if so, then how can anyone talk about things having any kind of meaningful existence at all once they have been refuted by reasoning?

Tsongkhapa has an interlocutor pose this very question (LRC 606). In response, he argues that this question comes about through conflating (1) the inability to withstand rational analysis with (2) invalidation or refutation by reason. While it would be foolhardy to claim that things are refuted by reason and nonetheless exist, he argues, things may very well exist although being unable to withstand rational analysis. To ask whether something can withstand rational analysis is to ask whether it is "found" or demonstrated by a line of reasoning that analyzes what exists ultimately. This kind of analysis is intent upon seeking out the essential nature that is the core reality behind an

6. The difference between Prāsaṅgika and Svātantrika, according to Tsongkhapa, is that Svātantrikas, while recognizing that nothing withstands ultimate analysis, regard things as having an intrinsic nature conventionally, while Prāsaṅgikas take intrinsic nature to be just that which *would* be found by ultimate analysis if it existed, concluding from the fact that nothing withstands ultimate analysis that nothing has any intrinsic nature at all, even conventionally.

appearance. When such reasoning analyzes a car, it does not find any such essential reality, and this is what it means to say that a car is "unable to withstand rational analysis" (LRC 606–610).

Thus, the unfindability of a car under ultimate analysis is not a sign of car's *nonexistence;* it is only a sign of a car's not existing in manner sought by this sort of analysis. That is, it is a sign of the utter nonexistence of an essentially real car. We do not expect to see Saturn looking through a microscope; we do not expect a sociologist to find quarks; we do not expect rational analysis to find conventional existence and so do not conclude that there is none just because it is not found thereby. As Tsongkhapa says, we cannot expect to see sounds even when we look with utmost care.

Weighing the Butter: Intrinsic Nature and Nominal Imputation

As we have seen, for Tsongkhapa the fact that cars and people lack any trace of analytically findable essence does not mean that they do not exist. They exist. But what *sort* of existence can they then have? How real can they be? In brief, the answer is that they are *dependent arisings,* phenomena that exist only through their interconnections with other (equally empty) phenomena. Things are often said to be dependent arisings in consideration of their dependence upon constituent parts and/or prior conditions. And the root of suffering according to all Buddhists is the failure to recognize interdependence. But Tsongkhapa argues that *deepest* root of all needless misery is neither the failure to recognize reliance on parts nor a notion that things might appear without relying on prior conditions. It is the failure to recognize another sort of dependence, dependence on conceptual imputation.

Fire arises in dependence upon fuel as a causal condition, but fuel is something that we have identified as burnable and on that basis think, "There is fuel." Cars depend upon auto parts, but auto parts are recognized and so designated in consideration of their connection with real or potential cars. Thus, the term "dependent arising" includes the notion that *all* things exist in dependence upon conceptual designation. In order to appreciate Tsongkhapa's position on intrinsic nature, we have to realize that it is *this* type of dependent arising that is most crucial. The "intrinsic nature" of which all things are empty is precisely things' existing otherwise. In other words, a conception of intrinsic nature is a thought that things have their own way of setting themselves up and existing apart from any cognitive perspective. Tsongkhapa says that the delusion at the root of all other faults is a consciousness superimposing intrinsic nature upon things, apprehending them as existing by way of their own intrinsic character

(LRC 654). To specify exactly what this means, he states that this conception regards things as having an "*ontological status or manner of being in and of themselves, without being posited by the force of an awareness*" (LRC 660).

Thus, things do exist precisely in consideration of their being imputed, while there is also a mode of consciousness—the root of all misery—that regards things as existing *without* needing to be posited in this way. We may then ask: Is the conventional awareness through the force of which things are posited as existing the same as the root delusion that sees things as existing without being so posited?

For Tsongkhapa, the answer is a resounding *no*. Take the situation of students looking up at a blackboard where the instructor has scratched out the shape of the letter *A*. In recognizing the letter, the students at least initially perceive the letter as being set up "out there," from its own side. It appears to be objectively established, and they experience themselves as attentive but passive recipients of the message it is sending out. Yet after a moment of reflection on the conventional nature of language, the lack of any "*A* nature" among the bits of chalk and so on, students come to see they are participating in the establishment of the *A*. The conventional consciousness that recognizes the shapes that can serve as a basis for imputing the *A*—and ascribes *A* rather than *B* in relation to the shape—is not wrong. It is *not* the basis of all misery; it is a practical and correct conventional mind. What *is* wrong is the habitual and usually unchallenged sense that the *A* is naturally or objectively *there*, on its own, without its "being posited through the force of awareness."

While the *A* utterly lacks any natural, independent identity from its own side, it is nonetheless fully capable of functioning. It works in words; it works as a grade. It does its job perfectly well even though it has no trace of the objective existence we unconsciously attribute to it. Likewise, a dollar bill pulled from my pocket at first appears to be, quite objectively and independently, a real dollar. Of course, like the letter *A*, dollars—and the paper or coins that carry dollar values—are all completely a matter of convention. Currency markets track the ever-shifting meaning of these conventions; there is no natural and objective value in them. Yet even without that sort of value and in fact precisely because they lack it, having only exchange value, dollars can still buy things.

To make this point, Tsongkhapa gives an ancient example a new twist:

> Take the case of an imaginary snake that is mistakenly ascribed to a rope. If we leave aside how it is ascribed from the perspective that apprehends a snake, and try to analyze what the snake is like in terms of its own nature, since a snake is simply not present in that object, its features cannot be analyzed. It is similar with regard to all

> phenomena. Suppose that we leave aside analysis [of] how they appear—that is, how they appear to a conventional awareness—and analyze the objects themselves, asking, "What is the manner of being of these phenomena?" We find that they are not established in any way (LRC 661).

It is absurd to leave aside anything we might know about the snake from the perspective of the person who sees the snake and then to ask about the snake on its *own* terms. Why? Because the snake obviously exists only in dependence upon the perspective, only in the perspective, of that mistaken observer. Analogously, we are not going to find anything to point at when we set aside consideration of how people and cars and tables appear to ordinary, valid conventional consciousnesses and ask, "Apart from all of that subjective stuff, how do these cars and people *really* exist?" We arrive only at emptiness, the utter absence of any such nature as would answer.

Unlike the hallucinated snake, people and cars *do exist*, but they do not at all exist on their own; they are ascribed, imputed, designated. They are sliced out (cf. Garfield 1995, 89–90), categorized, and named. However, they do not at all present their lack of independent existence to our senses. Instead, through the force of delusion they seem as though they were established on their own. Thus, Tsongkhapa says that delusion "apprehends each phenomenon as *having a manner of being such that it is comprehensible in and of itself*, without being posited through the force of a conventional consciousness" (LRC 661).

Whatever we know or talk about is already a thing so designated, a thing as pointed out or conceived by a mind. We cannot get at things as they are in and of themselves, apart from mind or in a way that is prior to any kind of conceptualization. For Tsongkhapa this is because things have no nature in and of themselves; they have no way of being apart from mental imputation. To understand just this, that things are empty in *this* way, is wisdom. Regardless of avowed philosophy, we habitually proceed as though the world is already fully real, independent of our minds, waiting to be revealed by the searchlight of consciousness, whereas, in fact, our minds are engaged in structuring the world, moment by moment.

This does *not* mean that hallucinated snakes have the same status as people and cars and tables. Snakes falsely imputed to ropes do not in fact exist, while tables and people do exist because they have a genuine *conventional* existence. To some, Tsongkhapa's emphatic validation of conventional reality pulls too hard toward affirming the ordinary way that things appear. However, as Tsongkhapa makes clear, actual snakes and rope snakes are *equally* devoid of the kind of snakes we habitually perceive, believe in, and fear. When a person sees a rope and imagines a snake, there is no snake at all in the rope. Nonetheless, even when there actually *is* a snake and we perceive a snake, the snake as we perceive it—the intrinsically existent snake—is also *completely* absent. It is just as nonexistent as the rope snake. Thus, all of the snakes with whom we feel ourselves involved are, in a sense, utterly nonexistent. Likewise, people exist, but people as we habitually apprehend them have *never* and could never exist even to the slightest degree. The world as we know it is certainly not left unscathed. The world just as it is, only nominally existent, has yet to appear.

Tsongkhapa does assert that there is a functioning external world. This world exists outside of our minds; it is not one entity with our minds. However, in the same breath Tsongkhapa emphasizes that this external world is dependent upon consciousness and that imagining otherwise is the source of endless misery. For example, when a god, a human, and a ghost each look at a bowl of fluid, the god sees nectar, the human sees water, and the ghost sees a mixture of pus and blood. These beings *correctly* perceive the fluid in accordance with *the constitution of their respective sense and mental faculties.* We cannot talk about what is really in the bowl apart from considering the perspectives of the various perceivers. While some Buddhist systems use this example to show that there are no external objects at all, Tsongkhapa argues that the nectar, blood, and water *do* exist externally but only in dependence upon the minds ascribing them. All three fluids can be simultaneously present, unmixed. They are each established by reliable epistemic instruments operating within diverse but equally correct perspectives.

We can reframe this old ghost story by considering how different species perceive their environments. If there is a spider on the desk as I type, we are present together here and now. We each have healthy minds and sense faculties. Our perceptions of the immediate environment are both correct—and yet so radically different as to be mutually incomprehensible. Which of us sees what is *really* there? As I walk my dog down the street, there is only a partial overlap between the dog's valid perceptions and mine. We inhabit functioning worlds that arise in dependence upon the operation of our diverse and equally sound mental and sensory faculties. These worlds are external to—but never independent of—our minds. Thus it is that the worlds of our experience intersect and overlap in astonishing ways, in infinitely complex patterns. This would be impossible if each thing actually existed objectively, out there on its own, by way of its independent and intrinsic nature. In that case, there would be only one right way to see each real thing—the way that corresponded most perfectly to its objective status. Someone, God perhaps, could rate each species according to how close its subjective world comes to mapping objective reality. What is the rainbow on its own side? What is true about the sky depends upon where you stand, what kind of eyes you have. Tsongkhapa's view asserts that all existing things, including emptiness, exist only in just this rainbowlike way.

There are two important theses bound up in this claim that must be distinguished: (1) What appears from an ultimate point of view does not appear in a conventional perspective and vice versa; and (2) Within the conventional, what is true from one point of view may not be true from another—there are different loci of conventional epistemic authority. But if the dependence of things upon mental imputation means that things are just constituted in the very act of being noticed, then how do we account for natural processes that seem to occur at times, places, or levels of scale unobserved by any living being—the tree falling in the woods, the radon seeping up into the house, or the Big Bang?

Neither Tsongkhapa nor his successors directly address this question. Many contemporary Geluk (*dge lugs*) teachers, if asked, will dismiss the problem by referring to the omniscient mind of the Buddha. But others share our dissatisfaction with this solution. Geshe Palden Drakpa (*dge bshes dpal ldan grags pa*) is one who has thought carefully about this. He told me that we should think of "being imputed by thought" as just being the "measure or limit" (*tshad*)[7] of how real things are. Kensur Yeshe Thupten (*mkhen zur ye shes thub bstan*) elaborates (Klein 1994, 129):

> When we sleep there are many things we do not see which are posited by the mind. Whether phenomena are seen or unseen, they can fulfill the measure of being posited by the mind. It is not essential for a mind to be present. For example, a thousand grams makes a kilo of butter. I may have a one-kilo stone by which, on a balance, I can ascertain that a particular lump of butter weighs one kilo. Even if the stone is not present, the measure [of the butter as one kilo] is still there. Analogously, even if the mind which is the positor of something is not present, the measure of positing is still there and it is sufficient that the measure of being posited is fulfilled. Thus, even if no one sees the production of a sprout [in a deserted forest] directly, it is still posited by the mind.

When we weigh the butter in a market on planet Earth and find that it is a kilogram, we roughly infer that it was a kilogram of butter when the cowherds churned it and it will be a kilogram of butter as we carry it home. The point of

7. Note that the term chosen by these teachers, *tshad*, strongly suggests *tshad ma*, the term for reliable means of cognition or epistemic instruments (*pramāṇa*). It is reliable minds that take or make the *measure* of the world.

this analogy is simply that *things do not have to be imputed each and every instant in order to have the ontological status of being mere imputations by thought.* When we look at a car and say, "There is a car," we establish it to be a car. The measure of the reality of objects is that they exist as imputations by thought; there is nothing one can point out that is naturally there, objectively present in them, apart from their being imputed as such. This remains true both at times when a mind is actively doing that imputation and at other times.

This means that—excluding consideration of omniscient minds—there in fact do exist *as yet unobserved* conditions that contribute to the arising of things. What conditions? As soon as we answer we are already observing, imputing, weighing out the butter. When we ask about what conditions may have been like in this or that case and form a notion about the possible identity and nature of said conditions, we are then doing the imputing. We are saying how things look from our point of view. To exist as an imputation in this way is the full extent, the limit, of the reality of things. It is in fact the only way of being such-and-such a thing.

Hence, while there are objects external to the mind, there are no things that exist by their own power apart from mind. Things exist, but we make an accurate account of this reality only when we recognize that they exist just as seen from a perspective, a point of view, in dependence upon which they are established as the things we take them to be.

Falsification and Conventional Knowledge

Tsongkhapa claims (1) that things are not established in the perspective of a mind examining their ultimate mode of being, and yet (2) they do exist in a robust way. How can this be so? It is because the existence of *everything* (even emptiness) is established only from the perspective of conventional knowledge—that is, via reliable conventional epistemic instruments (LRC 613–627, 638–639). Conventional epistemic instruments are cognitive processes through which we know and thereby establish or certify the conventional objects thereby engaged. Emptiness, the ultimate, is not a conventional object, but the *existence of emptiness* is a conventional object of knowledge.

As noted by Thakchöe (2007), many of Tsongkhapa's critics have claimed that, in adopting this view of conventional knowledge, he is falling from a Prāsaṅgika view. They argue that Tsongkhapa has imported from Dharmakīrti notions of conventional knowledge that are incompatible with Prāsaṅgika. In Prāsaṅgika, ordinary conventional minds are necessarily deceived and mistaken inasmuch as they are pervasively subject to a false appearance of their objects as intrinsically real. How, then, can they provide reliable information? How can they be instruments of actual knowledge?

Tsongkhapa's answer is that while conventional means of knowledge in fact do deliver false appearances, they nonetheless provide accurate information about the objects they observe. When I look at a car, for example, it falsely appears as though it were set up independently, from its own side. It falsely appears as though it had its own natural power to be there. Yet even though my conventional mind is deceived in this way, it can still be relied upon to know a car from a cat.

For Tsongkhapa conventional existence is the only kind of existence anything can have. Something exists conventionally when (1) it is acknowledged by ordinary people in the world, (2) it is not refuted by conventional means of knowledge, and (3) it is not refuted by ultimate means of knowledge. The *first* criterion should be understood in terms of the earlier discussion of imputed existence in the "weighing the butter" section. To exist conventionally involves being imputed or ascribed by a mind. The *third* criterion can be understood by reference to the first part of this chapter. Ultimate analysis refutes the existence of ordinary things as they now appear—that is, their existence by way of their own nature—but it does not refute their *mere* existence (LRC 627).

Here we focus on the *second* criterion. Conventional existence requires not being refuted, not being discredited or shown to be nonexistent by the conventional epistemic instruments. Conventional minds impute, ascribe, and name many things that, upon scrutiny in various ways, are found to be totally nonexistent. We may believe there is water in the distance but find upon investigation find that it was a mirage. Our conviction that there was water there, alas, does not make it so. That view is discredited by closer conventional examination.

In brief, then, Tsongkhapa's notion of valid conventional existence is *not* that there are epistemic instruments that reliably get at the essential, or intrinsic, nature of their objects, even at the conventional level. He explicitly refutes such a notion (LRC 699). Nor is it that we must accede blindly to whatever common sense or "conventional wisdom" dictates in a given social situation. It is rather that careful observation and analysis at either the conventional or ultimate level will discredit or falsify mental imputations (water in the mirage, face in the mirror, intrinsic nature) that are unsustainable. The data of sense experience and our ability to analyze allow us to challenge, discredit, and falsify a great many conventional imputations. *Those conventional imputations that cannot be thus falsified constitute what exists.*

For Tsongkhapa the basis for *all* analysis, including the ultimate analytical refutation of intrinsic natures, can only be reliable information provided by ordinary conventional consciousness (LRC 739). We see that a log is different from a flame, that a horse is different from a cow, that being accompanied is different from being unaccompanied, that a car is distinct from the parts of the car, and from this sort of ordinary factual knowledge Mādhyamikas develop arguments against intrinsic nature. Our ordinary cognitive states are mistaken in that cows appear to them as though they were intrinsically real when in fact they are utterly devoid of such a nature. Yet these same mistaken consciousnesses provide accurate and practical information that allows us to tell a cow from a bull. We can and must have this sort of information to do our herding and so on. Moreover, *we need this information even in order to formulate or understand the argument against the reality of intrinsic nature.* Without reliable information from our senses, how could we even infer that appearances even to those very senses are deceptive? In Tsongkhapa's system the foundation for the bridge between benighted ordinary existence and the awakening of buddhahood is the aspect of reliability in ordinary, healthy minds.

But what constitutes a particular consciousness as a conventional means of knowledge, a reliable epistemic instrument? Tsongkhapa's approach derives from Candrakīrti's (Mav VI.24–25) distinction between conventions that are real in relation to the world and those that are unreal in relation to the world:

> We maintain that there are two kinds of false perception:
> That by healthy and that by impaired sense faculties.
> The understanding of those with impaired sense faculties
> Is regarded as false by comparison with that of those with healthy faculties.
> Mundane knowledge is that which is apprehended
> By the six unimpaired sense faculties.
> That is true by conventional standards. The rest
> Is regarded as conventionally false.[8]

Tsongkhapa reads Candrakīrti as arguing that the criterion by means of which we distinguish what exists conventionally from that which only seems to exist but does not exist at all is the absence or presence of some type of defect in or

8.

mthong ba rdzun pa'ang rnam pa gnyis 'dod de//
dbang po gsal dang dbang po skyon ldan no//
skyon ldan dbang can rnams kyi shes pa ni//
dbang po legs 'gyur shes bltos log par 'dod//

gnod pa med pa'i dbang po drug rnams kyis//
gzung ba gang zhig 'jig rten gyis rtogs te//
'jig rten nyid las bden yin lhag ma ni//
'jig rten nid las log par rnam par gzhag//

Skt. of Mav VI.25 in chapter 9, n. 17.

impairment of the apprehending awareness. He explains that sensory impairment here refers to a *superficial* (*'phral*) cause of error (GRS 199.4–5). As examples, Candrakīrti (MavBh) and Tsongkhapa (GRS) list eye disease, jaundice, consumption of poisonous berries, a mirror held in front of the face, shouting into a canyon (producing an echo that sounds like another voice), mantric spells, hallucinogenic drugs, bad philosophical tenets, and dreams. A judgment about the reality of any object is always grounded in a judgment about the adequacy of the perspective from which the object is attested. If a cognitive process is impaired by an optical illusion or a mental illness, then it is not the measure of the existence of the certain objects to which it attests. In other words, it may be disqualified as a reliable epistemic instrument.

When Candrakīrti says that things are posited as either true/real or false/unreal in relation to a *mundane* perspective, what is that mundane perspective that takes the measure of things in this way? In other words, given that all things lack any existence ultimately, what is this "world" with reference to which some other type of existence may be attested? Gelukpa scholars have converged in agreement that this "mundane perspective" must be that in which a conventional epistemic instrument is not directed toward the ultimate nature of things (Newland 1992, 136–157). This means that it must be a reliable, conventional means of cognition that is not informed by or influenced by or acting in reliance upon an earlier realization of emptiness. That person either has never realized emptiness or else has realized emptiness but is no longer apprehending phenomena within the context of or under the influence of that prior realization. If such conventional epistemic instruments are utterly unable to undermine a thing's reality, then that thing exists. This existence is, of course, the only kind possible: conventional existence.

Here are a few examples: A table is a false, deceptive phenomenon because it appears to exist by way of an intrinsic nature but does not have a shred of such existence. At the same time, it is real from a mundane perspective because one cannot refute its existing just as it appears without relying on a realization of emptiness. Two moons in the sky over the earth are unreal even from a mundane perspective because a healthy visual faculty, without reference to emptiness, can falsify a claim that this appearance is real. Moreover, even though many in the world believe it to exist, a permanent personal soul is unreal from a mundane perspective because it can be falsified by analysis of the person's transitory nature, even without understanding emptiness.

Like color-blind witnesses to a traffic accident, we are all qualified to give reliable testimony just as long as it bears only on that within our ken and not on matters with regard to which we are incompetent. When their minds and sense faculties are not further impaired by some internal or external circumstance, spiders, dogs, ordinary humans, and advanced bodhisattvas all have equal right to give testimony about what does and does not exist from their point of view. Testimony about *how* things exist, apparently by way of their own natures, may then be rebutted by those who have carried out deeper analysis of all the evidence. Thus, what is true about conventional truth is just that which cannot be falsified through *the fullest use* of a healthy, unimpaired observer's faculties.

We falsify claims about things that are imputed by conventional minds, even things that are very widely believed to be real, through the use of conventional epistemic instruments—that is to say, through empirical evidence and analysis thereof. Through this process of elimination, a sort of epistemic survival of the fittest, we refine modes of practice better and (perhaps) best suited to our situation, including our bodies, minds, and total environments. Successful interactions (see chapter 12 in this volume) with other living beings and with the physical environment—interactions that effectively promote well-being—become established as conventional facts unless they are discredited by some further deployment of a healthy and unimpaired observer's conventional faculties.

In other words, by attentive conventional practice we can become gradually more skillful in acting to promote happiness. Never idling in the "dismal slough" of popular opinion or established custom (see chapter 9, this volume), we can refine our ways of working as cowherds, philosophers, and physicians. We can become deeply attuned in our responses, knowing quickly which cow needs tending, which question to pose to which student, and what dose to give which patient even though *all things are equally empty*. We can do that even when our choices are unpopular or counterintuitive, that is, even when they are unconventional.

5

Identifying the Object of Negation and the Status of Conventional Truth: Why the *dGag Bya* Matters So Much to Tibetan Mādhyamikas

Jay L. Garfield and Sonam Thakchöe

Emptiness as a Negation and the Object of Negation

Emptiness is the emptiness of intrinsic existence. It is, according to all of Nāgārjuna's canonical commentators in India and in Tibet, a negation and, more specifically, an *external* negation. To say that the statement,

(1) This person is empty of this intrinsic nature.

is a negation is to say that it is logically equivalent to

(2) This person does not have this intrinsic nature.

But that statement in turn is ambiguous. We could read the negation *internally* and paraphrase as follows:

(3) This person's intrinsic nature is not *this*.

Or we could read it *externally* and paraphrase thus:

(4) It is not the case that a person has this intrinsic nature.

No matter how much they affirm or deny the reality of that which is conventional, Buddhapālita, Bhāvaviveka, and Candrakīrti (as well as both Tsongkhapa and Gorampa, whose dispute regarding the import of this point will occupy most of this chapter) agree that (4) is the correct paraphrase of (1).

This might seem surprising, especially in the context of a discussion of the two realities/truths. After all, it might seem that (3), in virtue of its implication of another kind of intrinsic nature, presumably, is *conventional existence*. But that would be to miss the importance of the *identity* of the two realities/truths, not their mere *consistency*. The person has *no other intrinsic nature*, even its emptiness. The fact that the person exists only conventionally just consists in the fact that it *is empty of any intrinsic nature*. Statement (4), in virtue of implicating no *other* kind of intrinsic nature, gets things just right. Statement (3), on the other hand, despite its superficial plausibility as the best paraphrase, sneaks in an intrinsic nature as part of conventional reality *in addition to* the negative ultimate reality. This may be one of the subtlest issues in understanding the relations between the two realities/truths and the reason for so much emphasis on the *kind* of negation emptiness represents, as well as on its *object*. To see it as an internal negation is to lose focus on the important identity.

Nonetheless, as Candrakīrti emphasizes (see Mav VI.23 cited in chapter 1), the two realities are in fact two distinct natures of each phenomenon, each of which is apprehended by a different kind of cognitive process. For this reason, even though ultimate reality is an external negation and conventional reality is nondifferent from it in one respect, there must be another respect in which they are distinct. It is with regard to this respect that disputes arise in Tibet between those like Tsongkhapa, who regard conventional truth as a kind of *truth*, and conventional reality as a *way* of being *real* on the one hand, and those like Gorampa, who regard conventional truth as *entirely false* and conventional reality as *unreal* on the other.

Negations, in Indian and then Tibetan logical theory, always have *objects*. We can always ask *what* is negated. And whereas in most Western logical theory, this question is always asked in the *formal* mode, taking the object of negation to be essentially linguistic, in Indian and Tibetan theory it is asked in the *material* mode, with the object of negation taken to be in the extralinguistic world (except, of course, in the case of metalinguistic discourse). This difference has important implications for how the distinction is to be drawn between the two kinds of negation. In the West, the two are distinguished in terms of the respective objects that are negated. In India and Tibet, they are distinguished instead in terms of the way in which a single object is negated.

In the West, that is, we would think of the object of an internal negation as a predicate expression or a property (conceived as an intentional object) and the object of an external negation as a proposition or a sentence. The internal negation "my horse is not white" presupposes that I have a horse and denies that he satisfies the predicate *is white*. It follows (from the sentence together with appropriate discourse presuppositions) that I have a horse of another color. The negation operator applies to the predicate. The external negation, "it is not the case that I have a white horse," on the other hand, involves an operator that applies to the entire sentence. That is what is denied. There is no implication that I have any horse of any color. In India and Tibet, however, the *object* of the two negations is taken to be the same, but the manner in which they eliminate it is taken to be different. In each case, it is an extralinguistic fact, not a linguistic expression, and is the fact that is asserted to obtain by the sentence negated. The internal negation and the external negation each eliminate the fact that my horse is white. The whiteness of the horse is the object of negation in each case. The external negation eliminates it without implying that I have a horse of a different color; the internal negation eliminates it while implying that I do.

Given that emptiness is the negation of intrinsic natures in things, it is therefore important to answer two questions in order to understand just what that negation is and what it says about things: First, what kind of negation is it? Second, what is the object of negation? We have made it clear at least in a preliminary fashion that the *kind* of negation is *external*. We now turn to the question of the *object* of negation, the question that divides Tsongkhapa and Gorampa. We will first consider Tsongkhapa's account, according to which the object of negation is *intrinsic existence* or *intrinsic nature*. We then turn to Gorampa's, according to which it is *existence*, unqualified. We will show that Tsongkhapa's position on the object of negation leads to an understanding of conventional truth as in an important sense a *truth* and of conventional existence as a kind of *existence*, whereas Gorampa's account leads to a view of conventional truth as entirely *false* and of conventional existence as a kind of *nonexistence*.

Conventional Truth and that Negation: Two Models

Here is one possibility: The object of negation is the conventional phenomenon itself. Let us see how that plays out in an account of the status of conventional truth. Since ultimate truth—emptiness—is an external negation, and since an external negation eliminates its object while leaving nothing behind, when we say that a person is empty, we eliminate the *person*, leaving nothing else behind. To be sure, we must, as Mādhyamikas, in agreement with ordinary persons, admit that the person exists *conventionally* despite not existing *ultimately*. But, if emptiness eliminates the person, that conventional existence is a complete illusion: The ultimate emptiness of the person shows that the person simply does not exist. It is no more actual than Santa Claus, the protestations of ordinary people and small children to the contrary notwithstanding.

Here is another possibility: The object of negation is not the conventional phenomenon itself but instead the *intrinsic nature* or *intrinsic existence* of the conventional phenomenon. The consequences of taking the object of negation this way are very different. On this account, when we say that the person does not exist ultimately, what is eliminated by its ultimate emptiness is its intrinsic existence. No other intrinsic identity is projected in the place of that which was undermined by emptiness, even emptiness or conventional reality. But the person is not thereby eliminated. Its conventional existence is therefore, on this account, simply its existence devoid of intrinsic identity as an interdependent phenomenon. On this view, conventional reality is no illusion; it is the actual mode of existence of actual things. We now turn to Tsongkhapa's reasons for taking this second option and Gorampa's reasons for taking the first option and examine the implications for their accounts of conventional truth and of the relation between the two truths.

Tsongkhapa on the Object of Negation

In the *lhag mthong* (Special Insight) section of *Lam rim chen mo*[1] *(Extensive Exposition of the Stages of the Path)*, Tsongkhapa distinguishes between the soteriological object of negation (*lam gyi dgag bya*) and the epistemological object of negation (*rigs pa'i dgag bya*). The soteriological object of negation is something that exists as an object of knowledge (*shes bya la yod pa*); it comprises the obstructions to *nirvāṇa* and awakening, which are to be eliminated on the path, and will not concern us here (1993, 651).[2] The epistemological object of negation comprises two aspects: "erroneous apprehension" (*phyin ci log gi 'dzin pa*) and "the existence of intrinsic nature thereby apprehended" (*des bzung ba'i rang bzhin yod pa*). Of these, Tsongkhapa identifies the apprehended intrinsic nature as the *fundamental* epistemological object of negation since the reified object must first be negated in order to eliminate the erroneous subjective state.

1. We heavily relied on Cutler et al, and Newland (2002) for their translation of the text, although we have made changes wherever we thought they were appropriate.

2. *spyir dgag bya la lam gyi dgag bya dang rigs pa'i dgag bya gnyis yod do / de la dang po ni / . . . nyon mongs pa dang shes bya'i sgrib pa gnyis so / / 'di ni shes bya la yod pa'i dgag bya yin te / 'di med na lus can thams cad 'bad med du grol bar 'gyur ba'i phyir ro //.*

Although the soteriological and subjective epistemological objects of negation exist and are to be actively eliminated, the principal epistemological object of negation, the existence of an intrinsic nature (*rang bzhin yod pa*), is not an object of knowledge (*shes bya la med pa*); instead, it is erroneously reified (1993, 652).[3] The fact that intrinsic nature is purely a metaphysical fiction is central to Tsongkhapa's account. If it were to exist even conventionally, on Tsongkhapa's view, it could never be negated. This is because, argues Tsongkhapa, *epistemic* negation is not like eliminating a jar by hammering it. It involves only purging the mind of fictions. It is because intrinsic nature is a fiction that the error that takes it to be real can be effectively eliminated through philosophical practice (1993, 652).[4]

It follows that this object of negation (henceforth simply *the object of negation*) is not conventionally existent and that conventional truth is not an object of negation. In the same text Tsongkhapa provides us four key arguments defending his position that Madhyamaka's object of negation does not entail negating conventional existence.

The first argument is based on a distinction between "inability to withstand rational analysis" (*rigs pas dpyad mi bzod pa*) and "being undermined by rational analysis" (*rigs pas gnod pa*). This argument states that the investigation into whether conventional reality is capable of withstanding rational analysis does not result in its negation because, in spite of the fact that conventional reality does not withstand logical analysis and is established to be empty of intrinsic existence, conventional reality is nevertheless not undermined by the rational analysis:

> A proper analysis of whether these phenomena—such things as material objects—exist, or are produced in reality, is "a line of reasoning that analyses reality," or "a line of reasoning that analyses the ultimate." We do not assert that the production of such things as material objects can withstand analysis by such reasoning. Therefore our position avoids the fallacy that there are truly existent things. One might then ask: If these phenomena cannot withstand rational analysis, then what does it mean to be "rationally undermined" (*rigs pas khegs pa*)? This challenge mistakenly conflates the "inability to

3. *rigs pa'i dgag bya ni / . . . phyin ci log gi 'dzin pa la dgag byar gsungs pa dang des bzung ba'i rang bzhin yod pa la dgag byar mdzad pa gnyis yod do / 'on kyang dgag bya'i gtso bo ni phyi ma yin te / yul can phyin ci log ldog pa la des bzung ba'i yul thog mar dgag dgos pas so / . . . dgag bya 'di ni shes bya la med pa zhig dgos te / /yod na dgag par mi nus pa'i phyir ro / /.*

4. *de lta yin na'ang yod par 'dzin pa'i sgro 'dogs skye bas dgag dgos la / 'gog pa'ang tho bas bum pa bshig pa lta bu min gyi / med pa la med par ngo shes pa'i nges shes bskyed pa ste med par nges pa skyes na yod par 'dzin pa'i 'khrul shes ldog pa yin no //.*

withstand rational analysis" with that of "being undermined by rational analysis." (1993, 606)[5]

To ask whether something can withstand rational analyses is to ask whether it is found by a line of reasoning that analyses reality. As Candrakīrti's *Catuḥśatakaṭīkā* states: ". . . because our analysis is intent upon seeking intrinsic nature," it aims to discover whether such things as material objects have the intrinsic nature of being produced, of cessation, etc. Thus, the analysis is to discover whether such things as material objects have production and cessation that exist intrinsically; it *is not the case that this line of reasoning searches for mere production and cessation.* Therefore this line of reasoning is described as "that which analyses reality" because it analyses to discover whether production, cessation and the like are established in reality (1993, 607).[6]

When such a line of reasoning analyses or searches for such things as production, it does not find a trace of them; and this is what "inability to withstand analysis" means. However, the fact that this line of reasoning does not find them does not entail that it negates (*khegs pa*) them. Rather if they did exist [ultimately] this reasoning would establish them, and since it does not, they are negated [ultimately]. The production and cessation of such things as material objects are established by conventional consciousness. They do exist but rational consciousness does not establish them; it does not find them, so how could it negate them? This is similar to a *visual consciousness: while it does not find sounds, it does not negate them* (1993, 607).[7]

5. *gzugs la sogs pa'i chos 'di dag don yin lugs la yod dam med skye'am mi skye zhes pa la sogs pa'i sgo nas tshul bzhin du dpyod pa ni/ de kho na nyid la dpyod pa'i rigs pa dang mthar thug dpyod pa'i rigs pa zhes bya ba yin la / rigs pa des gzugs sogs kyi skye ba dpyad bzod par ni kho bo cag mi 'dod pas bden dngos su thal ba'i skyon med do / /gal te de dag rigs pas dpyad mi bzod na rigs pas khegs pa'i don yod par ji ltar 'thad snyam na / 'di ni rigs pas dpyad mi bzod pa dang rigs pas gnod pa gnyis gcig tu 'khrul ba ste //.*

6. *rigs pas dpyad bzod mi bzod kyi don ni de kho na nyid la dpyod pa'i rigs pa des rnyed ma rnyed yin la / de yang bzhi rgya pa'i 'grel ba las / kho bo cag gyi rnam par dpyod pa ni rang bzhin 'tshol ba lhur byed pa nyid kyi phyir ro / zhes gsungs pa ltar / gzugs sogs la skye 'gag la sogs pa'i rang bzhin yod med 'tshol ba yin no / / de lta na gzugs la sogs pa la rang gi ngo bos grub pa'i skye 'gag yod med btsal ba yin gyi / rigs pa des skye 'gag tsam 'tshol ba min no / /des na rigs pa de la de nyid la dpyod pa zhes bya ste de kho na nyid du skye 'gag sogs grub ma grub dpyod pa yin pa'i phyir ro //.*

7. *de lta bu'i rigs pa des dpyad pa'am btsal ba na skye ba la sogs pa cung zad kyang mi rnyed pa la dpyad mi bzod pa zhes zer la rigs pa des ma rnyed pa tsam gyis khegs pa min gyi / yod na rigs pa des 'grub dgos pa las des ma grub na khegs pa yin no / /gzugs la sogs pa'i skye 'gag rnams kyang tha snyad pa'i shes pas 'grub pa yin gyi / de dag yod kyang rigs shes kyis mi 'grub pas des ma rnyed pas de dag ji ltar khegs te / dper na / mig gi shes pas sgra ma rnyed kyang des mi khegs pa bzhin no //.*

> Therefore, if such things as production and cessation existed intrinsically, i.e., were established in reality, then reason would have to find them because it accurately analyses whether such things as material objects have intrinsically existent production and cessation. Since such analysis does not find production and the like, it negates essentially established or ultimately real production, cessation, and the like (1993, 607).[8]

Tsongkhapa's second argument is based on a distinction between the "conventionally existent" (*tha snyad du yod pa*) and the "conventionally nonexistent" (*tha snyad du med pa*). On this argument what is conventionally existent (production for example) cannot be regarded as an object of negation because it satisfies the triple criterion of conventional existence: (1) its existence is taken for granted by ordinary people, (2) its existence is not undermined by conventional epistemic instruments, and (3) its conventional existence is not undermined by critical rational analysis of its ultimate nature. Its intrinsic nature, on the other hand, is regarded as the object of negation because it does not satisfy these criteria.

Intrinsically existent production (1) is not taken for granted by ordinary people (although the production is real, we don't take it to be intrinsically real); (2) no conventional epistemic instruments reveal an intrinsic nature, and (3) the idea that production has an intrinsic nature is undermined by rational analysis. Hence, when considering the ultimate nature of the production, the object of negation is its *intrinsic nature*, not *the production* (1993, 607).[9] (See also 2003, 63 ff).

The third argument is grounded in his account of the negation of the four alternatives regarding production (*mu bzhi'i skye ba*). According to this argument, the Mādhyamika negates production from self, from another, from both, as well as causelessly, but this does not entail the negation of "mere production" (*skye ba tsam*) or "conventional production" (*tha snyad kyi skye ba*). This is

8. *des na skye 'gag la sogs pa rang gi ngo bos grub pa'am de kho nar grub na rigs pa des de rnyed dgos te / rigs pa des gzugs sogs la rang gi ngo bos grub pa'i skye 'gag yod med tshul bzhin du dpyod pa yin pa'i phyir ro / /de lta bu des skye ba sogs ma rnyed pas rang gi ngo bos grub pa'am de kho nar grub pa'i skye 'gag sogs 'gog pa yin te / rang gi ngo bos grub na des rnyed dgos pa las ma rnyed phyir ro / /dper na / shar phyogs su bum pa yod na rnyed par nges pa'i 'tshol mkhan gyis shar du bum pa btsal ba'i tshe ma rnyed na des shar na bum pa yod pa khegs pa yin gyi / bum pa yod pa tsam des ji ltar khegs / de bzhin du rang gi ngo bos grub pa'i skye ba yod na rnyed par nges pa'i dbu ma pa'i rigs pas btsal ba na skye ba ma rnyed pa des rang bzhin nam rang gi ngo bos grub pa'i skye ba khegs pa yin gyi / skye ba tsam ji ltar khegs //.*

9. *tha snyad du yod par 'dod pa dang med par 'dod pa ni ji 'dra ba zhig gi sgo nas 'jog pa yin snyam na / tha snyad pa'i shes pa la grags pa yin pa dang / ji ltar grags pa'i don de la tha snyad pa'i tshad ma gzhan gyis gnod pa med dang / de kho na nyid la'ang rang bzhin yod med tshul bzhin du dpyod pa'i rigs pas gnod pa mi 'bab pa zhig ni tha snyad du yod par 'dod la / de dag las ldog pa ni med par 'dod do //.*

because the four alternative kinds of production represent four distinct reificationist views of production. Inasmuch as each involves the superimposition of intrinsic nature on mere production, they are all conceptual fiction. They do not even reflect our ordinary conventional talk about production. Hence, to negate them is not to negate mere, conventionally existent production, which is nothing more than dependent arising:

> Suppose one argued as follows: Madhyamaka negates production from self, from another, from both and causelessly. Does this negate production? (i) If you claim that it does, then since these four alternative modes of production do not exist even conventionally in this system, there would be no need to qualify the negation of production. (ii) If you claim that it does not, then the negation of the four alternative modes of production would fail to negate ultimate production.
>
> We reply: We do not accept the former, so I will explain the rejoinder to the latter. Those who posit ultimate production must assert that it withstands analysis by reasoning that analyses reality. As this is so, they must use reason to analyse production so as to discover in which of the four alternatives it consists—production from self, from another, etc. Hence, those who posit ultimate production are definitely required to assert that it can be analytically identified as falling under one of the four alternatives. Because we assert mere production—the arising of particular effects in dependence on particular causes and conditions—we do not accept ultimately existent production. Since we do not accept ultimately existent production, why would we use reasoning that analyses ultimate reality to analyse production as to which it is—production from self, another, and the like? For, we are not required to assert that production withstands rational analysis (1993, 633–634).[10]

The fourth argument relies on the negative tetralemma. Tsongkhapa maintains here that the object of negation for Madhyamaka cannot exist in any of the ways

10. *rang gzhan dang gnyis ka dang rgyu med las skye ba bkag pas skye ba khegs na mu bzhi'i skye ba 'di pa'i lugs la tha snyad du'ang med pas skye ba 'gog pa la khyad par sbyar mi dgos la / mi khegs na mu bzhi'i skye ba bkag pas don dam gyi skye ba'ang mi khegs par 'gyur ro zhes smra ba'i snga ma mi 'dod pas phyi ma'i len bshad par bya ste / don dam gyi skye ba khas len na de nyid dpyod pa'i rigs pas dpyad bzod du 'dod dgos la / de'i tshe rigs pas bdag dang gzhan la sogs pa bzhi gang las skye dpyad dgos pas don dam gyi skye ba 'dod pas mu bzhi gang rung gi dpyad pa nges par khas blang dgos so / /rgyu dang rkyen 'di la brten nas 'di 'byung gi skye ba tsam zhig 'dod pas ni de kho na'i skye ba khas ma blangs la / de ma blangs pas de kho na nyid la dpyod pa'i rigs pas bdag dang gzhan la sogs pa gang las skye zhes ji ltar dpyod de rigs pas dpyad bzod du 'dod mi dgos pa'i phyir ro / /.*

specified by the tetralemma (existence, nonexistence, both, and neither). But this is not a problem for *mere* existence. This is because the negative tetralemma rejects only reified existence, reified nonexistence, reified existence and nonexistence, and a reified sense of neither existence nor nonexistence. It therefore denies neither the existence of conventional phenomena nor the nonexistence of conventionally fictional phenomena nor the fact that the previously existent can become nonexistent nor the fact that such entities as illusions and mirages are neither existent in any unqualified sense nor nonexistent in any unqualified sense (1993: 637–638).[11]

Moreover, to negate conventional truth, according to Tsongkhapa, would be to negate dependent arising, and to negate dependent arising would be to negate emptiness. To negate emptiness is to negate ultimate truth. Ultimate truth therefore makes sense only when it is understood simply as the ultimate nature of real conventional phenomena since emptiness is simply their dependent arising (see chapter 2 of this volume).

In the *rTen 'brel stod pa (Praise of Dependent Arising)*, Tsongkhapa makes this point clearly:

> 11. Since, as you have seen,
> The meaning of "emptiness" is *dependent arising,*
> Emptiness of intrinsic nature and
> Efficacy of agent and action are not inconsistent.
>
> 12. If it were seen to preclude them,
> One could make no sense of action in the context of emptiness.
> We say that since the efficacious would have to be non-empty,
> you would plunge into a terrifying abyss.[12]
>
> 15. Thus, since there are absolutely no phenomena,
> Other than the dependently arisen,
> There are absolutely no phenomena
> Other than those that are empty of intrinsic nature.[13]

11. *de 'dra ba'i khyad pa sbyar rgyu med par mu bzhi ka 'gog na dngos po yod pa dang dngos po med pa 'gog pa'i tshe de gnyis ka ma yin te zhes bkag nas / slar yang gnyis ka ma yin pa'ang ma yin zhes bkag na ni khas blangs dngos su 'gal ba yin la / de ltar yin kyang skyon med do zhes bsnyon na ni kho bo cag bsnyon pa dang lhan cig tu mi rtsod do //.*

12. *khyod ni nam gzhig stong pa nyid/ /rten 'byung don du mthong ba na/ /rang bzhin gyis ni stong pa dang/ / bya byed 'thad pa'ang mi 'gal zhing/11/ de las bzlog par mthong ba na/ stong la bya ba mi rung zhing/ /bya dang bcas la stong med pas/ nyam nga'i g.yang du ltung bar bzhed/12/.* See also Tsongkhapa (1994).

13. *de phyir brten nas 'byung ba las/ /ma gtogs chos 'ga' yod min pas/ /rang bzhin gyis ni stong pa las/ /ma gtogs chos 'ga' med par gsungs/ 15/.*

In the *Lam gtso rnam gsum (Three Principal Aspects of the Path)*, Tsongkhapa argues that things are able to appear to us as they do because that they lack intrinsic nature. Therefore, by accepting the conventional existence of mere appearance, Tsongkhapa argues, the Mādhyamika eschews reification without eschewing commitment to conventional reality; reificationism is a conceptual error, and its elimination requires a correct understanding— not the elimination—of conventional truth. Moreover, he argues, seeing things to be empty of intrinsic nature undermines nihilism because to see things as empty is to see them as they really are. Hence, emptiness alone resolves the problem of nihilism because only in the context of emptiness is causal efficacy possible and hence conventional existence.

Tsongkhapa hence delivers an account of the object of negation according to which while emptiness is an external negation, it is a negation of intrinsic nature, not a negation of conventional truth. This allows him to preserve a robust sense of the reality of the conventional world in the context of emptiness and to provide an analysis of the relation between emptiness and conventional reality that makes clear sense of the identity of the two truths. We now turn to Gorampa's account of the object of negation, according to which conventional reality itself is that object.

Gorampa on the Object of Negation

In the *Lta ba ngan sel (Elimination of Erroneous Views)*, Gorampa also distinguishes the soteriological object of negation from the epistemic object of negation. According to Gorampa, the soteriological object of negation, which will play a greater role in Gorampa's account than it does in Tsongkhapa's, "comprises all false appearances" (2001, 101–102; 1969b, 595f).[14] By "false appearance," Gorampa means anything that appears to our mind. Therefore, all conventional phenomena are false appearances. Appearances, he claims, are conceptually produced. So, when conceptual reification ceases, appearance also ceases. Insight into reality puts an end to conceptual reification and so to appearance. Therefore, Gorampa insists that the Mādhyamikas "should aim to develop a correct understanding of both the 'illusory-like conventional' (*kun rdzob sgyu ma lta bu*) and the 'ultimate freedom from conceptual fabrication'" (*don dam spros bral*) (2001, 101; 1969b, 594–594).[15] To achieve this cessation, the Mādhyamikas' "first priority should be the negation of the reality of appearances; thus the

14. *lam gyi dgag bya ni 'khrul pa'i snang ba mtha' dag yin na/.*
15. *bsgrub bya ni kun rdzob sgyu ma lta bu dang/ don dam spros dral* [sic] *gnyis yin la/.*

unreality of appearances is the principal thing to be established" (1969b, 594–595).[16] Appearance progressively disappears as one's naïve and false view of things disappears.

Gorampa refers to the epistemic object of negation as the "object of negation by scripture and reasoning" (*lung dang rigs pa'i dgag bya*). He distinguishes two types: the object (*yul*), comprising all conventional truths, and the subject (*yul can*), comprising all cognitions except an ārya's meditative equipoise. This distinction between the subjective and the objective epistemic objects of negation is fundamental to his framework. He emphasizes the distinction between nonerroneous nondual knowledge and erroneous dualistic appearance. All conventional knowledge is dualistic in virtue of being constituted by an apprehending subject and its apprehended object; it inevitably reifies the dichotomy between subject and object.

Gorampa claims that the object of negation consists in all conventional truth—subjective and objective. In the *Nges don rab gsal (Illumination of the Object of Ascertainment)* he writes:

> So, in the case of the first extreme, the basis of negation is this: the very basis of the debate (*rtsod gzhi*) for arguing about whether a thing exists or not is itself the basis of negation ('*gog gzhi*). (1969a, 388d; 2002, 163–164)[17]

> All phenomena which are apprehended as positive entities—characterized as "truly established" (*bden par grub pa*), "ultimately established" (*don dam par grub pa*), "really established" (*yang dag par grub pa*), "essentially established" (*ngo bo nyid kyis grub pa*), "intrinsically established" (*rang bzhin gyis grub pa*), "established through their own characteristics" (*rang gi mtshan nyid kyis grub pa*), "truly produced" (*bden pa'i skye ba*), "merely existent as true entities" (*bden pa'i dngos po yod pa tsam*), etc.—must be negated. This is because none of these are affirmatively established as positive phenomena when these bases of negation are subjected either to Prāsaṅgika or to Svātantrika forms of logical analysis. (1969a, 389a–b; 2002, 164–165)[18]

16. *de gnyis ka la yang thog mar snang ba la bden pa dgag dgos pas snang ba bden med bsgrub bya'i gtso bo yin no/.*
17. *des na mtha' dang po gang la 'gog pa'i gzhi ni gang zhig bden par yod med rtsod pa'i rtsod gzhi de nyid yin te/.*
18. *gzhi de dag gi steng du bden par grub pa / don dam par grub pa / yang dag par grub ba / ngo bo nyid kyis grub pa / rang bzhin gyis grub pa / rang gi mtshan nyid kyis grub pa / bden pa'i skye ba / bden pa'i dngos po yod pa tsam la sogs pa sgrub pa'i sgo nas gzung ba'i chos thams cad 'gog ste thal rang gnyis char gyis dgag gzhi de dag la rigs pas dpyad pa'i tshe yongs gcod du grub pa'i chos ci yang med par 'dod pa'i phyir ro /.*

Gorampa argues that since the Mādhyamika's investigation into whether things are "real/true" (*bden pa*), "existent" (*yod pa*), or "truly/really established" (*bden grub*), and so on purports to be an analysis of real phenomena rather than fictional entities, the failure to find the reality of things through such analysis entails that those things do not exist and so that so-called conventional reality is entirely nonexistent. Gorampa writes:

> Suppose someone replied: If that were the case, even conventional truths would have to be the object of negation from the perspective of the ultimate rational analysis.
>
> Precisely, absolutely. This is because they are not found at all when subjected to ultimate rational analysis. (1969a, 392c; 2002, 178)[19]

Gorampa also agues that the Prāsaṅgika Mādhyamika rejects the reality of all existent objects because s/he rejects the existence of any common object that can be a basis of philosophical debate between the Ābhidharmika and the Prāsaṅgika. He argues that since the Ābhidharmika is committed to the reality of things and because Prāsaṅgika and Ābhidharmika have no object that they accept in common, the Prāsaṅgika must be interpreted as rejecting the reality of things. If, as Tsongkhapa would have it, the Prāsaṅgika's negation of intrinsic existence did not entail negating the reality of the things themselves, then, in Gorampa's view, there could be an object accepted by both as the basis of the debate. But that would be contradictory to the Prāsaṅgika claim to positionlessness in virtue of the impossibility of such a debate:

> Otherwise, if one were debating whether or not appearances are real, the subject would have to be taken to appear in the same way to both the proponent and the opponent. Then if you agreed to this on the grounds of maintaining that only the reality of appearances is to be negated, but not the appearances themselves, you would fall from the Prāsaṅgika position. (1969a, 392c; 2002, 178)[20]

As we have seen, for Tsongkhapa, "mere appearance" is a conventional *truth* and is not the object of negation. What is negated is only appearance established as real, that is, *really established appearance* (*bden grub kyi snang ba*), a conceptual fiction superimposed on the mere appearance. However, for

19. *'o na kun rdzob bden pa'ang mthar thug dpyod pa'i rigs ngor dgag byar 'gyur ro zhe na shin tu'ang 'dod de / mthar thug dpyod pa'i rigs pas brtsal ba'i tshe mi rnyed pa'i phyir ro /.*

20. *de lta ma yin na snang ba'i steng du bden par yod med rtsod pa'i tshe rgol phyi rgol gnyis ka la mthun snang du grub pa'i chos can snang ba yod par 'gyur te / de'i tshe snang ba'i steng du bden pa tsam 'gog gi snang ba mi 'gog par khas blangs pa'i phyir 'dod na thal 'gyur ba'i lugs las nyams so /.*

Gorampa, Tsongkhapa's distinction between *mere appearance* (*snang ba tsam*) and *really established appearance* is of no significance. Neither is real. To endorse either is to reify and to provide a common object for debate, at least in the realm of appearance, hence undermining Candrakīrti's account of Prāsaṅgika.

Gorampa also argues that endorsing the conventional reality of conventional truth undermines soteriology:

> If there is grasping to the reality of phenomena, i.e., the [five] aggregates, then similarly grasping to the reality of person (*gang zag kyi bden 'dzin*) will surely arise, which is itself primal confusion, the first of the twelve links. And all of the subsequent links arise from this one. Thus the root of suffering is grasping to the reality of phenomena (*chos kyi bden 'dzin*). (1969a, 389b–c; 2002, 165)[21]

Gorampa also argues that awakening requires the denial of the reality of conventional phenomena:

> Those who seek to achieve awakening must negate reality: seekers of the awakening of the śrāvakas must negate the reality of the five appropriated aggregates; seekers of the awakening of the pratyekabuddha must, in addition to the former, negate the reality of the external objects and of afflictive defiled phenomena; and seekers of the awakening of the Mahāyāna must negate the fabrication *(spros pa)* of all four extremes. (1969a, 389c–d; 2002, 166–167)[22]

Since all forms of reality must be negated in order to attain full awakening, for Gorampa there is no room for conventional truth as reality.

Moreover, Gorampa argues, conventional realities are objects of negation because their existence is not verified by a buddha's enlightened gnosis. He asserts in *Yang dag lta ba'i 'od zer (The Bright Light of the True View):*

> From the perspective of that kind of cognition, dependently arisen things are the objects of negation; since they are essentially pacified, dependent arising itself too is termed "peace." (1969c, 292a)[23]

21. *chos phung po la bden par 'dzin pa'i bden 'dzin yod na dngos 'dras gang zag gi bden 'dzin nges par 'byung / de nyid yan lag bcu gnyis kyi thog ma'i ma rig pa yin zing / de las yan lag phyi ma rnams 'byung bas sdug bsngal gyi rgyu'i gtso bo ni chos la bden par 'dzin pa'i bden 'dzin yin te /.*

22. *byang chub thob par 'dod pa dag gis bden pa dgag dgos te / nyan thos kyi byang chub thob pa la nyer len gyi phung po'i steng du bden pa dgag dgos / rang rgyal gyi byang chub thob pa la de'i steng du gzung ba phyi rol gyi don dang kun nas nyon mongs kyi chos sogs la bden pa dgag dgos / theg chen gyi byang chub thob pa la mtha' bzhi char gyi spros pa dgag dgos pa'i phyir ro/.*

23. *blo de'i ngor rten 'brel de nyid dgag bya de dag zhi ba'i rang bzhin du gnas pas rten 'brel de nyid la yang zhi ba zhes bya'o /.*

In *Nges don rab gsal*, under the section called "Analysis of whether or not the two truths exist at the level of buddhahood," Gorampa is more direct:

> Conventional realities presented in the contexts [of Nāgārjuna's MMK XXIV.8–10 and Candrakīrti's Mav VI.23–24] are nonexistent [at the level of buddhahood] because where there is no erroneous apprehending subject, its corresponding object [i.e., conventional reality] cannot exist. (1969a, 446b; 2002, 399)[24]

Finally, Gorampa argues that conventional reality is the object of negation on the grounds that all conventional realities are fabrications and that awakening requires the transcendence of all fabrication (*spros bral*). Gorampa identifies fabrication (*spros pa*) and conventional reality in *Nges don rab gsal:*

> In short, the entire conventional and nominal framework, including the eight entities such as arising and cessation addressed in the homage verses of the *Mūlamadhyamakārikā*, as well as everything examined in the twenty-seven chapters, from the one on conditions to the one on views, plus what they present, is fabrication. (1969a, 447c)[25]

Given that fabrication must be negated to achieve awakening, it is clear that all of conventional reality must go. For Gorampa, therefore, there simply is no truth in conventional truth; to be conventionally real is to be completely unreal. To see things as they are is to see nothing at all.

The Central Insight: The Degree to Which Conventional Truth Is True Hinges upon the Understanding of the Object of Negation

Our task here is not to adjudicate the debate between Tsongkhapa and Gorampa. Thakchöe (2007) addresses that issue in detail. Instead, we wish to draw attention to an important refinement that Tibetan thinkers introduced into Madhyamaka philosophy's understanding of the nature of conventional truth and the relation between the two truths. Emptiness was always understood in Madhyamaka thought as a negation and always understood as an external negation. But

24. *zhes pa'i skabs nas bstan pa'i kun rdzob bden pa ni med de / yul can mthong ba brdzun pa med pas / de'i yul med pa'i phyir ro//.*

25. *mdor na rtsa ba shes rab kyi mchod brjod kyi skabs kyi skye 'gag la sogs pa brgyad dang/ rab byed nyi shu rtsa bdun gyis dpyad par bya ba'i rkyen nas lta ba'i bar nyi shu rtsa bdun dang/ des mtshon nas kun rdzob tha snyad kyi rnam gzhag thams cad spros pa yin . . ./.*

going this far does not allow one to determine precisely the status of conventional truth or the relation between the two truths.

By asking the more precise question concerning the object of negation, we can understand the ambivalence in Indian Madhyamaka philosophy and in subsequent traditions more deeply. If one takes the object of negation to be conventional phenomena themselves, conventional truth must be regarded as entirely false, truth only from the perspective of fools, and conventional phenomena as nothing at all. There is no correct perception of conventional phenomena. The only truth on this view is ultimate truth, and the apprehension of ultimate truth is the apprehension of emptiness; in virtue of the fact that emptiness on this view amounts to the nonexistence of apparent phenomena, this is the apprehension of nothing at all.

If, on the other hand, one takes the object of negation to be *intrinsic nature*, superimposed conceptually through primal confusion on conventional phenomena that are in fact empty of such natures, conventional truth is a kind of truth, correlative with ultimate truth. To understand conventional truth correctly is to perceive conventional phenomena as dependently arisen, as empty of intrinsic nature. Ultimate truth on this view is the truth about conventional phenomena, and without them, there would be no ultimate truth either. Perception of ultimate truth is not the perception of nothing but the perception that conventional truth is empty of anything more than nominal existence.

These are radically distinct views of the nature of conventional truth and of the relation between the two truths. Each view, as an account of Indian Madhyamaka thought, has scriptural support, and indeed each view can be supported by citations from different passages of the same text or even slightly different contextual interpretations of the same passage. But by directing our attention to the question of the object of negation, Tibetan scholars have developed a productive way of prosecuting debates about the status of the conventional that reveals more nuance than would have been available otherwise.

6

Can a Mādhyamika Be a Skeptic? The Case of Patsab Nyimadrak

Georges Dreyfus

One of the most puzzling and yet central notions in Madhyamaka philosophy is that of conventional truth. For Buddhist realists, this notion makes a great deal of sense, referring to the convenient ways we have of describing the interactions of the basic elements of reality (Siderits 2003). A pot can be said to fall within the domain of conventional truth in that its existence depends entirely on our convenient ways to describe the extremely complex interactions of the basic building blocks that make up the pot. But for a Mādhyamika, who denies the reality of such basic elements, what does it mean to say that a pot belongs to the domain of conventional truth? This question can be understood from various angles, as is noted in the introduction to this volume. Most important, however, this question interrogates the ontology entailed by the radical Madhyamaka critique and hence can be understood as raising this further question: What does it mean to say that phenomena such as pots and plants are conventionally real in a philosophy that rejects the very notion of reality?

Among the many possible answers available to the Mādhyamika, the simplest, though perhaps the most jarring, is the skeptical one: Nothing. There is nothing real about conventional phenomena because the very notion of reality is problematic and cannot be used without falling into a dogmatic and hence extreme position. Hence, the wise person who follows the middle way should remain satisfied with suspending judgment about all statements pertaining to how things are and be contented with living in accordance with the ways things appear and the conventions of the world. In this perspective, the idea of a conventional truth is merely a pragmatic and skillful way to explicate our responses to the exigencies of daily life and clear away metaphysical confusions, not a way to do constructive philosophy and find a place for distinctions between what is more and what is less real.

This skeptical answer may appear at first as being outside of the range of acceptable Madhyamaka interpretations. How can Mādhyamikas, who are after all committed to the truths of the Buddhist tradition, hold a position that rests on the suspension of all judgments about how things are? Should Mādhyamikas not be committed to some truth due to their belonging to a tradition that makes all kind of pronouncements about the deeper features of human existence and the nature of reality? Moreover, should Mādhyamikas not take seriously the doctrine of the two truths and use it to find a place for the truths that Buddhism is committed to? In this chapter, we answer some of these difficult questions by focusing on the works of Patsab Nyimadrak (*pa tshab nyi ma grags*, 1055–1145?), the translator and promoter of Candrakīrti's works in Tibet.

We begin with a review of some of the previous interpretations of Madhyamaka as a form of skepticism. We consider Matilal's analysis of Nāgārjuna's refutation of Hindu realist epistemology and Garfield's description of a broad cross-cultural skeptical family including Sextus Empiricus, Nāgārjuna, Hume, Tsongkhapa, and Wittgenstein. In criticizing these two interpretations, we focus on two related questions that are at the center of the skeptical interpretation of Madhyamaka. Should skepticism be taken as a doctrine making truth claims about the limits and even impossibility of knowing, or should it be approached in an entirely different way, as a radical suspension of any assertion? And if so, is such a radical suspension compatible with constructive philosophy?

To tackle *these* questions we turn to Patsab's defense of the Prāsaṅgika interpretation and his refutation of the Svātantrika. The problem with the latter, argues Patsab, is that, in suggesting that emptiness can be established through logically compelling autonomous arguments, it ignores Nāgārjuna's fundamental insight: Madhyamaka does not aim at rejecting particular views as false but seeks to overcome the very act of asserting or negating a thesis. We examine Patsab's understanding of this thesislessness and contrast his interpretation with that attributed to him by the later tradition. In the process, we will explore the therapeutic nature of his Madhyamaka, and we will see that his stance has significant parallels among ancient Greek skeptics. We will then examine the consequences of this skeptical stance for some of the key Madhyamaka doctrines, such as the two truths, and show how Patsab understands them pragmatically. We will also examine his conception of enlightenment, which he also understands pragmatically rather than cognitively. Finally, we explore some of the consequences of the skeptical approach for the various domains of human experience, particularly morality, where it would appear that the skeptic finds it difficult to overcome relativism.

Madhyamaka and Skepticism

Although the connection between skepticism and Madhyamaka may appear at first surprising, it is not new within modern Madhyamaka scholarship. For example, B. K. Matilal understands Nāgārjuna as offering a skeptical argument against his Hindu realist adversaries and their epistemology (Matilal 1986, 46–68). For Matilal, the skeptical argument revolves around a critique of our standards of proof as being logically defective. Our epistemic practices are based on criteria grounded in standards of proof. We do not just have impressions about reality but also hold these impressions to be true in relation to some criteria, which in turn can be assessed in relation to some standards of proof. For the skeptic, as understood by Matilal, these standards fail the test of being logically coherent and hence should be rejected by the rational person. Thus, for Matilal, skeptics understand their stance not just as a skillful attitude that happens to have positive consequences but also as the logical outcome of a sustained investigation into the nature of knowledge, investigation that exposes the true limits of human knowledge. We have all kinds of opinions, and we believe that some of them are true, but a searching inquiry into our justification for holding such a view reveals that we cannot make such claims without involving ourselves in fatal contradictions.

Within the Indian context, Matilal finds such a skeptical challenge in Nāgārjuna's *Vigrahavyāvartanī* (VV), a sustained critique of the Hindu realist (i.e., the Nyāya) epistemology, according to which our epistemic practices require the support of well-established means of reliable cognition (*pramāṇa*).[1] For Nāgārjuna, such a requirement is impossible since it either begs the question (presupposing the very standards that it seeks to establish) or it leads to an unacceptable infinite regress, in which every appeal to some standard presupposes

1. In this chapter we translate the difficult term of *pramāṇa* as "means of reliable cognition" or simply as "reliable cognition" (instead of "epistemic instrument"). The first term corresponds to its pan-Indian usage, where means of reliable cognition and reliable cognition are distinguished. In the Buddhist context, however, this distinction is dropped, and hence we use the term "reliable cognition" when referring to *pramāṇa* in the Buddhist context. I think that these translations have the advantage of avoiding jargon while at the same time capturing the reliabilist view of knowledge, or rather, its rough Indian equivalent, *pramāṇa*, which Buddhist thinkers share. For a translation of Nāgārjuna's VV, see Bhattacharya (1978, 1986). For a discussion of the Nyāya epistemology, see Matilal (1971, 1985).

another standard of justification. In either case, the requirement that every claim be supported by some well-established means of knowledge fails and leads to logical contradictions. The conclusion is that it is logically inconsistent to require every epistemic episode to be supported by some well-established means of reliable cognition. Hence, we should dispense with this requirement and realize that we do not have principled ways to distinguish veridical from nonveridical cognitions.

Nāgārjuna's refutation raises an immediate objection from his realist opponent (Matilal 1986, 64). If there are no well-established means of reliable cognition, what is then the epistemic status of this refutation? Is it itself reliable? If it is, it should be supported by some well-established means of reliable cognition in flagrant contradiction to the skeptical thesis. If it is not reliable, why should we give it any credence? This question raises another question that is both central to the understanding of the nature of skepticism and to both this chapter and the next: Is skepticism a doctrine that makes truth claims by asserting a thesis (in this case the fact that there are no well-established means of reliable cognition), or is it an altogether different approach that avoids the commitment to any claim through a complete suspension of judgment?

Matilal's answer seems unclear. In some passages, he seems to be taking Nāgārjuna's view as a philosophical doctrine asserting the universality of doubt and the unreliability of human knowledge (Matilal 1986, 54), much as Descartes and modern skeptics tend to do. As he notices, however, this stance would involve Nāgārjuna in a contradiction and would render his skepticism incoherent. Matilal is then tempted to understand Nāgārjuna's skepticism in a different way, not as a true doctrine, but as a radical suspension of any truth claim, much as Sextus Empiricus and ancient skeptics tended to do (Matilal 1986, 66–68), but this would make Nāgārjuna's stance deeply paradoxical. Matilal says:

> The upshot is that a radical skepticism of this kind is not, or does not seem to be, a statable position. For if it is statable, it becomes incoherent and paradoxical. (Matilal, 1986, 65)

If skepticism is not committed to any substantive truth, it becomes embroiled in the paradox that it cannot be stated. For any statement presupposes the assertion or negation of some point and hence entails some truth claim. The essay ends up ambiguously, giving the impression that Matilal has a hard time moving away from his Nyāya loyalties and remains wedded to the idea that skepticism is a doctrine and therefore deeply incoherent.

Although Matilal's understanding of skepticism is problematic, it has the merit of raising the fundamental question that skepticism faces. Is it itself a doctrine committed to some positive or negative truth claims, or is it an entirely different approach, and if it is so, what kind of approach is it? This question is examined by J. Garfield, another proponent of a skeptical interpretation of Madhyamaka. Contrary to Matilal, however, Garfield is clear that the skepticism that can be attributed to Nāgārjuna is not a substantive philosophical doctrine committed to the denial of the possibility of knowledge (like modern skepticism, which is often little more than a preliminary methodological stance to be overcome on the way to a more constructive position) but a suspension of all substantive claims. This is Nāgārjuna's famous thesislessness, about which we will have much more to say. This rejection of any position is taken by Garfield to be similar to Sextus Empiricus's Pyrrhonism and its suspension of belief. However, in delineating his approach to skepticism, Garfield argues that this kind of skepticism is compatible with a constructive philosophical agenda.

In comparing Madhyamaka to Pyrrhonism, Garfield paints with a broad brush, creating a large cross-cultural skeptical family that includes not just Pyrrho, Sextus, and Nāgārjuna but also Hume, Wittgenstein, Kripke, and Tsongkhapa. According to Garfield, such a family is bound by its commitment to giving skeptical solutions to the skeptical problems raised by the nihilist. Saul Kripke describes a skeptical solution in this way:

> A *skeptical* solution of a philosophical problem begins . . . by conceding that the skeptic's negative assertions are unanswerable. Nevertheless our ordinary practice or belief is justified because—contrary appearances notwithstanding—it need not require the justification the skeptic has shown to be untenable. (Kripke 1982, 66–67, quoted in Garfield 2002, 6–7)

The nihilist argues that we cannot make sense of our concepts such as substance, causation, and ethical qualities and that therefore we should repudiate them as unfounded. The skeptical solution is to grant the point that our notions are unfounded but to argue that, far from justifying their rejection, this absence of grounding allows us to proceed using these notions conventionally. Thus, far from substantiating the conclusion that the nihilist wants to draw, skepticism allows for a constructive agenda in which we are justified in using notions such as self, substance, and goodness as forensic devices or as conventional truths, that is, as making sense within the framework of our socially embedded practices.

For the purposes of the present discussion, we do not dispute the merit of drawing such a broad skeptical family for the purpose of initiating a cross-cultural philosophical conversation, but questions can be raised about Garfield's picture of a happy family united around Kripkean skeptical solutions. For, it is hard to ignore that, as in the best families, the alleged agreement between its members involves a fair amount of papering over differences. If we examine Kripke's description of a skeptical solution more closely, we realize that it raises questions concerning the scope of skepticism and its compatibility with constructive philosophy. There is no denying that the skeptical family is broad and includes various positions. Montaigne's idiosyncratic self-examination is not the same as Sextus's Pyrrhonism, which in turn differs from Philo's Academic skepticism. Hence, there is no difficulty in attributing a constructive agenda to some form of skepticism (Academics are often described in this way), but this is much more problematic in the case of those who propound a suspension of judgment, as did Sextus, who explicitly argues against the attempt by the Academy to formulate a constructive skeptical doctrine.[2]

Hence, when we scrutinize more closely the cross-cultural family drawn together by Garfield, we cannot but wonder whether it is as happily united as he wants us to believe. For if Tsongkhapa would enthusiastically take part in the gathering (he may be the thinker, with Kripke, to whom Garfield's description best applies), Sextus or the later Wittgenstein might be more reticent.[3] Moreover, it is problematic to understand skepticism as being based on the suspension of any truth claim while still attempting to find a place for constructive philosophy. To illustrate this point we now turn to Nāgārjuna's philosophy and its tradition.

In examining this tradition, we first need to recognize its complexity and plurality. Although most of Nāgārjuna's commentators partake in its deconstructive approach,[4] they differ in their understandings of its implications. These differences are the result of the interpretive choices made by these commentators and reflect the complexity and ambiguities of Nāgārjuna's textual corpus. Some commentators choose to privilege the more radically skeptical passages in Nāgārjuna's textual corpus, particularly the ones concerning thesislessness and the repudiation of all views. Others privilege more constructive and nonskeptical passages where Nāgārjuna seems to make substantive truth claims, as when he states that things lack any essence or intrinsic nature (*svabhāva*), that this esssencelessness is their ultimate truth, and that it is

2. We discuss alternative interpretations of Pyrrhonism and their relevance to Madhyamaka in chapter 7 in this book.

3. For a response to Kripke's interpretation of Wittgenstein, see Diamond (1991, chap. 1).

4. The use of this term may create an unfortunate impression of trendiness and wrongly suggest some exaggerated comparisons. It should be clear that we do not conflate Madhyamaka and postmodern deconstruction, two styles of thought that differ greatly in the outlook they recommend. Nevertheless, at the level of the philosophical method there are intriguing similarities between these two approaches, which do not seek to develop a critique concepts from the outside but rather from the inside, showing the contradictions they lead to. This critique is less a refutation of a particular thesis, which would "involve the setting-up, within the frame of binary alternatives, of a counter-thesis and the holding of a counter-position" (Seyfort Ruegg 2000, 151). Rather, it is a dissolution of the concept itself, a deconstruction that frees the mind from its grasping.

compatible with the basic Buddhist stance of dependent arising (MMK XXIV).[5] In other passages, Nāgārjuna also seems to make knowledge claims, as when he asserts that this ultimate nature can be known and that such knowledge brings about the freedom from suffering (YSV 22–23 in Scherrer-Schaub 1991, 203–209; SS 68–69a in Burton 1999, 35). Obviously these nonskeptical passages lend themselves to various interpretations, but this is precisely my point.

Nāgārjuna's texts are hence far from being unambiguous, lending themselves to various interpretations (skepticism being just one), which are reflected in the different approaches taken by commentators. This does not mean that we should not pursue the comparison between Madhyamaka and skepticism but that we may be in better position to do so if we narrow our focus and chose a single commentator who offers a less ambiguous Madhyamaka interpretation. Hence, instead of trying to determine "what Nāgārjuna really thought" (a highly dubious enterprise given the rich polysemy of his textual corpus), we here focus on a single thinker, Patsab Nyimadrak, the translator of Candrakīrti's works and the initiator of the Prāsaṅgika line of Madhyamaka interpretation in Tibet.

Up to now, Patsab had been known almost exclusively as a translator, his commentarial works having been lost. This situation has changed with the publication (in the *bKa' gdams gsung 'bum*) of three works attributed to him. There are obvious questions about the authenticity of these texts (Dreyfus 2009). For the purpose of this chapter, however, these questions do not matter. All we need to keep in mind here is that there is a well-established interpreter of Nāgārjuna who understands him to hold a stance comparable to Sextus's Pyrrhonian skepticism. In the context of this chapter, we assume that this author is Patsab, although it could turn out that the author of these texts is somebody else or that they are his but actually reflect the opinion of another author such as Mahāsumati, his teacher in Kashmir. It should be clear that the scope of this comparison is limited. We are not comparing Prāsaṅgika or Candrakīrti and his followers to Pyrrhonian skepticism but only Patsab.[6] For, although Candrakīrti and most of his later Tibetan interpreters may share some commonality with Sextus, they are also likely to differ in several respects

5. In this chapter we translate *svabhāva* as "essence" or "essential property," that is, what the thing really is, the property that really makes the thing what it is. Therefore, essence or essential property is not to be understood in the Aristotelian sense as being opposed to accidental properties but as synonymous with intrinsic property, the hypothetical construct that Madyamaka, as an antiessentialist philosophy, is arguing against.

6. This is not to claim that Patsab holds an original position. His interpretation comes from his contact with Indian pandits such as Mahāmati, his teacher. In fact, Patsab seems to be saying in the colophon of this text that he is merely repeating the opinions of his teacher Mahāsumati. Similar views are also found in Jayānanda (Vose 2008). Hence, it appears that Patsab's view was not just his but was shared by a group of Candrakīrti's followers in Kashmir. See Dreyfus (2009).

(as explained in the next chapter), particularly in their willingness to find some limited room within Madhyamaka for the notion of reliable cognition (*pramāṇa*).

Patsab's Prāsaṅgika

The texts considered here focus mostly on exegetical matters and are not philosophically very sophisticated. Nevertheless, they provide an interesting and thought-provoking picture of a consistently skeptical approach to Madhyamaka, as well as a historical document about the development of Prāsaṅgika interpretation. The gist of the Prāsaṅgika approach as understood by Patsab is that Mādhyamikas should not try to establish emptiness through reasoning demonstrating that phenomena are empty of intrinsic nature. Rather, they should take as their targets particular views asserting various possible candidates for articulating how things exist and show the internal contradictions these views lead to through *reductio* arguments (*prasaṅga, thal 'gyur*). Mādhyamikas should not attempt to prove a general thesis but should stick to the refutation of opinions relating to particular topics on the basis of their adversaries' assumptions, as Nāgārjuna did in his *Mūlamadhyamakakārikā*. This is the proper procedure that Mādhyamikas should follow, and this is what distinguishes the appropriate approach, the Prāsaṅgika interpretation, from that of the Svātantrika. Whereas the former are appropriately skeptical about the possibility of establishing the view of emptiness as true through logically compelling demonstrations, the latter attempts to do so, suggesting that it is possible to make substantive claims about how things are and hence that the view of emptiness is correct. Let us further explore this topic and appreciate its importance for our appraisal of a skeptical Madhyamaka interpretation (Patsab 2006, 38).

The question of the ways in which emptiness is established may seem arcane, but in fact it is not, for it connects to central philosophical issues. For Patsab, the Svātantrika approach is not just mistaken in determining the dialectical tools appropriate to Madhyamaka but ignores and even threatens Nāgārjuna's central insight that emptiness is not a view but the suspension of all views.[7] Understanding emptiness does not entail the adoption of a doctrine that asserts some essential truths about how things are and rejects other views as mistaken. Rather, it is an insight that frees us from the compulsion to make

7. The best known passage in which this insight is expressed is MMK XIII.8, where Nāgārjuna declares that emptiness is the relinquishing of all views and that the one who takes emptiness to be such a view is incurable. See Garfield (1995, 212).

such claims. Hence, it is completely self-defeating for Mādhyamikas to attempt to demonstrate emptiness through reasoning, for this reinscribes the very essentialism that Madhyamaka seeks to overcome. The very project of following the middle path that avoids any extreme—that is, any dogmatic position—is threatened by the attempt to set emptiness as the right view. To make his point, Patsab proceeds through a lengthy analysis following the usual lines of inquiry of Indian epistemology of the various means of reliable cognition, through which the doctrine of emptiness could be validated, showing how each possibility leads to contradictions.

One of the ways in which a thesis can be established for some Indian epistemologists is through verbal testimony (*śābda*). The Nyāya, for instance, argues that language is one of the four means of reliable cognition, for one can come to acquire knowledge in dependence on reliable testimony. Buddhist epistemologists, however, reject this view, arguing that language is not a sui generis means of reliable cognition. Following this standard Buddhist view, Patsab argues that language cannot establish the Madhyamaka view that all things lack a real essence as true, for the simple fact of stating such a view does not make it true. Otherwise, the thesis that things have a real essence would also be true since it can be stated.

In that case, can inference, another well-established means of reliable cognition, establish emptiness as true, like it does in the case of other theses and as Svātantrikas argue? For Patsab, this is not possible, for an inference requires a probative argument (*sbyor ba* = *prayoga*) whose terms (the subject, the reason, and the pervasion, *khyab ba* = *vyāpti*) are established by reliable cognitions in common to the two parties taking part in the argument. This is what is called an autonomous inference (*rang rgyud kyi rjes dpag* = *svātantrānumāna*), that is, an inference supported by an argument whose terms are established in common by the two parties independently of the particular ways in which they view things. For Patsab, such an inference is not possible within the context of a discussion of the ultimate nature of things, for if the terms of the argument were established by a reliable cognition, they could not be refuted or undermined by any other reliable cognition.

The requirement that the terms of the inquiry should be established in common by both parties and should not be undermined by the conclusion may seem unexceptional, but it creates a particular problem within the context of Madhyamaka inquiry. This is so because this inquiry is based on the investigation of the ultimate nature of things. In such an investigation, one looks for the essence of the examined phenomenon among, for example, its parts. Upon not finding it, one comes to realize that such a phenomenon lacks any true essence, that is, that its ultimate nature is that it lacks such an intrinsic nature.

For Patsab, the nonfindability of a particular phenomenon is not just a failure to find the phenomenon through a particular mode of analysis (as it is for Tsongkhapa, for example). Instead, it shows that the phenomenon itself cannot be validated. It undermines (*gnod* = *bādhā*) or invalidates the phenomenon itself. Hence, Mādhyamikas cannot use probative arguments to demonstrate the absence of ultimate essence without committing themselves to the very essentialist view that they are attempting to disassemble.

The Svātantrikas reply that the establishment of the terms of the reasoning by a reliable cognition does not entail that the objects to which they refer exist ultimately. The terms of the reasoning are established, they argue, by conventional reliable cognitions that do not differentiate whether things exist ultimately or not but merely ascertain them according to how they appear ordinarily. Hence, there is no problem in finding a common subject in reference to which Mādhyamikas and their adversaries can argue.[8] Mādhyamikas can deploy their arguments against their adversaries in reference to conventional phenomena, which are established on the basis of common appearances, much as Buddhists demonstrate to Vaiśeṣikas that sounds are impermanent on the basis of the common understanding of sound despite the fact that both parties have a different understanding of the nature of sound.

For Patsab, this example is inconclusive since in the case of the ascertainment of the impermanence of the sound, the common conception of sound is not negated by the realization that it is impermanent, whereas the insight into the lack of essence of the subject undermines the reality of the subject itself. This insight comes as a result of the search for the ultimate nature of the subject, a process through which one decides whether the subject really exists or not. One then comes to the provisional conclusion that it does not really exist. This conclusion does not mark, however, the end of the inquiry, for one should also realize that the subject does not not-exist either.[9] Nevertheless, it remains the case that it is the very subject of the inquiry that is negated in the Madhyamaka inquiry, not some other entity. Hence, if the subject were to be established by a conventional reliable cognition, its existence would be confirmed, and it could not be undermined by the search for its intrinsic nature. Hence, it would have to exist ultimately.[10]

8. *chos can la sogs pa'i yang dag du grub par 'gyur bas rang bzhin med pa nyams ces pa'i skyon mi 'ong ste chos can ji ltar snang ba tsam po gang gis kyang khyad par du ma byas la tha snyad pa'i tshad mas grub gtan tshigs gcig dang du ma bcad pa tsam yang tha snyad pa'i tshad mar mngon sum yod par 'dod pas grub/* (Patsab 2006, 43).

9. I am here obviously alluding to Nāgārjuna's famous tetralemmic approach. For a classical treatment of this question, see Seyfort Ruegg (1977).

10. *chos can snang ba dang gtan tshigs tshad mas grub na tshad mas grub pa la tshad ma gzhan gyi (gyis?) mi gnod pas na chos can la sogs pa don dam pa'i bden par grub par thal bas na rang bzhin med par mi 'thad do/* (Patsab 2006, 43).

The conclusion is then that emptiness cannot be established by an inference. Could it then be established by a yogic perception (*rnal 'byor mngon sum* = *yogipratyakṣa*)? No, replies Patsab, for any yogic perception is born from the habituation to and the enhancement of the insight that one gains through inference. But since emptiness is beyond the scope of inference, it cannot be made into an object of yogic perception (Patsab 2006, 48). Hence, emptiness cannot be established either by inference or by perception.

How then can Mādhyamikas proclaim emptiness if the assertion of the emptiness of things cannot be established as true? Patsab's answer is that the emptiness of things indeed is not established as true. Mādhyamikas do not have any thesis to establish, view to defend, or position to eliminate about how things really are. They merely proceed by consequences exposing the contradictions to which the views of their adversaries lead. Mādhyamikas are not in the game of demonstrating the truth or falsity of claims about how things are. They do not need to defend their position as true and criticize their adversaries as being mistaken, for they do not believe that it makes any sense to make claims about how things are. Since nothing can be found under analysis, no statement can be established as true upon being analyzed from an ultimate perspective or, for that matter, shown to be false. Even emptiness is not findable under analysis, and hence the statement that things are empty cannot pretend to be true since it sets up an object (emptiness) that fails to be confirmed by further analysis. Hence, even when they offer the proposition that phenomena are empty, Mādhyamikas should not be understood to hold this proposition to be true and to decry the opposite proposition to be false.

Similarly, for Patsab, Mādhyamikas should not take their "conclusions" to follow logically from unassailable arguments. The claim that phenomena are empty is not a conclusion that follows logically from the contradictions contained in their opponents' views. Rather, it is merely a provisional stance, a skillful slogan that aims at showing opponents the way to get out of the contradictions entailed by their own commitments. Hence, Matilal's depiction of Mādhyamikas as asserting that the realist view is logically inconsistent and that logic requires them to adopt an antirealist position misses the point. It assumes that Mādhyamikas are committed to the rules of logic and argue that their arguments conform better to the canon of sound reasoning than those of their opponents. But to say this, argues Patsab, would be to ignore the fact that Mādhyamikas should merely argue on the basis of their opponents' own ground and rules but should not have any other commitment over and above those necessary to the pursuit of the conversation.

It is precisely this lack of commitment that the realist opponents seem to miss when they argue that Madhyamaka arguments are self-stultifying. For if it is true that phenomena lack any essence and have merely conventional existence, is it not the case, ask the realist opponents, that the truth of this very statement becomes merely a matter of convention and hence lacks any validity? Nāgārjuna's famous answer is well known and illustrates the attitude that Patsab sees as being at the core of Madhyamaka:

> If I had any position, I would, in virtue of that, commit an error.
> But since I have no position, I commit no error at all.[11]

The realist objection would be true if Mādhyamikas were in the business of establishing some claims about how things are, but since they are not, it just misses the point. Mādhyamikas are neither in the business of defending true positions about how things are nor in that of exposing wrong ones. Hence, they cannot be assailed on the ground of being inconsistent since they do not hold to any view whatsoever. It is this stance of "thesislessness" (*khas len kun bral*), that is, of complete suspension of assertion and negation about how things are, that can be usefully compared to Sextus' skepticism.

Often skepticism is thought to be limited to a suspension of belief about knowledge claims. This is how it is often depicted in modern philosophy, where Descartes' method is taken to represent its quintessence. For the modern skeptic, we gain impressions at the contact of reality, and it is on this basis that we form beliefs about how things are. In doing so, we can be said to be justified, for these impressions help us to various degrees in our dealings with the world, but there is no way for us to know with certainty the things that give rise to these impressions.

This epistemological interpretation is, however, quite different from Sextus' skepticism. For one thing, it is dualistic, assuming a radical separation between the unknowable external reality and the internal domain of our subjective evaluations, which are given to us absolutely. It also assumes that although we can never know with certainty how things are in reality, we can form more or less informed opinions about them over and above how they appear to us. But it is precisely this possibility that Sextus rejects, suggesting that it makes no sense to attempt to think about how things are over and above how they appear to us. Hence, it is most judicious to suspend judgment not just about knowledge but also about any view concerning the way things are and limit our practices to appearances. We explore this reading further in the next chapter.

11. Nāgārjuna VV 29, quoted in Patsab (2006, 49). For a thorough examination of this statement, see Seyfort Ruegg (2000). Asimilar point is made in YSV 50–51; see Scherrer-Schaub (1991, 294–296).

Patsab recommends a similar stance, arguing that it makes no sense for Mādhyamikas to hold to any thesis, positive or negative. There are, however, crucial differences between his method and Pyrrhonism, which seeks to reach a suspension of belief by outlining the arguments for and against a thesis. In this way, a standstill is reached, and the mind is brought to suspend judgment concerning the application of a particular concept (Striker 1983). The Madhyamaka method does not satisfy itself with reaching such a balance but, rather, seeks to go beyond the concept by deconstructing it, showing the contradictions to which any of its uses lead. Hence, in some ways, its thesislessness can be said to go further than the skeptical *epochē*. It nevertheless remains that their stance (suspension of belief/freedom from view) and their goal (the peace and freedom that come about through such stance) is quite similar, thus revealing the nature and scope of their philosophy.

In Tibet, this topic of thesislessness animated numerous commentators, who debated over whether it should be taken literally or not. Patsab is often credited by later authors such as Gorampa with the view that although Mādhyamikas do not entertain positive theses, they hold negative ones.[12] But this does not appear to be Patsab's position. His assertion that Mādhyamikas do not hold any thesis elicits objections from an opponent, who argues that although Mādhyamikas have no positive thesis (*yongs gcod gyi bsgrub bya*), they must have negative theses (*rnam bcad dgag pa tsam gyi bsgrub bya*) since they refute the view of their adversaries. To this Patsab responds unambiguously that negative theses are not different from positive ones and hence that both are to be rejected. Patsab states:

> Objection: Although you do not accept positive theses, you must accept negative theses, i.e., mere negations. Hence, you must also accept reasonings establishing them. Answer: I do not even accept negative theses, for if the essence of that which is to be negated does not exist, its negation cannot hold either.[13]

As we can see here quite clearly, there is no ambiguity: Patsab rejects both types of thesis, for both presuppose that it is feasible to make claims about how things are. The use by Mādhyamikas of a negative dialectic does not seek to argue for the truth of their view or the falsity of other views. It also does not show that there are true contradictions. Rather, it aims at exposing the problems created by the attitude of asserting or negating a thesis. Hence, its actual

12. Seyfort Ruegg (2000, 48, 159–160).

13. *khyed yongs gcod kyi bsgrub bya mi 'dod kyang rnam gcad dgag pa tsam gyi bsgrub bya 'dod dgos pas de sgrub pa'i gtan tshigs la sogs pa khas len rgos so zhe na/ nged la dgag pa tsam gyi bsgrub bya'ang 'dod pa med de dgag bya'i rang bzhin ma grub pas na bkag pa yang mi 'thad de/* (Patsab 2006, 49).

target is not some thesis to be negated, either p or $\sim p$, but, rather, the assent to p or to $\sim p$ (or to both or to neither).[14] Hence, far from being a flippant neglect of the most basic rules of reasoning or a careless embrace of contradictions, this approach seeks to recommend a new attitude of suspension of all claims, positive or negative, for they both lead to dogmaticism and attachment to one's view.

Any description, either positive or negative, of how things are is bound to be problematic and hence ultimately to be suspended. We may want to approach the ultimate nature of things through various helpful descriptions of the type "things are devoid of intrinsic nature," but it is important not to lose sight of the fact that these statements are merely helpful indications of how to proceed in our quest for freedom from suffering rather than true descriptions of the ultimate nature of things since such nature is utterly beyond any description and radically ineffable. This is so not because reality is too much to be contained within our limited conceptual schemas but, on the contrary, because it is not enough. Things lack any core features that could be seized upon by descriptions, and hence language is bound to fail to capture the ultimate. All that language can do is to provide provisional accounts of how things appear to us (*snang ba*), and, as far as the ultimate is concerned, metaphors indicating the direction in which to proceed and helpful therapies to cure the habit of holding appearances to reflect the ways things are in reality.

Skepticism, the Two Truths, and Buddhahood

This rejection of both negative and positive theses establishes Patsab as a bona fide skeptic and differentiates him from a nihilist. The nihilist rejects the notion of truth to privilege that of falsity. Patsab does not just reject the truth of all propositions in order to assert their falsity. Rather, he argues that any opinion about how things are is problematic. Hence, Patsab recommends remaining without any thesis (*khas len kun bral*), an attitude of perfect nonabiding (*rab tu mi gnas pa*) that I take to be similar to Sextus' Pyrrhonian suspension (*epochē*) of all beliefs.[15] The dialectical tools used by Sextus differ from those recommended by the Madhyamaka, but their aim appears to be very similar. In both

14. We could say that the Madhyamaka negation should not be understood in the usual locutionary way (as asserting $\sim p$ and $\sim\sim p$) but as being illocutionary (I deny that either p or $\sim p$ can be asserted). Matilal himself considers this point but seems unable to see how it answers the realist objection. See Matilal (1986, 66–67). For an insightful discussion of this topic and thesislessness in general, see Seyfort Ruegg (1983, 1969).

15. This discussion of ancient skepticism follows the views expressed by Burnyeat (1983), Mates (1996), and Hallie (1964). For a discussion of the skeptical dialectic, see Striker (1983).

cases, reason examines all the possibilities to reach a point a point of complete suspension. Hence, Sextus compares his philosophy to a purge that first gets rid of the disease at which it is aimed before eliminating itself (Sedley 1983, 12). He also compares his arguments to a ladder to be thrown away once it has been climbed (Burnyeat 1983b, 139). Arguments are to be used to relinquish all views (to use Nāgārjuna's language), not to make some philosophical point, positive or negative. Hence, statements such as "we cannot know anything" and "all beliefs are false," which are usually taken to express the skeptical stance, are to be avoided except, perhaps, as skillful means (to use again a Madhyamaka term) to bring about the peace and detachment (*ataraxia*) that the skeptic aims for. Hence, skepticism is not a doctrine but a way of living philosophically one's life without being entangled in the web of beliefs that binds most people and creates much suffering.

This attitude differs from modern skepticism, which holds that we are forever enclosed within the limitations of our subjectivity. For the modern skeptic such as Descartes, there is a clear separation between the inner domain of beliefs, hopes, and desires and the realm of objective facts that we seek to approach through various sciences but which actually remains forever out of our reach. This dualism clearly differs from Pyrrhonian skepticism, which finds the problem not in the separation of the inner and the outer but in the very act of asserting or negating any proposition. It also clearly differs from Madhyamaka, for which the deconstruction of the inner-outer dichotomy is at the very core of its project.

Patsab is not a skeptic *because he is committed to* the Madhyamaka deconstructive approach but *because he understands this project as being incompatible with holding any thesis.* For Patsab, Madhyamaka is not a doctrine asserting some truth and refuting other positions. Rather, it is a middle way that avoids falling into any dogmatic extreme of "is" and "is not." This stance provides a therapeutic approach that seeks to overcome the problems created by the attachment to any particular view. It is this stance that differentiates Patsab from other Mādhyamikas and justifies the comparison with Pyrrhonian skepticism. We consider the degree to which this comparison can be extended to other Mādhyamika thinkers such as Candrakīrti, Tsongkhapa, and Gorampa in the next chapter.

As we can imagine, the wholesale rejection of any serious idea of true statement as far as how things exist has important consequences for several of the doctrines that are taken to be central to Madhyamaka. This is particularly so for the doctrine of the two truths, which seems to play such an important role for Mādhyamikas, particularly for later commentators. As we saw earlier in chapter 1, Nāgārjuna himself emphatically declared:

> The various buddhas' teaching of the Dharma relies upon two truths: the conventional truth of the world (*lokasaṃvṛtisatya*) and what is true from the ultimate perspective (*paramārthataḥ*).[16]

What can Patsab say about this schema, which seems so basic to the Madhyamaka? Is it not contradicted by the radical suspension of truth recommended by the skeptic? And is it not precisely this notion of conventional truth that needs to be preserved in order to find a place for constructive philosophy within the skeptical tradition? Patsab's answer is clear and unambiguous. The two truths should not be construed as a doctrine endowed with some intrinsic validity and opposed to that of other schools. This schema is not meant to create a place for constructive philosophy on the basis of the validity that worldly practices have, for it is merely a skillful means of providing pragmatic guidelines on how to go on living one's life. It is also a way to clear away metaphysical confusion. Asked by an opponent why the two truths are propounded, Patsab enumerates a list of wrong views to be eliminated, such as the denial that past and future lives exist and the view that things are permanent. He then concludes:

> [The two truths] were spoken to refute these views, not because they are established by reliable cognitions (*tshad ma = pramāṇa*).[17]

The two truths are not some autonomous doctrine, a way for Mādhyamikas to have their systematic philosophy while eating their skeptical cake, too. Rather, the value of the doctrine of the two truths is pragmatic and hence devoid of normative force. It simply points to the force and value of common sense, thus providing ways for the skeptic to interact with others and help them to free themselves from their dogmatic hangovers and metaphysical confusions. But such appeal should not be misconstrued for Patsab as offering the basis for a systematic Madhyamaka philosophy.

We may, however, wonder about the understanding of emptiness. Is it not true? Here again, Patsab's answer is quite clear. Even the direct realization of emptiness is not a reliable cognition, for its object, emptiness, is undermined when it is further analyzed. Hence, even yogic perceptions cannot be asserted to be true. We may wonder, however, how far we are to take this radical denial of the validity of transcendent wisdom. Does it apply to the Buddha as well? If so, how are we to understand his wisdom, which is at times described as omniscient? In the third text Patsab gives a very brief indication that seems to

16. Nāgārjuna MMK XXIV.8; Skt. and translation at the beginning of chapter 1; see also Garfield (1995, 296).

17. *lta de dag dgag pa'i don du gsungs kyi tshad mas grub nas bzhag pa ma yin no/* (Patsab 2006, 49).

confirm that the denial of validity does not concern solely ordinary beings but includes the wisdom of the Buddha as well. He says:

> As for the nature of conventional truth, it is the appearance to ordinary beings and the grasping to form and so on under the power of the passions and the obstructions to full knowledge. It is also the appearance free from grasping of the bodhisattvas who have entered the great stages [of the ārya bodhisattva] to the perceptions following [the direct realization of emptiness] due to their not having abandoned the obstructions to full knowledge. The appearance to the omniscient mind is the ultimate truth. This term "appearance to the omniscient mind" should be understood to refer merely to the cessation of the stream of consciousness and mental factors like the cessation of fabrications (*spros pa = prapañca*) due to the absence of the way of looking of ordinary beings with grasping and of that of bodhisattvas free from such grasping. This term should not be [understood to refer to] a seeing taking something as an object, much like the double moon and falling hairs appear to someone with ophthalmia, despite their nonexistence, but not to those free from such disease.[18]

Patsab follows Candrakīrti precisely in his understanding of buddhahood as consisting of the elimination of all the obstacles to the full realization of emptiness. The buddha's wisdom is not a panoramic omniscience in which all phenomena are perceived in their particularities. Rather, it is the actualization of the full potential of the realization of emptiness through which the Buddha is enabled to help other beings in exactly the appropriate way. Moreover, this realization should not be understood to be cognitive in the usual sense of the word, for it does not cognize any object, positive or negative. This wisdom is not a cognitively active state engaged in figuring particular objects but, rather, is the cessation of any attempt to cognize reality.[19]

Although this description of the realization of emptiness is short, it reveals quite clearly Patsab's understanding of the implications of what may

18. *ngo bo ni nyong mongs pa dang shes bya'i sgrib pa'i dbang gis gzugs la sogs par zhen cing byis pa la snang ba dang sa chen po la zhugs pa'i bo des shes bya'i sgrib pa ma spang pas rjes kyi shes pa la zhen pa dang bral ba'i snang ba la yod pa ni kund rdzob kyi bden pa yin la/ tham cad mkhyen pa'i snang ba ni don dam pa'i bden pa ste tham cad mkhyen pa la snang ba zhes bya ba'ang byis pas zhen pa dang bcas par mthong ba dang bo des zhen pa dang bral bar mthong ba de ltar mthong ba med pas chos nyid spros pa dang bral bzhin du sems dang sems las byung ba'i 'jug pa rgyun chad pa tsam la tha snyad gdags par zad kyi yul du byas pa'i sgo nas mthong ba yod pa ma yin ste dper na rab rib la zla ba gnyis dang skra shad la sogs pa med snang gi rab rib med pa la mi snang ba zhin no/* (Patsab 2006, 146).

19. For an excellent discussion of the views of Candrakīrti and Śāntarakṣita concerning omniscience, see McClintock (2000).

be called *Madhyamaka skepticism* for Buddhist soteriology. It is true that Patsab's main concern in the works we examine here is not Buddhist soteriology but the elimination of the reification of knowledge. It is in this perspective that he sees Svātantrika as an example of how this reification can infect and corrupt the very Madhyamaka that is supposed to provide the antidote to this disease. Hence, his main concern is to counteract this tendency toward reification, not to provide an analysis of the epistemic status of transcendent wisdom. Moreover, he is ready to draw radical consequences from his views and does not exclude the transcendent wisdom from the deconstruction of knowledge. Even the direct realization of emptiness is not true in the sense that it does not have an object that can be confirmed by further investigation. Such wisdom is true, however, in the sense that it is the final realization of the futility of looking for such a form of knowledge. For Patsab, this is the only wisdom that is available.

What Skeptics Can and Cannot Do

This response shows the radical nature of Patsab's interpretation and his commitment to the skeptical idea of suspension of all belief, positive or negative. It is in this perspective that we may want to consider the question of the possibility of constructive philosophy within skepticism. We recall Garfield's description of the happy family united around Kripkean skeptical solutions. It should come as no surprise that Patsab would find it difficult to take part in such a gathering, for he refuses to find any place for knowledge or, rather, its Indian counterpart, reliable cognition, within Madhyamaka philosophy, even on the conventional level. He says:

> As for the first point concerning the answer to five questions about reliable cognitions, one could ask: do you accept that there are objects of reliable cognitions (*gzhal bya = prameya*)? Answer: I do not accept reliable cognition, since both reliable cognitions and their objects have been refuted [by Nāgārjuna] in [his] VV. This is so because reliable cognitions require objects but no such objects exist. Some hold both that conventional reliable cognitions realize [their objects] in accordance with what is renowned and that the ultimate is realized [by ultimate reliable cognitions]. This is incorrect, for anyone who accepts conventional reliable cognition [has to accept that] inasmuch as a reliable cognition realizes its object, it cannot be undermined by another reliable cognition and hence [its object] would have to be

> real. Therefore, if either a so-called conventional reliable cognition or a nondual [i.e., ultimately] reliable cognition were established, then its object would have to be real. Hence, there are no reliable cognitions whatsoever, and so we do not accept [this notion]. Objection: If there were no reliable cognitions, there would be no distinction between the two truths. Answer: I accept that ultimately the distinction between the two truths does not exist. It is not established in reality but has been taught by Buddha and the Noble Ones (or the two Noble Ones, i.e., Nāgārjuna and Āryadeva) conventionally to meet some [particular] need.[20]

Patsab rejects completely the notion of reliable cognition and suggests a clear and thorough skepticism that seems to exclude the possibility of a constructive program. For Patsab, it does not make any sense for a Mādhyamika to try to find a place for reliable cognition, either on the ultimate or on the conventional level. For cognition to be reliable, it must be uncontradicted by other cognitions; that is, its object cannot be undermined by any subsequent inquiry. But this is precisely what happens when the object of cognition is examined within the context of Madhyamaka inquiry. There, upon searching for its essence, the inquiry leads to the realization that the object does not really exist and that our idea of an object existing really independently of our conceptions is deeply incoherent. Hence, the cognition of such an object, which posits such an object as really existing, cannot be true. Even the direct realization of emptiness is not, as we have just seen, true. Hence, for Patsab, there is no place whatsoever within Madhyamaka for the notion of reliable cognition, for it threatens to reintroduce the very extremes that this approach seeks to overcome.

Patsab hence takes a very radical position that differentiates him from many other Mādhyamikas, even perhaps from Candrakīrti, who seems to want to find some place, however limited, for reliable cognition.[21] This radical rejection of reliable cognition has fatal consequences for the project of a constructive Madhyamaka philosophy. For to get off the ground, this project would

20. *gnyis pa tshad ma la dri ba lnga'i lan gdab pa las dang po ni khyod gzhal bya khas mi len na tshad khas len nam ma yin zhe na/ nged tshad ma khas mi len te tshad ma dang gzhal bya gnyis ka rtsod zlog du bkag pas te/ tshad ma la gzhal bya yod rgos la gzhal bya med pa'i phyir ro/ kha cig tha snyad pa'i tshad ma grags tshod du 'jal ba dang don dam 'jal ba gnyis yod zer na/ myi 'thad de tha snyad pa'i tshad mar 'dod pa des rtogs pa'i don la tshad ma yin phan cod tshad ma gzhan gyis mi gnod pas de yang dag du 'gyur bas na tha snyad pa'i tshad ma ces pa dang gnyis med kyi tshad ma gcig grub na de'i don bden par 'gyur bas na tshad ma gang yang med de khas mi len to/ tshad ma med na bden pa gnyis kyi dbye med par 'gyur ro zhe na/ bden pa gnyis kyi dbye ba don dam par med par thal ba 'dod thog yin pa la/ don do 'chad bka' tha snyad du rgos pa'i dbang gis bu ta dang 'phags pa dag gsung bas so/* (Patsab 2006, 49).

21. In such a short chapter it is impossible do justice to this topic, which has already been well examined by Siderits (1980, 1981).

require a principled way to differentiate reliable from nonreliable cognitions. But since this differentiation is not feasible, there cannot be any principled way to distinguish what can be validly asserted from what cannot be, and hence the very idea of a Madhyamaka constructive philosophy becomes untenable.

Sextus seems to entertain a similar approach when he decries the attempt to find a place for constructive philosophy within skepticism by some of the members of the Academy in their debate against Stoic opponents. Carneades, for example, is depicted as advocating a fallibilism based on the distinction between more or less convincing impressions.[22] We are subject to experiences, things appear to us in certain ways, and this can be taken as a basis for a constructive program that differentiates between more or less reliable impressions, the former being those that are not contradicted or reversed by any other impression.[23] This absence of contradiction provides only a fallible criterion that allows for the distinction between the convincing impressions that are to be assented to provisionally and those that are to be rejected. However, as Sextus argues following Aenesidimus, once the skeptic enters into the game of sifting through appearances to decide which one is the best guide for understanding how things are, she is in danger of reintroducing the very dogmatism that she sought to dispense with. Convincing impressions may be only provisional or probable truths, but they are truths nevertheless, that is, opinions about how things really are over and above the ways they appear to this or that person and hence clear departures from the Pyrrhonian ideals advocated by Sextus of sticking to appearances and living free from *doxa* (Mates 1996).

This does not mean that the skeptic remains cognitively or morally inert, for she lives in accordance with how things appear. Sextus offers a fourfold scheme of life that illustrates how the skeptic can lead a perfectly normal life. First, the skeptic is guided by nature, following natural dispositions, perceptions, thoughts, etc. She also follows the inclinations of her body, appetites, etc. Hence, there is no problem for the skeptic to avoid putting her hand in the fire, to eat when hungry or to take a medicine when sick (Sextus was a doctor). The skeptic also has no problem in engaging in normal social intercourse. She is acutely aware that her appearances are not those of an isolated individual but those of a social being who follows the rules and laws of the community in which she lives. It is in such a context, that she earns a living, learns a trade,

22. The *pithanon* doctrine of convincing impressions is apposite here. It appears, however, that Carneades did not hold this view but merely used it as an argument against the Stoics. Nevertheless, it remains true that this idea was adopted by later skeptics, such as Philo, as the official doctrine of the Academy. See Sedley (1983, 18).

23. There is here an obvious comparison with Tsongkhapa's attempt to provide criteria to distinguish nominal existence from pure fictions. The main criterion that he suggested for an object to exist nominally is for its cognition to remain uncontradicted by other cognitions. See Cutler and Newland (2000, 163–184). See also chapter 5 for Tsongkhapa's three criteria.

performs some function, etc., in conformity with the rules and standards of her community in ways appropriate to her situation (Burnyeat 1983b). Hence, there is no problem for the skeptic to live a normal active life in accordance with *sensus communis.*

Patsab is not explicit in discussing the implications of his approach for daily life and Buddhist practice. It appears that he would be sympathetic to Sextus's recommendations of living according to common sense. This is after all what Candrakīrti already recommended, a way of life that follows the common sense of cowherds while keeping an important place for Buddhist practice understood as an extension of what humans naturally seek, namely, well-being and freedom from suffering. Hence, as we shall see in the next chapter in more detail, we can use Sextus's discussion of the skeptical way of life to clarify the implications of Patsab's Madhyamaka for the various domains of human practice, topics not directly addressed by our author, who is mostly preoccupied by the task of differentiating his Prāsaṅgika approach from the Svātantrika.

We must now examine the skeptic's commitment to Buddhist tradition, for one may wonder how she can claim to be Buddhist, given her commitment to a total suspension of belief? Isn't such an attitude antithetical to the faith necessary for religious commitment? For it may seem that without some belief in the validity of core doctrines such as the four noble truths, it would be difficult to imagine that a reflective person, which skeptic is bound to be, will be committed to the Buddha, Dharma, and Sangha. And without such commitment, any claim of allegiance to the Buddhist tradition remains hollow.

Here again, the assumption that skepticism is antithetical to commitment is mistaken. Historically, skepticism has often served as a way to argue for religion, for example during the sixteenth and seventeenth centuries, when Catholic apologists were fond of using skeptical arguments for emphasizing the weaknesses of human reason and the need for relying on faith and church (Penelhum 1983). Conceptually, skepticism does not contradict faith, which is not identical to belief. The skeptic is prevented by her commitments from entertaining opinions about the way things really are. But she acknowledges that things appear in certain ways to her depending on the situation in which she finds herself. Hence, there is no problem in entertaining commitments as long as they remain based on the way things appear to her. Skepticism does not entail a denial of appearances but a suspension of the assent to these appearances, so as to find freedom within the confines of the situation in which the skeptic finds herself. Hence, a skeptic is in no way committed to mental blankness and can appraise the way things appear to her and make commitments on this basis.

For example, the skeptic notices that she experiences suffering, that her body seems to get sick, become old, that it seems to her that all people around her die at some point. She also notices that it appears to her that her suffering is largely due to the fact that she clings to her body, herself, etc. She also notices that it seems to her that detachment promotes greater peace and long-lasting satisfaction. She can assume from this that were she to strengthen this attitude through spiritual exercises she might well get to a state where it would appear to her that she is free from being affected by the troubles of human existence. In fact, it is precisely such a peace (*ataraxia*) that the ancient skeptics were seeking. Hence, far from being incompatible with a commitment to Buddhism, skepticism appears to be germane to this tradition and in no way incompatible with Buddhist commitments, which are less based on the belief in a creed than on the trust that the tradition provides the resources necessary for self-transformation.

The skeptic can even entertain doctrines such as rebirth and the law of karma provided that she understands them pragmatically rather than dogmatically. The skeptic finds it difficult to believe pronouncements about multiple lifetimes and the ethical consequences of various actions in this extended framework, but she has no problem with the ethical recommendations of these central doctrines. As for their metaphysical dimension, the skeptic does not feel any need to reject them. Because her attitude of suspension of belief entails a suspension of disbelief, she does not need to decide whether such doctrines are true or not, but can continue to inquire into these doctrines while taking very seriously the ethical commitments that they recommend.

Thus, one can see that skepticism creates no problem for living one's life in the normal way with all the commitments that this implies, including religious ones. Things appear in certain ways, and it is on this basis that the skeptic can make decisions concerning all the spheres of life, not just the most immediate ones. Nonetheless, it is important to keep in mind that these criteria are just guidelines for practical living, not ways to distinguish the true from the false, the more probable from the less so. Hence, such criteria do not provide the basis for a constructive philosophical program, which, for the Pyrrhonian skeptic, is in fact nothing but a way to reintroduce through the back door the idea that we can makes sense of claims about how things are. Within the Madhyamaka context, we may want to take these criteria as explicating the notion of conventional truth, but we should remember that this notion is not a philosophical position to be defended even on the conventional level. Rather, the idea of conventional truth is just a skillful means for pointing out the ways in which metaphysical positions confuse common sense. It also provides a convenient way of talking about how the skeptic lives and interacts with others based on the way things appear to her in accordance with common sense. But there is one thing that the skeptic cannot do, namely, to hold that what appears to her is true, that is, that it has any normative force, even conventionally. For this would contradict the basic Madhyamaka insight that things do not exist the way they appear ordinarily.

The question is often raised of whether the skeptic can draw ethical distinctions. Can she, for example, avoid becoming embroiled in atrocities if she has no belief about whether it is good or not to torture people? I think that the answer is not particularly difficult. Although the skeptic may have no belief about how things really are, she can make decisions on the basis of how things appear to her. It appears to her, for example, that when she is waterboarded she becomes greatly distressed. She can also notice that it appears to her that other people exposed to the same treatment are greatly distressed too. On this basis she can make a decision to abstain from treating people in this way.

She cannot, however, argue that her decision is right and should have any binding force on others. When confronted by those who would defend the use of torture, she cannot hold them to be mistaken and argue that it is wrong to torture other human beings. All she can do is to make recommendations, arguing that not torturing other people has worked well for her, that torturing others appear to her not to promote well-being in herself and others, etc., but she will find it difficult to come up with stronger arguments. All that she can provide are skillful rhetorical exhortations to entice people to reform themselves and try other ways. From her perspective, all moral commandments are merely rhetorical recommendations to entice people to give up behaviors that appear harmful to her.

This suspension of normativity may seem a nihilistic unleashing of the specter of complete moral relativism. It appears to the skeptic that torture is not a good thing, but things appear differently to John Ashcroft. Can the skeptic do anything to advance her discussion with Ashcroft and argue against torture? I believe that she can, though I am not sure how far this possibility can take her. What she can do is to argue on Ashcroft's own ground that as a Christian he should not do to others what he does not want to undergo himself. This type of argument is actually quite important for the skeptic, for she has often no other recourse but to argue on others' grounds. Many of the arguments provided by the ancient Greek skeptics, particularly those directed at the Stoics, must be read in this way, as arguing from the others' premises rather than providing what Prāsaṅgikas would describe as autonomous reasoning.

Similarly, for Patsab and the Prāsaṅgika tradition, Madhyamaka arguments should proceed on this basis, for any other way would entangle

Mādhyamikas in the extreme views from which they seek to free themselves. Hence, for Patsab, Mādhyamikas should not provide autonomous arguments proving that things lack intrinsic nature but, rather, argue on the opponents' ground, using the rules and premises they accept. The skeptic has the same recourse in the moral domain, where she can mount arguments to persuade her opponents to try the attitudes and behaviors that she recommends on the basis of their own commitments. Hence, the skeptical approach does not entail a conservative stance, as it is often claimed. The skeptic is quite free to advocate for radical changes. It is also not true that skepticism entails a nihilistic denial of the validity of moral distinctions. The skeptic can draw such distinctions. What she cannot do, however, is hold her recommendations as moral imperatives that are true regardless of whether we recognize them as such. Hence, it would seem that the skeptic is committed to a certain form of relativism inasmuch as she can never claim to go beyond the ways things appear to her and this may be, in the long run, a more restrictive stance than it may first appear.

Whether this is true or not is not a question we can tackle here. Our more modest goal is to examine Patsab's approach and its implications for our understanding of Madhyamaka, its relation to skepticism, and the doctrine of the two truths. This has allowed us to make at least two significant points. First, Patsab has provided us with a clear and unambiguous skeptical interpretation of Nāgārjuna based on the radical suspension of all theses and the repudiation of any form of reliable cognition. In doing so, he has allowed us to refine the comparison between Madhyamaka and skepticism (particularly in its Pyrrhonian form) while raising questions about its scope. For if it is true that Patsab can be described as a Pyrrhonian skeptic in that he completely rejects any position and any idea of reliable cognition, it is not clear to which degree this description applies comfortably to other Mādhyamikas (even to Candrakīrti), in that they do not seem to be as ready as Patsab to deny any role to reliable cognition and seem more favorably inclined toward the project of a constructive Madhyamaka philosophy.

Second, in rejecting the notion of reliable cognition, Patsab makes it clear that the project of a constructive Madhyamaka philosophy is deeply problematic, for it threatens to reintroduce the extremes that this middle way seeks to deconstruct. This warning against the dangers of constructive philosophy also concerns the Pyrrhonian skeptic, whose suspension of belief may well be jeopardized by the reintroduction, through the back door, of dogmatic positions under the guise of constructive philosophy. Instead, the skeptic should remain content to suspend judgment and follow *sensus communis*, using its resources without attempting to go beyond how things appear to her. It is a similarly skeptical approach that Patsab seems to recommend to his fellow Mādhyamikas, who, in his eye, too often succumb to the temptation of using the two truths to elaborate a constructive Madhyamaka philosophy. For Patsab this represents a reintroduction of extreme positions within Madhyamaka and hence a direct threat to the deconstructive approach that is at the heart of this tradition.

Whether he is right or not is a question we cannot settle here. Instead, what we have done here is to take seriously his challenge and raise this question. Can Mādhyamikas use the notion of conventional truth without reintroducing the very essentialism that they seek to overcome? This is a question that every Madhyamaka interpretation has to face. Hence, Patsab's skeptical interpretation may not be the final word in Madhyamaka philosophy but it certainly offers a challenge that cannot be ignored.

7

Madhyamaka and Classical Greek Skepticism

Georges Dreyfus and Jay L. Garfield

A Tension in Madhyamaka and in Skepticism

There is much to be said for reading Madhyamaka in the context of Western Pyrrhonian skepticism, and the earlier discussion of Patsab's exposition of Madhyamaka demonstrates once again the fruitfulness of this particular cross-cultural juxtaposition (see also Garfield 1990, 1996; McEvilly 1981, 2002; Kuzminsky 2007; Matilal 1985). But there are notorious disputes about how to understand Pyrrhonian skepticism on its own terms and how to understand the difference between Pyrrhonian and Academic skepticism. This is obviously not the place to dwell on these hermeneutical issues in detail, but some of the issues that dog the understanding of Greek skepticism are directly relevant to understanding Madhyamaka. A brief detour through these issues will prove fruitful in our endeavor to understand more precisely the notion of conventional truth within Madhyamaka and provide some clarification of the notoriously vexed distinction between Prāsaṅgika and Svātantrika.

The central issue revolves around the paradoxical statements made by Mādhyamikas and skeptics alike. Sextus Empiricus in *Outlines of Pyrrhonism* makes pronouncements such as "I assert nothing" (I: 192–194),[1] "I have no position" (I: 197), "I suspend

1. All references to the *Outlines* are from Mates (1996).

judgment" (I: 196). These assertions startlingly parallel Nāgāruna's assertion of thesislessness (see VV 29, MMK XIII.8, XXVII.30). For neither Nāgārjuna nor Sextus is philosophy in the business of characterizing the fundamental nature of reality; instead, it is in the business of providing therapy for those suffering from extreme views—views about the fundamental nature of reality. Indeed, Sextus and Candrakīrti each compares the skeptical method to a laxative that purges itself along with the dogmatic doctrines against which it is mobilized (see *Outlines* I, 206–207; PP 227, quoting the *Ratnakūṭasūtra*, i.e., *Kon brtsegs* cha 132a–132b).

We recall that Nāgārjuna was accused by his realist opponent of contradicting himself in his refutation of the realist view that things have real essences or, in other words, real intrinsic natures. The opponent argues that if the Mādhyamikas are right to deny the realist tenet, they must assume that there is some independent standard in relation to which the realist mistake can be demonstrated. We also recall Nāgārjuna's famous answer:

> If I had any thesis, I would thereby commit that error. But since I have no thesis, I do not commit any error.[2]

At first sight, this paradoxical statement may seem a glib way for Nāgārjuna to get out of a difficult situation. This is in fact how many thinkers, traditional and modern, have understood his statement, which they see as an illustration of the sophistry that they think is characteristic of his philosophy (Robinson 1972). Mādhyamikas, however, argue that this dismissal is too hasty: It misses the central Madhyamaka insight that the ways in which we habitually conceive reality and truth may be deeply incoherent. For Mādhyamikas, this incoherence issues from the fact that it makes no sense to think of how things really are in abstraction from how we engage them. Mādhyamikas reach this conclusion by showing that their opponents' views implicate that idea and in virtue of doing so are incoherent. They therefore claim that there is no ultimate mode of existence of things and that in fact it makes no sense to speak of things existing intrinsically. Nevertheless, Mādhyamikas are obliged to use reason to reach this goal, and in the process of arguing, their appeal to canons of proof seems to contradict their claim that it makes no sense to think about how things really are—they at least seem to think that arguments are sound or unsound, and this

2. Nāgārjuna, VV 29, quoted in Patsab (2006, 49): *gal te ngas dam bcas 'ga' yod/ des na nga la skyon de yod/ nga la dam bca'i med pas na/ nga la skyon med kho na yin//*. See Yonezawa (2008, 269); Skt. in Bhattacharya (1986, 61). For a thorough examination of this statement, see Seyfort Ruegg (2000, 115–156). Asimilar point is made in YSV 50–51. See Scherrer-Schaub (1991, 294–296).

distinction presupposes the ability to decide which argument is sound and which is not.

Mādhyamikas also seem to come to positive conclusions, as, for example, when they claim that things are empty of intrinsic nature and are dependently originated. There are hence deep tensions in Madhyamaka, not unlike those that beset classical Greek skepticism—a tension between a critique of positive philosophy and a commitment to that critique and between a critique of independent standards and an appeal to standards of reasoning in mounting that critique.[3] These tensions are not due to some oversight on the Mādhyamika's part but are built into the Madhyamaka project, which seeks to show from the inside that it makes no sense to attempt to describe how things really are but in the process seems forced to suggest that things do exist in some ways or, at least, that they do not exist in the ways assumed by the realists. It is this fundamental tension that Nāgārjuna's statement of thesislessness foregrounds, and it comes as no surprise that the clarification of this statement has been a central concern of later commentators.

Two Madhyamaka Strategies

Two broad Madhyamaka strategies have emerged in response to this challenge. Some Mādhyamikas have opted for a moderate approach, arguing that the claim to positionlessness cannot be taken at face value and that we need some way to modify or, at least, reduce the scope of the apparently paradoxical claim and make Madhyamaka safe for philosophical discourse, particularly by appealing to a strong distinction between the ultimate and the conventional. Tsongkhapa is a clear example of such a thinker, as are Svātantrikas as we shall see shortly (see *Ocean* 26–29, 37–38; Eckel 1987, 70–71). Others have taken a more radical stance, arguing for a literal interpretation of Nāgārjuna's statement. As we saw in chapter 6, Patsab is clearly in the second camp, offering a radical embrace of the paradoxical nature of thesislessness.

According to Patsab, Madhyamaka is incompatible with any commitment to the truth of one's claims, for such an idea presupposes that the objects of some statements can withstand ultimate investigation and thereby constitute standards for truth. Since this is not possible, he argues, no statement has any designated (in the technical sense) truth value. That is, from the ultimate point of view, every statement is false since no object can withstand analysis. But to

3. See, for instance, Sextus's worries about proof (II: 134–204), criteria (II: 14–96), the mode of assertion of skeptical formulae (I: 13–18, 206–209), and the nature of the skeptic's refutation of the dogmatist (II: 1–12).

say that all statements are false leads to an obvious paradox. Is the statement "all statements are false" true or false?

This apparent paradox is not a problem for Patsab, however. The role of Madhyamaka arguments, according to him, is not to establish truth—or even falsity—but rather simply to debunk our naive realist assumptions that things exist the way they appear to us and that it makes sense at all to speak about the truth or falsity of particular assertions about how things are. The Madhyamaka refutation of the realist is, from this perspective, not intended to provide some higher truth but to get us out of the game of ascribing truth and falsity without committing ourselves to any standpoint, positive or negative, on the grounds that any commitment to truth and falsity as polar semantic opposites leads us to contradiction. Thus, according to Patsab, even the claim that all phenomena are empty is not a conclusion, even one derived from the contradictions entailed by their opponents' views that things are nonempty. On his view, it is merely a rhetorical stance, a kind of slogan useful in showing opponents the way to get out of the contradictions entailed by their own commitments. On this reading, the Mādhyamika doesn't even actually say that he has no position, and even his professions to accord with mundane convention are to be distrusted.

According to Patsab, any other strategy is bound to reintroduce a notion of reality that contradicts Nāgārjuna's fundamental contribution, the deconstruction of essentialism. It is in this context that Patsab understands the distinction between Svātantrika and Prāsaṅgika: The Svātantrika Mādhyamikas are willing to characterize what the nature of reality is conventionally and are willing to offer arguments to defend their views. In that willingness they are not unlike the Academic skeptics refuted by Sextus (I: 220–235). The Prāsaṅgika Mādhyamikas, on the other hand, according to Patsab, refute opponents only by using their own presuppositions. Hence, they do not even endorse the conclusions of their own *reductio* arguments. They won't even characterize the nature of reality conventionally or defend their own practice, even conventionally. (Compare to Sextus in *Outlines* I: 13–16.) Any attempt to describe the world from their own perspective opens the door to an assertion of how things exist independently of our own perspectives and schemas. For Patsab, this is exactly what the Svātantrikas are doing when they assert that the conventional can be established by reliable cognition, that is, epistemic instruments (*pramāṇa*), and that there can be epistemic authority for the refutation of the realist position.

Obviously, the Svātantrikas see this somewhat differently. According to them, Mādhyamikas must draw a principled distinction between ultimate and conventional truths. Without such distinction, they argue, Nāgārjuna's dialectic is prone to descend into an incoherent position in which everything can be equally negated or affirmed, an Indian equivalent of the night in which all cows are black. To avoid this danger, Svātantrikas recommend that Nāgārjuna's statement be understood as concerning only the ultimate. Mādhyamikas, they agree, should not hold any position about the ultimate nature of things since any attempt to hold Madhyamaka statements about the ultimate to be true is bound to reify phenomena by attributing to them a negative intrinsic nature. Therefore, they argue, the best that Mādhyamikas can do is to make statements that approximate the ultimate without ever claiming to grasp it fully. This, then, is what Svātantrikas take Madhyamaka arguments to be all about: using the conventional to bring opponents to provisional conclusions that will lead them to understand the ultimate. This conceptual understanding is not, however, a fully accurate realization of the ultimate but merely an understanding of the ultimate through concepts. Hence, inasmuch as it is taken to be the ultimate, the object of realization can be only the represented ultimate (*rnam grangs pa'i don dam*). The actual—nonrepresented—ultimate (*rnam grangs ma yin pa'i don dam*) is beyond the reach of language and thought, which implicates the dualities that are to be transcended at the ultimate level.[4]

These Svātantrika arguments are based on the assumption that while we cannot find any ultimate intrinsic nature, we can still draw conventional distinctions. If we analyze things as they are taken conventionally, we will find, in our conventions, sets of necessary and sufficient conditions for their identities; if we ask about the nature of our conventions, we will find definite rules that determine our practices. Philosophical analyses of the *conventional* world, on this view, yield results, albeit *provisional* ones. There are, for example, principled distinctions that can be drawn between what is conventionally real and what is completely imagined and hence has no reality whatsoever (see Eckel 1987, 75–80).

Of course, Svātantrikas deny that any of what this *conventional* philosophical analysis yields survives *ultimate* analysis. That is why they still are Mādhyamikas. The criteria that we find in our conventional analyses, they concede, do not apply to anything independently of our practices and schemata; instead, they are useful only within the context of these practices. For instance, when we say that things are produced in dependence on causes and conditions, we are not attempting to capture how things really are but merely to describe how they appear to us. We are the kind of beings for whom it is not possible but to organize our experiences through a schema such as causality. Hence, we are justified in claiming that things are produced conditionally, but only conventionally, that is, within the context of our own practices and schemata.

4. This discussion of the represented and nonrepresented ultimate is found in several Svātantrika texts. See, for example, Eckel (1987, 71–75) and Ju Mipham (2004, 495–523). See also Tsongkhapa's discussion in *Ocean* 495–496.

Patsab vigorously rejects this Svātantrika position as a reintroduction through the back door of the notion of the real intrinsic natures that Nāgārjuna threw out of the front door. Hence, Patsab downplays the importance of the doctrine of the two truths, rejecting the idea that it provides the architectural structure that prevents the Madhyamaka system from descending into incoherence. (See preceding chapter.) Patsab's interpretation also leaves little room for other important Madhyamaka ideas such as dependent arising. In MMK chapter XXIV, Nāgārjuna argues that the Madhyamaka view is not only compatible with the assertion of the conditionality of phenomena but is also necessary to make this assertion viable. (See especially the conclusion at MMK XXIV.40) It is only because things do not have any abiding intrinsic nature that they can arise and cease in dependence on causes and conditions. Nāgārjuna summarizes his position in this well-known statement:

> Whatever is dependently arisen, that we explain as emptiness. That, being a dependent designation, is itself the middle way. (XXIV.18)

This statement is taken by many Mādhyamikas to provide the basis of the entire tradition and to connect to the doctrine of the two truths (PP 441–443, 450–45; *Ocean* 480–498, 503–505). Although things are not dependently produced ultimately, they are conventionally so, and we are justified in asserting them as such within the limits set by our practices and ways of perceiving the world. For Patsab, this is to read too much into this verse. On his view, it merely represents a way to engage those beings who cannot give up on the search for truth at the conventional level, not an articulation of a kind of Madhyamaka theory about reality, even conventionally speaking, for this would suggest that we can provide systematic accounts of how things are for us over and above the fragmented and confused accounts found in common sense.

This account of the debate (as understood by Patsab) between the Prāsaṅgikas and the Svātantrikas raises another question relevant to our comparison to Greek skepticism: Is there another, more constructive reading of Prāsaṅgika Madhyamaka? That is, can we find an interpretation according to which Madhyamaka provides a constructive philosophical account that merely describes mundane practices, accords with them, and argues (using, as the Pyrrhonian skeptic might put it [I: 17, 23–24], the discursive conventions of his community and the instructions of the arts of philosophy) that those practices are *not more* (I: 188–189) than merely mundane?

According to this interpretation, all that philosophy can and should do is to explore the conventional, not to find the contextually valid necessary and sufficient conditions that are taken by Svātantrikas to be integral to our practices but to explore the implications of conventionally accepted practices without falling into the philosophical dogmatism that issues from taking the objects of these practices to be more than merely transactional. This is where we may want to come back to our comparison with Greek skepticism. For this discussion of whether there is an alternative to Patsab's reading of Prāsaṅgika, we turn to another parallel discussion regarding whether Pyrrhonian skepticism can be interpreted as being consistent with constructive philosophy.

Sextus's Pyrrhonism

We recall that Sextus draws the distinction between his Pyrrhonian skepticism and Academic skepticism with respect to the skeptic's attitude toward skepticism itself: The Academic skeptic takes the skeptical critique to be self-exempted, whereas the Pyrrhonian takes it to be reflexive. That is, on Sextus's account, the Academic skeptic takes skeptical arguments to warrant skepticism; to establish that it is the best way of taking up with the world; and to establish that its critiques of dogmatism are sound and so that all dogmatic positions are false. (See especially I: 226–230.) The Pyrrhonian, he asserts, takes Academic skepticism to be dogmatism in disguise inasmuch as it *asserts* the falsity of dogmatic positions and the probity of skepticism itself, thereby maintaining a set of, albeit distinctive, theses, theses that survive skeptical critique. For the Pyrrhonian, Sextus insists, even the skeptical formulae and skeptical method are subject to *epochē*. They are not asserted; the skeptic is not even committed to the probity of skepticism or to the success of the skeptical arguments. (See also I: 206–207.) That is why Sextus's Pyrrhonism is so radical.

This point is particularly apposite in the context of Sextus's critique of deductive and inductive logic, a critique to which we will have reason to return later. Sextus points out that induction cannot be validated deductively; that any inductive validation would be circular (II: 204); that the validity of deduction cannot be validated inductively in virtue of the failure of any justification of induction; and that any deductive justification would be circular (II: 134–203). Moreover, since any premises of any argument must be justified either deductively or inductively, the failure to demonstrate the warrant of the two methods of argument undermines the warrant of any premises. So, he argues, neither argument form nor argument content has any warrant.

How, then, does the skeptic justify his own use of arguments, including the skeptical tropes? Sextus has two answers to this question. First, he argues, they are used purely *ad hominem*. The dogmatist relies on these arguments, and so they are probative for her (I: 164–186, II: 18–47). She will give up her dogmatic commitment because of them, even if the skeptic, despite using them, has no confidence in their warrant. Second, they simply appear to the skeptic to work, and skeptics follow appearances (I: 15). So, despite not having any confidence in the arguments, the skeptic goes on using them, as they, for reasons none can articulate, loosen dogmatic commitment and lead to *ataraxia*, just as throwing the sponge at the canvas just happened to represent the foam of the horse (I: 25–30).

All of this suggests one very plausible way of reading Pyrrhonian skepticism: The Pyrrhonian skeptic, unlike the Academic skeptic, *really* asserts nothing, uses no arguments as probative, and does not even have reasons to recommend his own skepticism, his refusal to assert, his *epochē*. This reading, which has been entertained by scholars such as Burnyeat (2001) and Barnes (1983), will remind us of Patsab's own reading of Madhyamaka. The question worth raising is whether there is another plausible interpretation, one that focuses not only on the relentlessly negative skeptical dialectic but also on the positive side of skepticism?

In Sextus, this positive account is found in the Fourfold Prescription presented in *Outlines*. Sextus asks how the skeptic is to live his skepticism, and replies that the skeptic follows his appetites, appearances, the laws and customs of his culture, and the instructions of the arts. The key passage from the *Outlines* is worth quoting in full here:

> Holding to appearances, then, we live without beliefs but in accordance with the ordinary regimen of life since we cannot be wholly inactive. And this ordinary regimen of life seems to be fourfold: One part has to do with the guidance of nature, another with the compulsions of the *pathé*, another with the handing down of laws and customs, and a fourth with the instruction in arts and crafts. Nature's guidance is that by which we are naturally capable of sensation and thought; compulsion of the *pathé* is that by which hunger drives us to food and thirst makes us drink; the handing down of customs and laws is that by which we accept that piety in the conduct of life is good and impiety bad; and instruction in arts and crafts is that by which we are not inactive in whichever we acquire. And we say all these things without belief. (I: 23–24)

Sextus's deep insight is that all of this is *practice* and that none of it involves commitment to deep theses about the nature of things. (See especially I: 18.) The fourfold prescription is the *positive* side of Pyrrhonian skepticism, and it is important to Sextus that it is possible to follow this prescription without falling into dogmatism, without making assertions, in the relevant sense; without taking positions, in the relevant sense. How is this possible? After all, many of our customs and many of the arts require us to speak in declarative sentences, and Sextus does not recommend total aphasia. (See I: 192–193 for his nuanced discussion of this issue.)

Sextus's answer is that we can do this by speaking "imprecisely," "neither affirming nor denying," "saying what appears to us and not asserting, as something firmly maintained, anything about the nature of the external objects" (I: 207–208). This we might call *skeptical assertion.* But what does he mean? What is skeptical assertion? It is, if we take the Fourfold Prescription seriously, to take our assertions not as representations of the nature of reality but rather as actions taken in the context of social praxes. It is to take a statement like "rooks move down the rank and file" to be the same kind of speech act as "Thank you." The former looks like an assertion of a convention-independent fact, and the latter looks like a mere conversational convention. But attention to the constitutive, as opposed to descriptive, force of rules of chess leads us to see these statements as on the same footing. And it is to take "The earth revolves around the sun" as the same kind of act as "rooks move down the rank and file." Both have descriptive content; both are true. While the conventional ground of the second is obvious, that of the first, the skeptic maintains, is only more subtle, not absent. While "thank you" feels worlds away in function and ontological weight from "the earth revolves around the sun," to say the latter *without prejudice* is to take them to be fundamentally the same kind of acts—acts of social coordination accomplished through *flatus vocis.* The skeptic can *say* whatever he wants, then; he just doesn't take any of it to have any ontological import.

Let us return to logic. We noted earlier that reasoning is a practice, a practice common in daily life and in philosophy and, of course, a discursive practice. So there is another account of how a skeptic can use reasoning and make philosophical statements: he can participate in the customs of local philosophers; he can follow the instruction of the art of philosophy, even though these practices are discursive. But when he speaks in the context of the practices, he does so *skeptically,* not making claims about the nature of reality or about the probity of those practices, not even negative claims, when refuting dogmatists, but engaging in discursive practices and offering arguments in order to dissuade others from claims about the fundamental nature of reality. To reject a dogma hence is precisely *to reject a dogma* but not to take its rejection as an alternative claim about fundamental ontology; it is to recuse oneself from that enterprise. To engage in a practice is not to give it a *privileged* position (to take it to be the *true* practice as opposed to a *false* one) but simply to engage in it—to play cricket is not to deny the reality or the beauty of baseball.

This alternative account offers us a way to think of skepticism as *constructive*, as offering an account of our ordinary life, including our epistemic and discursive practices, but a merely descriptive, or philosophically shallow, account. Such an account does not involve a commitment to how one *ought* to think or act, all things considered. But that does not mean that it has no normative content whatsoever. Instead, an account like this provides descriptions of local practices and norms, as well as (admittedly defeasible) arguments for taking these as merely descriptive. (Again, if one plays cricket, one accepts the Laws of Cricket together with their local normative force, but one is not thereby committed to extending them to baseball or denying the rules of baseball their place in the world.) *Epochē* need not entail *aphasia*.[5]

Prāsaṅgika and Svātantrika

This suggestion of an alternative reading of Pyrrhonian skepticism is valuable not just for clarifying the scope of this important tradition but also for understanding the scope of the Madhyamaka deconstructive method and the possible interpretations of Nāgārjuna's claim to positionlessness. We have seen Patsab's radical embrace of the paradox suggested by that claim. In this interpretation, he may reflect a stream of later Prāsaṅgika (or proto-Prāsaṅgika) Indian interpreters of Candrakīrti's Madhyamaka.[6] But what about the master himself, Candrakīrti, who is usually presented as the founder of the Prāsaṅgika? Does he fit Patsab's description of the Prāsaṅgika? And if he does not, where might he stand on the spectrum of Greek skepticism? Is he a skeptic? If so, is he an Academic or a Pyrrhonian skeptic? If the latter, is he a negative or a constructive Pyrrhonian? We may also wonder about Svātantrikas. Are they really Indian Academic skeptics, as suggested by Patsab's description of their positions?

Let us consider the first question. This is obviously not an easy task since it involves the appraisal of the works of a complex, prolific, and at times elusive philosopher. But our previous discussion of the scope of skepticism enables us to come to a provisional understanding of how his position compares to Greek skepticism. If to be a Pyrrhonian skeptic is, like Patsab, to refuse to assert anything, even that one refuses to assert anything, then it would appear that Candrakīrti is not a Pyrrhonian skeptic. For even a cursory examination of his

5. This view of skepticism is defended, for instance, not only in Garfield (1990) but also in Mates (1996) and Hallie (1985).

6. For a historical discussion of the place of Patsab in Madhyamaka, see Dreyfus (2009).

works shows that Candrakīrti is not shy about advancing a number of philosophical theses, particularly about the Madhyamaka method. (See, for instance, PP 54–56.)

Of course, he says that he asserts no theses and offers no autonomous reasoning establishing the emptiness of phenomena. But Candrakīrti does offer other types of argument such as statements of consequence and inferences established on the opponent's own ground. (PP is replete with examples, but chapter 1 is an excellent example, especially 10, 12–15.) More important, he extensively *defends* this methodology and criticizes Bhāvaviveka for advocating a different argumentative methodology, the use of autonomous reasoning (PP 12–38). Hence, on a restrictive Pyrrhonian notion of skepticism, we would have to conclude that he is not a consistent skeptic.

Moreover, Candrakīrti seems to want to keep a role, albeit a modest one, for the notion of means of reliable cognition (*pramāṇa*). He faults the Buddhist logicians, particularly Dignāga, for offering an overly pared down epistemology and argues that in these matters we should follow common sense rather than a revisionist epistemological program. In this perspective, the notion of means of reliable cognition is not to be rejected completely but relieved of its philosophical weight. Hence, Candrakīrti is quite happy to accept the Nyāya epistemology as reflecting the ways in which we use the concept of knowledge in daily life, and he clearly does not qualify as a skeptic in the same sense as does Patsab. (See also Siderits 1980 and 1981.)

But as we have already seen, the purely negative reading of skepticism is very restrictive, and there is another plausible and perhaps philosophically more fruitful way to read skepticism. According to this less restrictive reading, skeptics are not prevented from advancing their own theses as long as what they say is said *skeptically*. On this broader view, the skeptic is merely one who refuses to commit to a thesis regarding the nature of reality with regard to things being any way independent of convention and of our social, linguistic, and cognitive practices. And this may well be Candrakīrti's position—that it is impossible to speak coherently about "the nature of reality." Hence, all phenomena can be said to be empty of any such nature, and conventional truth is all the truth that we can ever express. By those lights, he is indeed a skeptic. But what kind?

One might tempted to argue that Candrakīrti is an Academic skeptic, as several passages might suggest. An Academic skeptic takes skepticism itself to be defensible on independent philosophical grounds and hence exempts skepticism from its own critique. When Candrakīrti criticizes Bhāvaviveka and defends Buddhapālita, and when he defends the Nyāya epistemology in *Prasannapadā*, and when he so carefully distinguishes the ultimate from the conventional in *Madhyamakāvatārabhāṣya*, explaining so explicitly the deceptiveness of conventional cognitive faculties and the falsity of their objects, he certainly sounds like he is making straightforward assertions about the limits of our cognitive faculties, and these assertions do not seem to be qualified in the way that one would expect a Pyrrhonian to qualify them.

But not so fast. There is always the danger of reading these passages out of context, and the context here is Candrakīrti's own metatheoretical account of his own practice. Here, as Huntington (2007), for instance, argues, and as Gorampa would certainly agree (Thakchöe 2005), Candrakīrti at least talks the talk of a negative Pyrrhonian. He *claims*, at least on one very straightforward reading, especially in *Prasannapadā* XVIII and XXVII, not to defend any thesis; he claims, in his account of Prāsaṅgika methodology in chapter 1 of *Prasannapadā*, to differ from Bhāvaviveka precisely in that the latter *does* take Madhyamaka to be a position at least conventionally, whereas Candrakīrti claims that he and Buddhapālita understand Nāgārjuna's purport to be that the Mādhyamika takes on and refutes the positions of others, on their own terms, but defends no account of his own.

Moreover, Candrakīrti also refuses the Svātantrika idea that Madhyamaka should be in the business of arguing for the truth of their views on conventional grounds through arguments that demonstrate that phenomena are empty. As we saw earlier, Svātantrikas do not believe that the conclusions reached through such arguments fully capture the nature of things or that they truly correspond to reality, but they do believe that they are better approximations of ultimate truth. Hence, they believe that it makes sense to discuss the ultimate in relation to probative arguments and to argue that the arguments establishing the ultimate are correct. This is precisely what Candrakīrti refuses. For him, ideas of an approximation of the ultimate truth or of represented ultimate truth are dangerous nonsense that delude us into thinking that the view of emptiness is a view like any other view, one that can be reached by sound arguments. Hence, Candrakīrti can hardly be taken to be an Academic skeptic.

But as we saw, there may be a middle way to understand Pyrrhonian skepticism, a way that may allow us to locate Candrakīrti between these two extreme readings. In this alternative reading, Candrakīrti is a constructive Pyrrhonian, who reconciles his practice and his account of that practice. A Constructive Pyrrhonian, we recall, offers us a description of our epistemic practices *just as practices*, that is, without defending them, as well as a critique of any possible defense of those practices. When discussing conventions, she remains resolutely descriptive, as opposed to normative, allowing herself to describe norms that in fact govern our lives but depriving them of any normative force independent of the conventions that institute them. This is also, by the way, a possible way to read Hume and Wittgenstein.[7]

Candrakīrti, as Garfield argues in (2008) and in chapter 2 of this volume, often does argue, just as the proponent of a nonskeptical or an Academic reading would charge, for positions regarding the emptiness of phenomena, the two truths, the nature of convention, and so on, and he both endorses and uses customary forms of argument. But he also argues that all language and all discursive practices fall within the domain of convention, including his own, and that all are deceptive, including presumably his own. While one might argue that this simply demonstrates either that Candrakīrti is trying to have his Madhyamaka cake and eat it, too, or that he is just confused about what he is doing, there is a more charitable and a deeper reading: When describing dialectical practices, as in *Prasannapadā*, or when describing conventional reality, Candrakīrti is doing just that, describing. His metaphilosophical claims on this reading provide the context for his ground-level claims. He accords with the world because, as a skeptic, he adopts the fourfold prescription; he is more than a mere cowherd, though, because in doing so, he knows that that is all he is doing, participating in a practice, and because he understands the significance of that knowledge.

On this reading, Candrakīrti hence does not satisfy the more radical, negative description of Pyrrhonian skepticism. Patsab, who takes Nāgārjuna's thesislessness literally, does: Candrakīrti's position is more nuanced. Nuance, of course, is but one philosophical virtue: We may wonder whether his position is *coherent*. It is at least prima facie unstable. But even instability in this context may not necessarily be a fault; it may in fact provide precisely the kind of subtlety necessary to Madhyamaka, which seeks to characterize reality while destabilizing our usual ways of conceiving of reality. For as we saw, although Patsab's reading of Nāgārjuna's claims to positionlessness is straightforward, he never reconciles it with other important aspects of Nāgārjuna's thought, such as his doctrine of the two truths and his insistence on the centrality of dependent arising. This is not to say that a negative skeptic such as Patsab has nothing to say about these doctrines. Nonetheless, their explanations that these points merely express the way the world appears to a fool at least seem not to take seriously their apparent centrality to Nāgārjuna's texts and enterprise.

7. Kripke (1982) defends this reading of Wittgenstein's *Philosophical Investigations*. Baier (1985, 1991), Wright (1983), and Coventry (2008), among others, as well as Garfield (1990), have defended this reading of Hume. Of course, there are other readings of Hume's and Wittgenstein's enterprises, and we do not want to enter into the complex debates about Hume and Wittgenstein exegesis here but only to point out that this kind of positive skepticism has offered one influential way of understanding a very important strand in the Western philosophical literature.

We hope to have shown that there is great benefit in using classical Greek skepticism as a lens for examining Madhyamaka. In doing so, we come to appreciate some of the nuances of the Madhyamaka tradition and the hermeneutical space opened by Nāgārjuna's texts. The vocabulary of skepticism helps us to capture these differences and highlight their significance. But this juxtaposition is not only a way to gain a better understanding of Madhyamaka: It also sheds new light on the possibilities and tensions within Greek skepticism. We can see that the mainstream interpretation of Sextus as a straightforward negative skeptic is not the only possible one and that his stance may offer more resources to the philosopher than is usually thought. Finally, we may also come to a greater appreciation of thinkers who are often dismissed as being insufficiently radical to be of interest. In the context of skepticism, this is often the case of Academic skeptics, who are presented as dogmatic. But were they really, or is this only a description given by their Pyrrhonian adversaries?

It is here that a comparison with Madhyamaka may be helpful. For as we have seen, the Buddhist philosophers who seem most comparable to Academic skeptics are not Candrakīrti and his followers but the usually neglected and maligned Svātantrikas such as Bhāvaviveka and Śāntarakṣita, whose Madhyamaka credentials are often dismissed by Tibetan commentators.[8] But this dismissal misrepresents their view. The Svātantrikas are not arguing that Madhyamaka reasonings can capture ultimate reality and provide a true depiction of the nature of reality. They are too steeped in Nāgārjuna's dialectic and Indian Buddhist nominalism to be tempted by such a form of epistemological realism. They seek instead to rein in the paradoxical nature of Madhyamaka so as to resolve or at least attenuate the fundamental tension that is at the heart of this tradition. They want to make sense of a doctrine that claims to show that it makes no sense to talk about the fundamental nature of reality precisely in virtue of the fact that the fundamental nature of reality is just as they characterize it, that is, natureless. (See Garfield and Priest 2003.) For the Svātantrikas, the tension can be relieved by arguing that Madhyamaka reasonings do not aim at providing a true description of reality but at providing the most justifiable way of thinking about reality, the one that is least misleading and most likely to foster a healthy attitude toward practice.

This way of arguing for Madhyamaka starts by taking the idea of conventional truth very seriously. It is not just the way deluded beings conceive of reality (as Patsab and negative Pyrrhonians think) or even a kind of concession that the skeptic makes to participate in the conversation (as the positive

8. For a discussion of the evolution of the Tibetan reception of Madhyamaka and the rise of Candrakīrti in the estimation of Tibetan scholars, see Vose (2008).

Pyrrhonian or Candrakīrti may think) but also an articulation of the presuppositions of our practice. Obviously, such articulation does not aim to provide a description of how things really are but just of how we assume them to be when we engage them in our practices. Hence, this articulation is merely conventional and is to be set aside when we attempt to think about how things really are. There, we need to embrace the Madhyamaka deconstructive strategy and relentlessly undermine any characterization we may come up with.

Nonetheless, such a strategy must start from the provisional knowledge that we have of the world as assumed by our practices. The world we experience does not exist outside of our interests and conventions but is also not completely determined by these considerations. Our assumptions about reality are also largely determined by our embodied condition. We see the world of experience in certain ways not just because of our interests and conventions but also because of the kind of perceptual apparatus that we have. Our embodied condition and the perceptual apparatus that this entails significantly constrain the kind of conventions that we can adopt. Hence, for Svātantrikas, Madhyamaka should base the idea of conventional truth on these fundamental perceptual constraints and the objects that they yield.

This is so not because the objects given in perception exist in reality just as they appear but because they reflect our most fundamental mode of interaction with the world. It is on this basis that Mādhyamikas can then proceed to show their fundamental point that it makes no sense to think of reality in abstraction of our modes of interaction with the world, as if we could take the view from nowhere. This conclusion may not strictly correspond to reality but is the best way, the most useful, and the least deceptive way of thinking about reality. Once we adopt this healthy skepticism toward any attempt to characterize how things really are in abstraction from our interactions with them, we come to realize that all that we have is what is provided by our interactions with the world.

On this Svātantrika view, this is what conventional reality is, and we need to realize that this is all that we have. This does not mean, however, that this level of reality is going to be determined just by our interests and conventions. There are ways in which our experiences are significantly determined by our embodiment, and we may be wise to start from this basis to show how we are justified to go from there to the fundamental Madhyamaka insight.

Pyrrhonian skeptics see this strategy as being misguided. They think that the attempt to try to find some provisional bedrock on which our conventional practices rest is misguided and even dangerous. The claim to rest on even a provisional ground suggests that although we may never be right to hold that things really exist in certain ways, we can at least be justified in holding certain views about reality, conventional or ultimate. For the Pyrrhonian—whether

Greek, Indian, or Tibetan—this temptation must be resisted at all cost; it is the symptom of the onset of the very disease of dogmatism that Madhyamaka and skepticism seek to cure. On this account, we should not distinguish between levels of truth or justification over and above common-sense practices. Rather, we should just rest happy with these conventions and focus on relentlessly undoing the knots that our mind creates. On this view, this is all there is to the two truths. To engage reality conventionally is to live in accordance with common sense. To think about things as they really are is only to create confusion by reintroducing ontology.

Does that mean then that the Pyrrhonian skeptic and the Prāsaṅgika cannot engage in constructive philosophy, as Patsab would have it? Perhaps not, but the question of what kind of constructive philosophy the Pyrrhonian or the Prāsaṅgika can aim for remains open. It is clear, however, that the various approaches to Madhyamaka and to skepticism are divided not by some substantive doctrine but rather by their divergent views about the implications of a doctrine they share for philosophical practice. Ancient skeptics and Mādhyamikas agree that it makes no sense to attempt to conceive of how things really are in abstraction from our own perspective and that we should stick to what is presupposed by our conventional practices. They differ regarding how we reach such skeptical wisdom and what, if anything, we can say about it.

8

The (Two) Truths about Truth

Graham Priest, Mark Siderits, and
Tom J. F. Tillemans

In this chapter we address the semantic side of the Buddhist distinction between the two truths. As was pointed out in the introduction to this volume, the Sanskrit word that we here translate as "truth" (*satya*) is sometimes also used to mean "reality," "the real," that is, the things that are existent/real. Here we concern ourselves with truth, a property that some statements, ideas, beliefs, theories, propositions, and representations may have and others lack, but that cannot properly be ascribed to simple things like pots and chairs. Though the issue of what sort of things are the *primary* bearers of truth is important, nothing we say here depends on a determination of this question. We therefore adopt a "tolerant attitude to truthbearers" (Kirkham 1995, 59–63). Readers are free to reformulate what we say into their preferred terminology.

If we take the semantic perspective, then among true statements, there are some that Buddhists claim to be conventionally true and others that they claim to be ultimately true. This raises two questions. First, is there something that both types of statement share? Second, how do they differ? To answer the first question we should look at some of the different theories of truth that have been developed in the Western traditions and see which of these might best capture the conception of truth behind the Buddhist distinction. This may also suggest some possible answers to the second question.

We will start by reviewing the standard views about the nature of truth in Western traditions. Matters, of course, are contentious. Our aim here is not to enter into the contention. It is simply to chart the geography of the area for subsequent application. Much more detailed discussion can be found in standard references, such as Kirkham (1995) and articles in the *Routledge Encyclopedia of Philosophy* and the online *Stanford Encyclopedia of Philosophy*. All the views of truth we will put on the table come in many varieties. Generally speaking, we will ride roughshod over the differences since it is only the core ideas that are relevant to our discussion.

Theories of Truth

Let us start with a truism about truth. Aristotle enunciated it as follows (*Metaphysics* 1011^{b} 25):

> To say of what is that it is not, or of what is not that it is, is false, while to say of what is that it is, and of what is not that it is not, is true.

The view was canonized some two and a half thousand years later by Tarski (1936) in what has become known as the T-schema:

> <*p*> is true iff *p*

where *p* is some proposition, and <*p*> is a truthbearer expressing it (and "iff" means "if and only if"). Thus, if *p* is the proposition that Kathmandu is in Nepal, <*p*> might be "Kathmandu is in Nepal." It would be a bizarre theory of truth that did not endorse the T-schema. It would seem incoherent, for example, to endorse the thought that it is true that Kathmandu is in Nepal, yet to deny that Kathmandu is in Nepal or vice versa.[1]

According to a currently popular theory of truth, there is nothing more to truth than that it satisfy this schema. An early form of the theory was proposed by Ramsey (1927). A more modern version is presented in Horwich (1998). This view deflates the notion of truth; there is nothing more to truth than the T-schema. We will therefore refer to it as the *deflationary theory* of truth. A crucial question about the view is whether, if there is no more to truth than the T-schema, it can accommodate all the things that a notion of truth is required

1. Having said that, there are some instances of the T-schema that appear to give rise to paradox—for example, the instance concerning the proposition that this very proposition is not true (the liar paradox). Those who are not prepared to accept the truth of this paradoxical proposition—Tarski included—have often, therefore, restricted the T-schema in such a way as to exclude such propositions. This is a sophistication we ignore here since it is irrelevant to the issues at hand.

to do in epistemology, semantics, and elsewhere. However, this is not the place to go into these matters.

For those who have felt that there is more to truth than the T-schema, perhaps the most popular view is a *correspondence theory* of truth. According to this theory, what makes a statement true is its correspondence to reality. Statements represent the world as being a certain way. For instance, the statement "A pot is on the ground" represents the world as having at least one pot on the ground. According to the correspondence theory, to say of this statement that it is true is to say that the world is as the statement represents it as being. This is sometimes expressed by saying that the statement correctly pictures how the world is. Since "correct" looks like a synonym for "true," this cannot be a proper analysis of truth. But it is useful in suggesting that we look at the picturing relation to understand how correspondence might work. In a picture, various elements (e.g., blobs of color) stand in certain relations to one another—for instance, a yellow blob being above and to the right of a green blob. There are also projection rules, whereby the relations that may obtain among pictorial elements are correlated with relations that may obtain among entities in the world outside the picture. To call a picture accurate is to say that when individual elements are taken to stand for particular entities in the world, then the real-world relations that one gets by applying the projection rules to the picture-relations actually do obtain among those entities.

A deflationist view of truth can be seen as a correspondence theory in a certain sense. After all, "Nepal" stands for Nepal, "Kathmandu" for Kathmandu, and Kathmandu does indeed relate to Nepal by being in it. However, typical defenders of a correspondence view have had something stronger in mind. A true sentence is to be made true by reality (that is, reality has a "truthmaker" in it) in a more robust way. This is explained by Armstrong, a proponent of the view, as follows (2004, 5):

> To demand truthmakers for particular truths is to accept a *realist* theory for these truths. There is something that exists in reality, independent of the proposition in question, which makes the truth true. The "making" here is, of course, not the causal sense of "making." The best formulation of what this making is seems to be given by the phrase "in virtue of." It is in virtue of that independent reality that the proposition is true. What makes the proposition a truth is how it stands to this reality.

This goes beyond a deflated correspondence in two ways. First, there are *entities* in reality in virtue of which true sentences are true. Different versions of the theory characterize these in different ways: They may be facts, situations, states of affairs, or whatnot. We will simply call them "facts." Second, we are to be a realist about these entities; that is, they are mind/language independent.[2] When we talk of a correspondence theory of truth, we shall have this kind of robust correspondence in mind. Perhaps the most famous theory of this sort is Wittgenstein's in the *Tractatus* (Wittgenstein 1922).[3] A major problem of the correspondence theory has been to give a satisfactory account of the nature of facts and the correspondence relation between facts and propositions. Thus, we speak of the fact of there being a pot on the ground as what makes it true to say that a pot is on the ground. And here it is natural to think of this fact as something in the world. But we also say that it is a fact that 2 + 2 = 4 and that it is a fact that there are no horned hares. These look rather less like inhabitants of what most people think of as "the world" and more like abstract objects. Some philosophers bite the bullet on this and posit facts as entities that exist in a third realm that is neither physical nor mental. Others find this ontological commitment hard to swallow, but the alternatives seem to end up making facts look rather like linguistic entities; in that case, correspondence fails to be of the robust kind.

If we cannot, in the end, make sense of a robust language-world correlation and yet wish to have more to truth than the mere T-schema, the next obvious thought is that we should locate this more in the relationship among the linguistic things themselves. Thus, we might take a set of sentences—let us call this a theory—to be true if all its members cohere. This is the *coherence theory* of truth, endorsed by idealists such as Blanshard (1939) and some of the logical positivists, such as Neurath (1983). What exactly coherence amounts to is a much-debated point. Consistency is usually taken to be a necessary condition, but more than this is required: The members of the theory should mutually support one another in some sense. Assuming that the notion of coherence can be spelled out satisfactorily, the coherence theory of truth faces a problem, noted, for example, by Russell (1907). It would seem that there can be any number of distinct coherent theories, and on some of these a given statement will count as true, whereas on others it will count as false.[4] We thus end up

2. In general, that is. Since it is true that Churchill thought about Hitler, there must, on this account, be a fact of Churchill's thinking of Hitler. This is obviously not mind-independent. However, this is a special sort of case.

3. In fact, Wittgenstein's view is slightly more complex than this. Atomic sentences are made true by facts. The truth of a complex sentence is reduced, via its truth conditions, to that of atomic sentences.

4. Note that this does not involve changing the language being used as we move from one theory to another. Take the statement "Mt. Everest is taller than Mt. Washington." The claim is that this statement will cohere with one theory but not with another, even when we keep fixed what is meant by "Mt. Everest," "taller than," and so on. One might think that the facts must tell in favor of the theory with which the statement coheres and against the theory with which the statement does not cohere. But this involves appeal to facts independent of theoretical framework. The coherence theorist has no truck with such things.

with the dismal view that truth is always relative to a theoretical framework. This is dismal because truth then appears to lose its normative force. We take it that one ought, *ceteris paribus*, to tell the truth. Truth functions for us as a norm. If any statement whatsoever may be both true and false, depending upon which framework we adopt, it is no longer clear how truth could serve that function.[5]

Another way in which one may attempt to go beyond the T-schema is to suppose that truth must answer to action in a certain way. This gives us (versions of) the *pragmatic theory* of truth, as espoused by Peirce (1905), James (1909), and others. This is the view that truth is the property of being conducive to successful practice. So to say that the statement "A pot is on the ground" is true is just to say that accepting this statement leads to success in one's pot-seeking and pot-avoiding behavior. It is important to distinguish this view from the view that successful practice is a *test* for truth. On the latter view, the way we tell whether a statement is true is by looking to see whether it leads to successful practice. But one may accept a pragmatic criterion of truth while believing that the property of truth is not this but something else, such as correspondence or coherence of some kind. One difficulty with the pragmatic theory of truth is that by "true" we seem to mean something other than "conducive to successful practice." Thus, we can imagine statements that are true but have no practical oomph whatever. For example, that there are *exactly* $10^8 + 17$ grains of sand on a particular beach would seem to have no practical import at all. Any number of Indian philosophers, including Buddhist philosophers such as Dharmakīrti, subscribe to a pragmatic criterion of truth. But it is not clear that any of them would accept the view that being such as to lead to successful practice is what truth *is*.[6]

The final theory of truth on our list locates what goes beyond the T-schema in one particular kind of activity, namely verification. Thus, a sentence is true if it is verifiable or maybe even verified. This gives us the *verifiability theory* of truth. Some (e.g., Ayer 1936) have held verifiability to be a theory, not of truth, but of meaning. So things that are not verifiable are literally meaningless. However, that truth in mathematics is itself verifiability was held by mathematical intuitionists, such as Brouwer.[7] And the intuitionist account has been extended to a completely general account of truth by philosophers such as Dummett (1976). A verificationist theory of truth would appear to be problematic due to

5. Chapter 9 of this volume takes up "dismal relativism" and the Svātantrika-Mādhyamikas' worries about it.

6. See Kirkham (1995, 212, 215) on the difference between pragmatic theories of truth and justification; Tillemans (1999, 6–12) on Dharmakīrti's supposed pragmatism.

7. See the papers by Brouwer translated into English in van Heijenoort (1967).

the fact that there appear to be statements that are true but not verifiable—for example, that the physical world will (or will not) continue to exist after the death of all sentient creatures (due to excess heat or excess cold, depending on whether the cosmos expands indefinitely or collapses back into itself). No doubt a verificationist would say that this begs the question: There are no such truths since they cannot be verified. But the verificationist is vulnerable to a difficult *ad hominem* argument. It would seem that the claim that truth is verifiability cannot itself be verified. It hardly seems true by definition; neither is it the sort of thing for which one can collect empirical evidence.

Abhidharma

So much for our whistle-stop tour of the Western alethic lands. Now to Buddhism. Buddhist philosophers claim that among the statements that can be said to be true, some are conventionally true, while others are ultimately true. What do they mean by "true"? The answer depends on which formulation of the theory of two truths we are discussing, for there are several. The first, historically, is the one developed by the Abhidharma schools. There, the distinction between the two truths turns on another distinction, that between two ways in which something might be said to exist: conventionally and ultimately. Among the things that might be thought to exist, some are partite (i.e., wholes composed of parts) and others are impartite. Ābhidharmikas argue that no partite entity can be real. Something must be real, however, so the reals must be impartite. Those impartite entities that do exist are then said to exist ultimately, to be ultimately real. Statements correctly representing the way that ultimately real entities are may then be said to be ultimately true. Here the sense of "true" is most naturally thought of as a robust correspondence, impartite things with their properties playing the role of genuine truthmakers.

Most of the things that we ordinarily suppose to exist are not ultimately real. Pots, trees, mountains, and persons, being wholes composed of parts, cannot ultimately exist if the Abhidharma argument against partite entities is sound. It would, though, be odd to say that such things are utterly unreal, like the horns of a hare. For there are atoms arranged potwise, while there are no atoms arranged horns-of-hare-wise. Since it is frequently useful for us to be able to refer to collections of atoms arranged potwise, and the atoms are many, while life is short, we have come to employ the concept of a pot as a shorthand way of referring to such collections. Habitually employing this concept, we come to think that there actually are things such as pots that somehow exist over and above the atoms of which they are composed. Since this useful fiction grows out of our use of a certain concept, we can call it a "conceptual fiction."[8] And some of the statements we make concerning conceptual fictions, such as the statement that there is a pot on the ground, may be said to be conventionally true.

Uniformity would seem to require that the "true" in "conventionally true" be understood, like that in "ultimately true," along the lines of the correspondence theory. But things cannot be so straightforward. Since the things referred to in conventionally true statements are mere conceptual fictions, they cannot serve as truthmakers in the sense of a robust realist correspondence theory of truth. And it turns out to be extraordinarily difficult to state the truth conditions for "A pot is on the ground" in terms of relations among atoms. (For instance, there is considerable elasticity in the number of atoms required for something to be a pot: As we remove randomly selected atoms one by one from a pot, there is no clear line beyond which there simply is no longer a pot.) This appears to rule out correspondence. Since conventional truths are statements that guide us to successful practice, one might suppose that conventional truth should be understood in terms of the pragmatic theory of truth. But this does not seem to be how Abhidharma philosophers see things. They appear to want to retain something like a correspondence account for this kind of truth as well. One way to understand how this might be involves thinking about what we mean when we say that something is true "in the story," such as that Hamlet killed his stepfather. There is no Hamlet. There are only the sentences that make up the story. But were those sentences true, then there would be whatever truthmakers are required to make "Hamlet killed his stepfather" turn out true. Likewise, there are no pots, only atoms, including some atoms that are arranged potwise at a certain location. But given those atoms arranged in those ways, if there were things such as pots, then there would be the requisite truthmakers for "A pot is on the ground." Thus, we still have correspondence in some sense. For then conventionally true statements are ones that correspond to arrangements of the fictions with which we populate our everyday world through conceptual construction (*kalpanā*).

At this point, a word is in order concerning the truthmakers for the ultimate truth in the Abhidharma scheme. Abhidharma adopts a robustly realist form of correspondence theory with respect to the ultimate truth. From what was just said about conventional truth, we can see why this should be.

8. There are several widely used terms expressing the Buddhist idea of a conceptual fiction: *kalpanā* "conceptual construct," or *prajñaptisat* "[merely] designated existent." They express the idea that such and such a thing is fabricated or "thought up," that is, is an invention of language and thought for which no corresponding real entity can be found under analysis.

Conventionally true statements "work" for us, yet they are about things that do not really exist. The thought is that explaining this fact requires that the truth of conventionally true statements be grounded in facts about things that are not mere fictions but are genuinely, that is, ultimately, real. But what are these ultimately real truthmakers like? The claim of Abhidharma is that the ultimately real things are things with *svabhāva*. As used in ordinary Sanskrit, this term has about the same meaning as "essence." That is, it denotes whatever nature is characteristic of an entity, whatever it is about that entity that makes it be the sort of thing it is. So being hot would be identified as the *svabhāva* of fire but not of water. Water continues to be water whether it is hot or cold. When water is hot, its being hot is said to be a *parabhāva* or "other nature" of water, a "borrowed" property that it has in dependence on something else. The ordinary uses of *svabhāva* and *parabhāva* correspond roughly to "essential nature" and "contingent nature." But when *svabhāva* is used in this way, then pots and trees can be said to have *svabhāvas*, yet these are said to be mere conceptual fictions. Abhidharma uses *svabhāva* to mean something other than what we ordinarily mean by "essence."

The reason for this is not far to seek. When we distinguish between a thing's essential nature and its merely accidental or contingent properties, we are thinking of a thing as an entity with a multiplicity of properties—some of which are properties that it must continue to have in order for it to continue to exist, and others, properties that it can acquire and shed over the course of its history. This shows that we are thinking of the thing in question as an aggregate entity. And Abhidharma claims that aggregation is always something superimposed on reality through conceptual construction. Entities that are not conceptually constructed can have but a single nature. And this nature must be intrinsic to that entity; it cannot be a borrowed nature that the entity has in dependence on other things. It is the hallmark of what is a mere conceptual construction that its nature be wholly extrinsic or borrowed from other things, typically the parts of which it is composed. The ultimately real, by contrast, can have only a nature that is *intrinsic*, or its very own. This is why in the Abhidharma context *svabhāva* is best translated as "intrinsic nature." And Abhidharma says that the truthmakers for ultimate truth are just the things with intrinsic nature.

An Interlude

Before we move on to other schools, it is necessary to digress briefly and take up problems that arise when the T-schema is combined with two truths.

Abhidharma denies that wholes like pots have intrinsic natures. So there are not the sorts of truthmakers for conventionally true statements that a robustly realist form of correspondence would require. So which notion of truth is appropriate for conventional truth in Abhidharma? Not a robust correspondence notion. Perhaps the most natural would seem to be a deflationary notion, which, as we noted, can be thought of as a weak sort of correspondence theory. But here we face a nasty little problem. That the pot exists is a conventional truth; that it does not exist is presumably an ultimate truth. All the notions of truth we discussed satisfy the T-schema, so whatever the notions of truth are, it seems to follow that the pot both does and does not exist. But there is no evidence of the Abhidharma endorsing this kind of contradiction. What is to be said about this?

First of all, it should be said that Buddhist traditions were themselves faced with a comparable accusation of contradiction and that they saw it as a serious problem, generalizable to various schools' (not just the Abhidharmas') talk about two truths. There were three basic Buddhist strategies to avoid those potential contradictions:

1. Maintain that there is strict insularity between two kinds of statements, one kind treating of conventional matters and one ultimate matters.
2. Reject the idea that conventional and ultimate statements are both equally true (i.e., both true in the same context of discourse). The conventional might, for example, be true only in a lesser sense of "true" (e.g., true for ignorant worldlings but not true properly speaking), or it might be true in a fictional context and not true in a context of talk about what is really so.
3. Allow that both statements are equally true but build in qualifiers so that contradiction is avoided; the same statement is not both true and not true.[9]

Ābhidharmikas adopted mainly strategy (1) to circumvent these problems. Their response to the problem of the pot that both exists and does not exist is to deny that the statement "A pot exists" is ultimately false. As a statement that uses the convenient designator "pot," it can be neither ultimately true nor ultimately false. Only statements that use terms designating impartite entities (things with intrinsic nature) can be ultimately true or ultimately false. In effect, they propose that we use two distinct discourses, one for those entities

9. For an example of Tibetan use of this strategy to defuse contradiction between the two truths, see Tillemans (1999, 133–138).

that are thought to be ultimately real, the other for the conceptual fictions with which we populate our common-sense world. Thus, the language of conventional truth concerns pots and people; the language of ultimate truth concerns the ultimately real entities with *svabhāva*. Their reason is that if we allow a single discourse that contains terms for both sorts of entity, then the question can always be raised whether, for instance, the pot is identical with or distinct from the atoms of which it is composed. There being good reasons to reject both horns of this dilemma, such a discourse would quickly lead to contradictions.

Strategy (2) is very widespread in Buddhism. It was used by the Buddhist logicians, Mādhyamikas, and at least some Ābhidharmikas; many types of Buddhists saw conventional truth as fictional truth or in some way not properly speaking true, merely "truths" for pedagogical purposes and so on.[10] One way to look at the payoff of this move is to maintain that "It is conventionally true . . ." is going to behave like "In the story . . ." This operator does not satisfy the T-schema. Thus, consider the following:

> In Shakespeare's story there was a prince of Denmark called "Hamlet" iff there was a prince of Denmark called "Hamlet."

The left-hand side is true; the right-hand side is false. Another strategy is to distinguish between normal contexts and pretense contexts. The T-schema then remains intact. An instance such as:

> "Apot exists" is true iff a pot exists.

is true since both sides are false. However, in the relevant context, we can pretend that both sides are true. Discussing the details of these proposals would, unfortunately, take us too far afield. Strategy (2) will be taken up in the Madhyamaka section, where the pros and cons of fictionalism will be looked at in more detail.

Still, what about the third strategy to avoid contradiction, that is, explicitly putting qualifiers into the two kinds of statements? Historically speaking, it is

10. Cf. Āryadeva, cited in PP 370 (ed. LVP): *nānyabhāṣayā mlecchaḥ śakyo grāhayituṃ yathā // na laukikaṃ ṛte lokaḥ śakyo grāhayituṃ tathā //* "Just as one cannot make a barbarian understand by any language other [than his own], so too the world cannot be made to understand if we do not use what is worldly."

11. It seems to be what Bhāviveka advocated and Candrakīrti rejected in their debate in the first chapter of the *Prasannapadā*, where the former insisted upon the need to add "ultimately" (*paramārthatas*) in sentences concerning the ultimate status of things and the latter saw it as dispensable. Whether the goal was to preserve consistency, however, is not sufficiently clear. The strategy becomes especially prominent in the Tibetan Madhyamaka, particularly in the philosophy of Tsongkhapa, who clearly does use it to preserve consistency. The strategy is opposed by Tsongkhapa's critics, like Gorampa, who in effect prefer unqualified statements and rely on strategy (2). See Cabezón and Dargyay (2006).

to be found primarily in the Madhyamaka.[11] But arguably this strategy, too, is quite general. It could be used by any Buddhist commentator, including even an Ābhidharmika, who feels the need to be explicit about kinds of truth at stake in order to make ambiguous or potentially misunderstood statements safe from contradiction. Indeed, many Tibetan doxographical textbooks (*grub mtha'*, *siddhānta*) did regularly seek to ensure precision and consistency by slipping qualifiers into their formulations of the four major Buddhist schools' key positions. It is instructive to examine briefly what the prospects and perils would be for this approach when it meets the T-schema. Let us first look at the perils, that is, at applications of (3) that may well have been seductive in traditional contexts but will probably *not* work updated.

Suppose we qualified the right-hand sides of the T-schema uniformly in the manner of the following examples:

> "The pot exists" is ultimately true iff ultimately the pot exists.
> "The pot exists" is conventionally true iff conventionally the pot exists.

Note that if we do this we have actually *given up* the T-schema. The truth predicate does not simply strip off quotes: It also *adds* material. But the move also has some philosophical plausibility. Western theories of truth have not traditionally had to cope with the thought that there are two truths. Once this is on the table, it is not unnatural to generalize the T-schema:

> <p> is true, ultimately, iff p, ultimately.
> <p> is true, conventionally, iff p, conventionally.

Nonetheless, it is not clear that this proposal is workable. The utterance of a bald proposition, p, now becomes ambiguous. It can mean "conventionally p" or "ultimately p." But what of, for instance, "conventionally p" itself? This is just as ambiguous as p. It could mean "conventionally conventionally p" or it could mean "ultimately conventionally p." But each of these is itself ambiguous in exactly the same way. We are clearly launched on a vicious regress.

The culprit is the ambiguous status of p.[12] Indeed, it seems likely that many Indo-Tibetan advocates of strategy (3) did take simple statements as ambiguous and thought that one had to specify the perspective in which they are to be taken by the qualifiers conventionally and ultimately. Arguably, there

12. Horwich (2006, 190) has a similar argument against leaving p ambiguous and qualifying it along the lines of "relative to such and such, p," "according to such and such people, p," and so on.

could be attempts to distribute the two qualifiers differently that may jibe better with Indian and Tibetan textual evidence. No matter. The essential point is that *if* these or other applications of strategy (3) leave *p* itself ambiguous, the regress will remain.

The lesson is as follows: A Buddhist who relies on qualifiers to disambiguate *p* may well go from the frying pan into the fire. The better and simpler course is to take *p* as itself unambiguous, keep a unitary sense of truth for all statements, but capture the special case of ultimate discourse with an operator like "REALLY." In the context of Madhyamaka, we will sketch such a simpler application of (3). But let us leave the consistency problems there for the moment and move on to take up Madhyamaka in detail.

Madhyamaka

It is within the Abhidharma schools that the distinction between two truths first developed. With the rise of the Madhyamaka schools, however, things changed. They agree with much of what Abhidharma says about conventional truth. They agree, for instance, that most of what people say about pots, trees, mountains, and persons is conventionally true. They also agree that the things such statements are allegedly about are some type of conceptually constructed fictions. Indeed, this idea of language and thought pertaining to fictions is present across the board in the Mahāyāna: It is in the Yogācāra and in the Yogācāra-Sautrāntrika school of Buddhist logicians.[13]

What is distinctive of Madhyamaka is that it argues, through the use of a large battery of arguments (many of them *reductio ad absurdum* arguments), that nothing could possibly have intrinsic nature, *svabhāva*. At the same time, Madhyamaka never disavows the Abhidharma claim that only things with intrinsic nature could have the sort of mind-independent existence necessary for something to be an ultimate truthmaker. The upshot is that there can be no things for ultimately true statements to be about. Even the property of being

13. These two Mahāyānist schools are realist in that they accept that ultimately existing entities must and do have intrinsic natures (*svabhāva*); those natures are, however, ineffable. The Indian Yogācāra school of Asaṅga and Vasubandhu, as represented in texts such as the *Bodhisattvabhūmi* and *Trisvabhāvanirdeśa*, places surprisingly little emphasis on the two truths. Instead, the contrast between conventional fictions and the ultimately real is brought out in an intricate theory of three natures (*trisvabhāva*). Of these three, the thoroughly imagined nature (*parikalpitasvabhāva*) is indeed fictional in nature due to language and conceptual thought (*vikalpa*); it is to be contrasted with two sorts of ineffable, real natures. In the Yogācāra-Sautrāntrika of Dignāga and Dharmakīrti, on the other hand, the doctrine of two truths is very significantly emphasized in the theory of *apoha* (exclusion), with conventional truth being concerned with fictions, that is, so-called universals (*sāmānyalakṣaṇa*) fabricated by language and thought, and ultimate truth being about real, ineffable particulars (*svalakṣaṇa*).

empty is, we are told, devoid of intrinsic nature. Consequently, it would appear that it could not be ultimately true that emptiness is the nature of all things. On the other hand, Mādhyamikas do take it as ultimately true that all things are empty. The question as to whether paradox results from this will be briefly taken up further on. It is difficult to juggle with all these balls in the air at the same time.

Let us start with conventional truth for Madhyamaka. This certainly cannot be a robust correspondence notion. If there is any kind of correspondence, this has to be with mind-dependent entities. This leaves us with a number of options. One is to endorse a pragmatic theory of truth. This approach gives no answer to the question of why statements concerning purely fictitious entities should nonetheless prove efficacious. But someone who takes this option might reply that the demand for an explanation of efficacy is illegitimate since it presupposes the correspondence theory of truth. Only someone who thinks of truth as a relation between statements and mind-independent reality will think that statements about fictions require grounding in things with intrinsic natures. The second option is to reject the correspondence theory in favor of the coherence theory of truth. In response to the same objection, the coherence theorist can give a similar answer. But there is a third option: Retain correspondence as our understanding of the "truth" in "conventional truth" but go deflationary about correspondence. In that case, the absence of robust truthmakers to stand behind our acceptance of conventionally true statements need not be an embarrassment. For then when we are asked what makes it true that there is a pot on the ground, we can simply reply that there is a pot on the ground. The absence of things with intrinsic nature is neither here nor there.

As we saw earlier, a deflationist theory, like that of Horwich, does *not* involve anything metaphysically charged. It might then seem that the deflationist's version of truth, purely along the lines of *<p> is true iff p* and stripped of the excess baggage of truthmakers and ontology, would give an elegant reconstruction of Madhyamaka's own oft-repeated principles. It might seem tailor-made for Buddhists who advocate a quietism that eschews ontological commitment or theses (*pakṣa, pratijñā*) about real entities (*bhāva*) and that just acknowledges as true what the world acknowledges (*lokaprasiddha*) without subjecting it to further analysis. Nonetheless, linking deflationism and Madhyamaka Buddhism is not that simple. The problem is this: Many Mādhyamikas (i.e., those whom Tillemans in chapter 9 dubs "typical Prāsaṅgikas") simply maintain that the world's beliefs and statements are actually *completely* wrong and false (*mṛṣā*) and that those beliefs/statements are "right" or said to be "right" only from the point of view of the world (i.e., within the world's erroneous belief system).[14] These Mādhyamikas thus accept what the world acknowledges unanalyzed, much as if it were a story that is actually false but qua story can be admitted unquestioned.

This position seems best accommodated by the fictionalist account, which we considered in the case of Abhidharma.[15] The approach enables a person to reject commitment to some or perhaps even all kinds of entities by adopting a type of *pretense* or *make-believe* stance, "according to such and such a story . . . ," or, to put things in Buddhist fictionalist terms, "according to the world (who have got it all wrong) . . . ," "conventionally . . ." To be more exact, for the typical Prāsaṅgika, conventional truth is fictionally true for spiritually realized Mādhyamika philosophers themselves, who know that it is all make-believe, but it is just error for worldlings, who wrongly buy into it being grounded in the real. Note, too, that whereas other Buddhist schools are arguably fictionalist in a restricted fashion (e.g., about partite things), Madhyamaka holds that all without exception is conceptual construction; in other words, even allegedly ultimately real entities are themselves just conventionally established fictions. In what follows let us therefore speak of this version of Madhyamaka as "panfictionalism"—the term was often used by Matilal (see, e.g., Matilal 1970) in his characterizations of Madhyamaka Buddhist views.

Fictionalism and panfictionalism can take several forms, and some ideas initially put forward in the 1950s before the term *fictionalism* had entered the analytic philosopher's vocabulary can be seen in this light, taking seemingly serious discourse as ontologically bracketed. Such is the case for Carnap's distinction between internal and external existence questions. In this volume, Finnigan and Tanaka extensively refer to this distinction to offer an interpretation of Madhyamaka's avoidance of ontological commitment. Internal existence questions about entities of type X are those said to presuppose compliance with "rules for forming statements [about Xs] and for testing, accepting or rejecting them" (Carnap 1956, 208). We can in this way remain *within* a linguistic framework and ask whether it recognizes the problematic types of entities. Or we can take a perspective *outside* the framework and ask whether those weird entities *really* exist independently of or even in spite of the framework's rules and procedures—though such questions are literally meaningless for Carnap and can be interpreted only as at best questions about how pragmatically useful it is to adopt the framework in question. Some of the contemporary advocates of fictionalism, like Stephen Yablo, have no problem in using

14. See chapter 9 of this volume.

15. Note that deflationists such as Paul Horwich dislike fictionalism quite intensely. See Horwich (2006). For a defense of a fictionalist interpretation in Buddhism, see Garfield (2006).

something like Carnap's internal-external distinction to their anti-ontological ends (see Yablo 1998). Remaining within the framework is respecting the story, adopting a make-believe stance, describing metaphorically, and so on and is ontologically uncommitted in any realist sense; stepping outside is asking what is true really, literally, and so on. A Madhyamaka fictionalism could be articulated in these directions. The central thought is that truth is truth within a framework; the ultimate truth is that nothing is *really* true (i.e., true in virtue of some real, intrinsic properties that are independent of frameworks). Since the Madhyamaka is rigorously panfictional, there is no such thing.

Panfictionalists are easily charged with the dismal problem that truth-in-a-story or truth-in-a-framework risks engendering relativism and stripping truth of its normative force. This would be a problem, for widespread beliefs and even the procedural rules and validation procedures in such belief systems often *do* need major reforms, and belief systems are not all equally right. Some Mādhyamikas (especially the Svātantrikas) saw these negative consequences as following from the typical Prāsaṅgika's panfictionalism. As they put it, the Prāsaṅgikas' confusion was to replace truths gained through reliable epistemic instruments (*pramāṇa*) with what is established through mere acceptance (*pratijñāmātreṇa siddha*) and then arrive at the conclusion that pretty much anything acknowledged by the world (*lokaprasiddha*) in the going belief system of the time—false as it actually is—would just have to be accepted as a conventional truth.

There are ways out of this impasse that nonetheless keep to the fictionalist strategy. One does not have to hold that all fictions are equal, so that the acceptance of the world's framework entails endorsing any old set of beliefs, even the dumbest kind, as many typical Prāsaṅgikas or their Svātantrika critics seem to think. Arguably, indeed, there are ways to significantly critique an accepted worldview while staying within it. First, considerations of coherence go a long way. One could propose reforms, some of them quite far reaching, by showing better coherence with other theories and with deep-seated epistemic rules and practices that the world accepts.[16]

Second, one could maintain a more pragmatist line. Indeed, the Svātantrikas deliberately adopt the Buddhist logicians' pragmatic criterion of truth-testing, that is, practical efficacy (*arthakriyā*), and apply it to testing conventional truth. Jan Westerhoff, in his chapter in this volume, uses ideas from David Lewis's

16. Candrakīrti does appeal to coherence with respect to people's normative beliefs, arguing that inconsistency with basic principles demands that people change many of their ethical views. What is perhaps odd is that he doesn't use that coherentist approach to significantly challenge popular beliefs concerning the nonnormative realm.

game-theoretic account of convention to explain how objects—not just humanly created national borders, stock markets, and the like but also physical things like mountains, trees, and so on—can be purely conceptual constructs that owe their existence only to conventions. But certain such conceptual constructs will yield effects, and others won't: Water that is conventionally existent and the conventionally illusory water in a mirage are both fictional conceptual constructions, but only the former quenches thirst. Finally, following Finnigan and Tanaka, one could maintain that the Mādhyamika replacement of whole frameworks is possible but that this is (as it is for Carnap) for purely practical reasons rather than theoretical reasons. Practical efficacy would then be understood in terms of progress toward enlightenment.

All this having been said, one will nonetheless want further explanation as to why certain effects occur and are as they are. We often look for a reductionist account: Medical science works because of facts about biochemistry that explain the effects of substances on organisms. And in such explanatory contexts, what happens on a molecular level will be regarded as more fundamental than the macroscopic phenomena—indeed, the latter consist just in certain types of events on the microscopic level. Macroscopic objects have properties that are borrowed from others—for example, their weight, size, and so on are determined by features of their microscopic parts and thus are extrinsic properties. The component parts to which the object is reduced may be provisionally admitted to have intrinsic properties in a certain way. Madhyamaka, too, could harmlessly endorse intrinsic natures in specific contexts, like reductive explanations, where an Abhidharma-like approach is deployed, all the while recognizing that under further analysis those same natures will be seen to be mind dependent and empty.[17] Instead of a final Madhyamaka position based on a master argument—that is, a proof that would settle things once and for all, a bit like a Thomistic proof of God supposedly does—we have a Madhyamaka program of acceptances of intrinsic natures that are subsequently annulled in an unending dialectical series. In chapter 10 of this volume, Siderits develops this idea in detail.

We have seen how conventional truth in Madhyamaka can be seen as a species of fictionalism. However, there are reasons that push toward deflationism as a Madhyamaka account of conventional truth instead. To put things

17. There are Mādhyamikas whose positions can be characterized this way. Tibetan dGe lugs doxographical literature (*siddhānta, grub mtha'*) depicts Svātantrikas as accepting that things are established via intrinsic natures (*svabhāva, rang bzhin*) on the conventional level (*tha snyad du rang bzhin gyis grub pa*). In effect, it looks like a Svātantrika's conventional intrinsic nature is taken by the dGe lugs as tantamount to a weak kind of truthmaker. There are intrinsic natures in virtue of which statements are true, but these natures are themselves only conventional entities and ultimately unreal.

roughly, the problem with Madhyamaka panfictionalism—and with fictionalism in general—is that it fails to take affirmations of truth as earnest, sincere, and literal. Everything has to be qualified with hedges and disclaimers about nonliteralness, pretense, "true from the point of view of . . . ," "in the world's story . . . ," or what have you. Deflationism does take truth very earnestly, literally, straightforwardly, and without hedges about stories even if at the same time it streamlines away any semblance of metaphysical profundity. This is very much in keeping with aspects of Madhyamaka thought, especially a Madhyamaka that recognizes full-fledged means of reliable cognition or epistemic instruments (*pramāṇa*) for determining conventional truth and hence does not see such truths as lesser or merely pretend truths.[18]

In order to see how deflationism might get us further ahead in reconstructing an acceptable Madhyamaka position, let us adopt an *atypical* Prāsaṅgika stance[19]—one that does *not* hold that the world is completely wrong about truth and what is true but holds that worldlings and spiritually realized beings alike are earnest, share an innocent/banal notion of truth in common, and share many literally true beliefs about what is so. There is a radical way to be a Buddhist deflationist that would be something like the following. When the Madhyamaka dialectic has done its difficult job of ridding us of realism, and when we then realize that nothing is established other than conventionally, we will see no reason to keep two distinguishable truths. We are thus left with a unitary sense of "true," and although the various truths we investigate may be complex and sophisticated, truth per se is not. This may be not all that far from the "mountains are mountains" perspective in Buddhist thought from Chan to Dzogchen (*rdzogs chen*), which aims at a lucid, nondichotomizing return to the ordinary. In any case, whatever be the historical schools that it approximates, alethic nondualism and deflationism would be what remain when two truths are no longer needed.[20]

We could thus maintain, in radical fashion, that talk of two truths will be left behind when finally it is no longer needed to counter realists. But then how is such talk to be interpreted *before* we get to that lofty stage? In particular, how are we to talk about ultimate truth on a deflationary approach? We can, in fact, accommodate the notion while remaining deflationist, provided we have a little extra machinery. Thus, we may borrow an idea from Fine (2002). Here is how Horwich (2006, 193–194) puts it (before he argues against it!):

18. See chapter 4 of this volume for a Madhyamaka philosophy that fits this bill.

19. Tsongkhapa, in his own way, is an atypical Prāsaṅgika, as are certain Dzogchen (*rdzogs chen*) writers like Rongzom Chökyisangpo (*rong zom chos kyi bzang po*) in their own ways. See chapter 9.

20. For an extended attempt to lay out what that might look like, see chapter 8 of Siderits (2003).

> [A] common move has been to assume a distinction between, on the one hand, so-called *robust* facts—facts that are REAL (with capital letters)—and, on the other hand, merely *deflationary* facts—facts to which we are committed merely by virtue of making assertions and accepting the trivial equivalence of "*p*" and "It's a fact that *p*." These deflationary facts are certainly taken to be *real* in the *ordinary* sense of that word (since everything that exists is real, in that sense), but not REAL (with capital letters), not robust. The point of this distinction is supposed to be that it's not so unpleasant, metaphysically speaking, to have to swallow weird facts, as long as they are merely deflationary. It's only weird *robust* facts that are hard to stomach . . . So far so good, perhaps. But we are owed an account of the robust/merely deflationary distinction. And no satisfactory way of drawing it has yet been established. Not that there is any shortage of competing candidates.

To implement the idea in the present context, we suppose that the language is augmented by the adverb REALLY, to be understood as a philosopher's term of art. We still have a single deflationary notion of truth. (So, in particular, "REALLY *p*" is true iff REALLY *p*.) Ultimate truths are of the form "REALLY *p*"; conventional truths are simply of the form *p*—where this does not contain an occurrence of "REALLY". A virtue of this proposal is that it also resolves the "nasty little problem" we noted in connection with Abhidharma and other Buddhist schools. When ultimate and conventional truths apparently contradict one another, the "REALLY" operator intervenes to defuse a literal contradiction: We will have, instead, something of the form "*p* but not REALLY *p*" or "REALLY *p*, but not *p*." However, note that because *p* itself does not ambiguously alternate between "conventionally *p*" and "ultimately *p*," the vicious regress described earlier in connection with strategy (3) will not occur.

The obvious problem with this approach is, as Horwich indicates, to give an account of what, exactly, "REALLY" means. Explaining this is no doubt an elusive matter. Thinkers, East and West, who would want to endorse this approach will probably see its elusiveness as a sign of genuine subtlety;[21] others may be tempted to take it as a sign that we have gone down the wrong path. But short of giving up entirely on the notion of ultimate truth, there does not seem much alternative. Moreover and in any case, the Madhyamaka, it may be

21. The problem of what REAL truthmakers amount to is, in effect, a problem closely connected with one that faces the Tibetan Madhyamaka of the dGe lugs school, namely, the difficult matter of recognizing the object of negation (*dgag bya ngos 'dzin*). (See Garfield and Thakchöe's joint chapter on this subject in this volume, chapter 5.) For Tsongkhapa there is an ascending scale of subtlety correlated with the difficulty of recognizing the various objects to be negated.

thought, owes us an account of ultimate reality.[22] So it is natural to hand-ball the problem off in this direction: We may look to this to tell us how "REALLY" is to be understood.

A final comment on a controversial matter. While using "REALLY" defuses the contradiction that loomed in maintaining distinct notions of conventional and ultimate truth, we may not be in the pure land of consistency yet, at least if we accept that the Madhyamaka means literally that there are no ultimate truths. Indeed, both panfictionalism and deflationism of the kind just described effectively dispense, in their own ways, with anything being ultimately so. Anatural move from this is to say that because nothing is ultimately so, there are no ultimate facts (i.e., there are no ultimate *satya* in the sense of things), and there also can be no ultimately true statements about how those facts are. This move and its consequences are contestable; the present authors have differing views.[23] But, prima facie at least, there would seem to be a problem, for in spite of there being nothing that is ultimately so, we find Mādhyamikas regularly saying things that do not look like conventional truths: There is no way, no path, no Buddha.[24] Of course, we could say that talk of the ultimate is all actually false but just skillful means (*upāya*) to be sloughed off when we return to mountains being mountains. But this is not very plausible if we remain within the Madhyamaka philosophy and take what it says seriously. As Deguchi, Garfield, and Priest (2008, 400) put it:

> It could be said that such descriptions are simply *upāya*, to be jettisoned as soon as one can appreciate the nature of ultimate reality directly. Although they might be seen in this way, this would not do justice to the texts. The texts in question are simply too carefully reasoned; too explicit; and are read by their commentators as correct.

Brushing aside consistency problems by invoking the idea of skillful means underestimates how rigorously philosophical the Madhyamaka is. Siderits

22. As, for example, in chapter 13 of this volume.

23. Priest sees the Madhyamaka stance on the ultimate as dialetheist (i.e., an acceptance of true contradictions about the ultimate). Siderits, who is responsible for characterizing the Madhyamaka stance by the phrase "The ultimate truth is that there is no ultimate truth," takes the point to be that the realization that brings about liberation from suffering (= one sense of "ultimate truth") is that there is no way things are ultimately. He thus rejects the imputation of dialetheism. See Siderits (2008, 127). See also Tillemans (2009) for his views. On the Tibetan Gelukpa (*dge lugs pa*) scholastic's differentiation between ultimately established/existent and ultimate truth, see Newland (1992, 92–94). The Geluk would contest the key move and the true contradictions it might be thought to imply.

24. The situation is, in fact, a standard one for any theory according to which something is ineffable but which then goes on to say something about those things (perhaps by way of explaining why they are ineffable), such as Neoplatonism, Kantianism, Heideggerianism, and indeed the Wittgenstein of the *Tractatus*. This matter is taken up in Priest's contribution to this volume.

and Tillemans would take Madhyamaka argumentation seriously but seek ways out of the apparent inconsistency. Priest would go in a different direction and argue that the contradictory nature of the ultimate even appears to be explicitly recognized and argued for, such as when the *Aṣṭasāhasrikāprajñāpāramitāsūtra* states:[25]

> By their nature, things are not a determinate entity. Their nature is a non-nature; it is their non-nature that is their nature. For they have only one nature, i.e., no nature.

Further reflection on this matter, as for all the topics we have broached in this chapter, will have to be left to the reader. In this chapter we have been able to do no more than sketch an engagement between an aspect of Western philosophy and an aspect of Buddhist philosophy. We hope, however, that it has provided the reader some kind of enlightenment, if only of a very conventional kind.

25. *prakṛtyaiva na te dharmāḥ kiṃcit. yā ca prakṛtiḥ sāprakṛtiḥ, yā cāprakṛtiḥ sā prakṛtiḥ sarvadharmāṇām ekalakṣaṇatvād yad utālakṣaṇatvāt* (p. 96 in the *Aṣṭasāhasrikāprajñāpāramitāsūtra*, ed. P. L. Vaidya 1960). Translated and discussed in Bhattacharya (1986, 113, n. 2) in connection with VV 29. See, further, the discussion in Garfield and Priest (2003) and Deguchi, Garfield, and Priest (2008).

9

How Far Can a Mādhyamika Buddhist Reform Conventional Truth? Dismal Relativism, Fictionalism, Easy-Easy Truth, and the Alternatives

Tom J. F. Tillemans

I

A famous passage of the *Ratnakūṭa*, cited in Candrakīrti's *Prasannapadā Madhyamakavṛtti*, goes like this:

> *loko mayā sārdhaṃ vivadati nāhaṃ lokena sārdham vivadāmi / yal loke 'sti saṃmatam tan mamāpy asti saṃmatam / yal loke nāsti saṃmataṃ mamāpi tan nāsti saṃmatam /*
>
> The world (*loka*) argues with me. I don't argue with the world. What is agreed upon (*saṃmata*) in the world to exist, I too agree that it exists. What is agreed upon in the world to be nonexistent, I too agree that it does not exist.[1]

1. *Trisaṃvaranirdeśaparivarta* (chapter 1) of the *Ratnakūṭa*. The source is traceable back to *Saṃyuttanikāya* III, p. 138. Sanskrit found in Candrakīrti's PP ad MMK XVIII.8 (ed. LVP 370.6–8).

Clearly the passage is taken as an account of conventional truth (*saṃvṛtisatya*) by the Mādhyamika; that is, it is cited by at least certain Mādhyamika philosophers, who were notoriously antirealist about everything, to show the sūtra source for their view that one should accept "conventional truth," or truths for the world, as being only as the world accepts them. But what does *that* mean, and what does it imply? It might well seem to imply an extreme conservatism that nothing the world ever endorsed could be criticized or rejected and that, on the conventional at least, a Mādhyamika's principal epistemic task was just to passively acquiesce and duplicate.

Let's adopt a shorthand for this version of conventional truth and characterize it and views like it as the "dismal slough." Most of us would agree that the potential flattening of the normative roles of truth and knowledge that such duplication brings is indeed quite dismal. It is a trivialization of the idea of truth to think that we could somehow settle what *is* true by periodically taking inventories of what people believe to be true at given times and places. Indeed, brute reliance on polls and inventories for determining truth has to remain unacceptable whether we are being democratic and counting each person as one or whether—supposing we are a bit snooty about the education of the masses—we prefer canvassing the opinions of a socially respectable group of clerics, academics, or other such experts.

Who, if anyone, held such an uninviting position on conventional truth? Something close to it was repeatedly *criticized* by the eighth-century Mādhyamika, Kamalaśīla, as being the view of some anonymous opponents who held that things were established as such and such because people simply accepted that they were established in that way (*dam bcas pa tsam gyis grub pa* = *pratijñāmātreṇa siddha*).[2] Kamalaśīla appears to have been duly horrified by the consequences that ensue when, instead of justifying one's views with "means of reliable cognition" or, in other words, "epistemic instruments" (*tshad ma* = *pramāṇa*), we are satisfied with simple *belief*. As he puts it, "it would follow absurdly that everything whatsoever would be established by everything" (*thams cad kyis thams cad 'grub par thal bar 'gyur ba*).[3]

For Buddhists, the worry about the negative outcomes when people collapse the distinction between things being so and merely being believed to be so goes back at least to Dharmakīrti and possibly further. As we see in

2. "Acceptance" and "belief" are sometimes differentiated in antirealist philosophies (e.g., that of Bas van Fraassen's *Scientific Image*); We're not using these terms technically here and am treating them as interchangeable.

3. See, for example, *Sarvadharmaniḥsvabhāvasiddhi*, p. 327b 7–8: *dam bcas pa tsam gyis ni 'dod pa'i don 'grub pa ma yin te / thams cad kyi(s) thams cad 'grub par thal bar 'gyur ba'i phyir ro //* "The intended point is not established simply because of being accepted (*dam bcas pa tsam gyis* = *pratijñāmātreṇa*), for [if it were,] then it would follow absurdly that everything [whatsoever] would be established by everything."

Pramāṇavārttika IV.9, Dharmakīrti was concerned that any discrimination between good and bad reasoning would be just "wiped out" (*lupta*) if we established things as so or not so (*tattvātattvavyavasthiti*) "by the force of people's thoughts" (*puṃsām abhiprāyavaśāt*).[4] (Note that Dharmakīrti seems to have been quite familiar with going accounts of different cultures' weird ideas and sexual mores; he often alluded to them sardonically in *Pramāṇavārttika* and other works in order to argue that social acceptability didn't give any claim to truth or goodness.) In fact, the flaws in basing justification purely on what people think is a theme that is often repeated by Buddhist epistemologists. Their fears about us plunging headlong into the slough are probably also, if pushed a little bit further, fears about relativism. While the failure to distinguish between *p* being so and *p* being believed to be so does not by itself constitute or entail relativism, the additional move comes quite easily. In effect, we get relativism when we accord equal truth status to opposing statements because we hold that truth is not a one-place predicate but a two-place predicate like "*p* is true for . . . ," "*p* is true in such and such a mindset/culture," and so on. Although it's difficult to be categorical, it seems plausible that Dharmakīrti and Kamalaśīla did also reject such a move to a two-place truth predicate that relativizes truth and gives different people with their different mindsets *equal* claims.

While Kamalaśīla does not explicitly give the name of a particular individual or school in India as the holders of the method of *pratijñāmātreṇa siddha*, some important aspects of his depictions do suggest that he might have been thinking of the sixth-century Prāsaṅgika-Mādhyamika (*dbu ma thal 'gyur ba*) philosopher Candrakīrti or at least (to be even less committal) someone like him. What Kamalaśīla rails against, in the *Sarvadharmaniḥsvabhāvasiddhi*, is someone who relies exclusively on what is acknowledged (*grags pa = prasiddha, pratīta*) by the world. Here is what Kamalaśīla says in that text:

> One should analyze the production of entities logically (*rigs pa = yukti*) and scripturally (*lung = āgama*). Suppose it were thought, "Why should we analyze it, when such things as the production of sprouts being conditioned by seeds and so forth is just simply acknowledged (*grags pa = prasiddha, pratīta*) by everyone from cowherds on up? Judicious people (*rtog pa dang ldan pa = prekṣāvat*) should not analyze in order to ascertain the natures of entities (*dngos po = vastu, bhāva*) because it would follow that [such an analysis] would be endless and that it would not be judicious." This is not right, for they would not ascertain anything through epistemic instruments (*tshad*

4. See Tillemans (2000, 18).

> *ma* = *pramāṇa*), and moreover it is possible that what is [generally] acknowledged is wrong. Otherwise [if analysis using epistemic instruments were unnecessary], no one who applied himself to what he had himself acknowledged would ever end up being unreliable about anything at all. To take some examples: it is acknowledged that cessation is something that has a cause [although this is actually wrong], and although people acknowledge that such things as matter are external objects, these ideas can be undermined (*gnod pa* = *bādhā*) by epistemic instruments when subjected to analysis. In the same way here too [with regard to the production of entities], what people acknowledge could also turn out to be false, and hence one really should analyze it. As for scripture without any logic, it would leave judicious people discontent. It is scripture grounded by logic that cannot lead one astray, and so first of all we should analyze logically.[5]

Indeed, Candrakīrti does seem to have been someone who held the position about the conventional being what is "just simply acknowledged" (*grags pa= prasiddha, pratīta*); he is, no doubt quite rightly, depicted by Tibetan scholastics as a "Mādhyamika who proceeds in accordance with what is acknowledged by the world" (*'jig rten grags pa ltar spyod pa'i dbu ma pa*).[6] There are a number of other tell-tale indices that strike one immediately in the *Sarvadharmaniḥsvabhāvasiddhi* passage, notably the admonition by Kamalaśīla's adversary to avoid analysis of causality and in particular to leave the relationship between seeds and sprouts philosophically untouched and just as "acknowledged by everyone from cowherds on up." This naturally brings to mind the famous argument in the first forty verses of Candrakīrti's *Madhyamakāvatāra* VI, where we find dismissed in

5. *Sarvadharmaniḥsvabhāvasiddhi*, p. 312a 8–312b 6: *rigs pa dang lung dag gis dngos po rnams kyi skye ba dpyad par bya'o // gal te 'di snyam du myu gu la sogs pa'i skye ba sa bon la sogs pa'i rkyen can gnag rdzi yan chad la grags pa kho na yin na de la dpyad par bya ci dgos / dngos po'i bdag nyid gtan la phab pa la ni rtog pa dang ldan pa rnams dpyad par rung ba ma yin te / thug pa med par thal bar 'gyur ba'i phyir dang / rtog pa dang mi ltan pa nyid du thal bar 'gyur ba'i phyir ro snyam du sems na / de ni rigs pa ma yin te / tshad mas gtan la ma phab pa'i phyir dang / grags pa yang log par srid pa'i phyir ro // de lta ma yin na rang la grags pa'i ngor byas te 'jug pa rnams su yang gang la yang bslu bar mi 'gyur ro // de la dper na 'jig pa yang rgyu dang ldan pa nyid du grags la / gzugs la sogs pa yang phyi rol gyi don nyid du grags zin kyang / dpyad pa byas na tshad mas gnod pa srid pa de bzhin du 'di la yang grags pa brdzun pa'i ngo bo yang srid pas dpyad par bya bar rung ba nyid do // de la lung rigs pa dang bral ba ni rtog pa dang ldan pa rnams rangs par mi 'gyur la / rigs pas brtan por byas pa'i lung yang don gzhan du drang bar mi nus pas de'i phyir re zhig rigs pas dpyad par bya'o //.*

6. = *'jig rten grags sde pa, 'jig rten grags sde dang mthun par spyod pa, 'jig rten grags sde spyod pa'i dbu ma pa.* See Mimaki (1982, 27 et seq.). The 'Jig rten grags sde pa and so on are regularly considered to be the Prāsaṅgika, that is, Candrakīrti and his school, but sometimes certain other thinkers, like Jñānagarbha, are also included. On the terms for Mādhyamika subschools, including the Sanskritizations of Tibetan terms (e.g., thal gyur ba = *Prāsaṅgika and rang rgyud pa = *Svātantrika) see Mimaki (1982, 53): "Tous les termes utiles pour classer les sous-écoles des Mādhyamika, tels que Sautrāntika-mādhyamika, Yogācāra-mādhyamika, 'Jig rten grags sde spyod pa'i dbu ma pa, Svātantrika et Prāsaṅgika sont une invention des auteurs tibétains."

detail the claims of Svātantrika-Mādhyamika Buddhists that cause and effect were essentially different things even if this variant on the pan-Indian debate about causes being nonexistent at the time of the effect (*asatkāryavāda*) was said by them to be only conventionally and not ultimately so. Candrakīrti, as is well known, saw as utterly misguided any such philosophically inspired attempt to analyze causal processes in terms that would go beyond ordinary notions like "This did that," "I planted such and such a tree," "I fathered this boy," "When wood, strings, and manual effort are present, sounds arise from musical instruments," "Rice comes from rice," and the other such deliberately simple and philosophically noncommittal characterizations.[7]

So, if the ghostly presence of Candrakīrti or of some such Prāsaṅgika very much like him is discernible in the *Sarvadharmaniḥsvabhāvasiddhi* passage that translated earlier, as as it appears to be, we see that for Kamalaśīla the case against the Prāsaṅgika is clear: The Prāsaṅgikas fail the basic standards of a rational, intellectual approach—they are not *judicious* (*prekṣāvat*), as they simply *copy* the world and eschew epistemic instruments (*pramāṇa*) that can confirm or correct the world's beliefs. This yields the unacceptable consequence that sufficiently widespread beliefs would be right ipso facto about the conventional.

II

We now jump about twelve hundred years ahead. Mark Siderits gives a somewhat more forgiving depiction of Candrakīrti's acceptance of *lokaprasiddha*, "what is acknowledged by the world." What Siderits (1989) attributes to Candrakīrti's Prāsaṅgika-Madhyamaka—as opposed to the Svātantrika-Madhyamaka of Bhāviveka, Śāntarakṣita, Kamalaśīla, et alii—is not the hopelessly dismal view that *everything whatsoever* that people say/believe is so is indeed so (at least conventionally). Rather, he attributes to him the view that the customarily accepted practices and community standards in terms of which people assess truth and falsity admit of no rational criticism or reform and have to be taken as given. He sees Candrakīrti as rejecting any and all theorizing about the conventional and thus advocating only mere description of the practices people do accept:

7. See Mav VI.32–33. On Prāsaṅgika-style music making, see MavBh ad VI.35 (ed. L. de la Vallée Poussin, p. 121): *dper na shing dang rgyud la brten byas la / lag pa rtsol ba byas pa gsum tshogs na / sgrog byed pi wang gling bu la sogs pas / de dag las skyes sgra yang 'byung bar 'gyur /*. The passage is quoted from the *Lalitavistara* XIII, verse 114 (ed. P. L. Vaidya): *yathā tantri pratītya dāru ca hastavyāyāma trayebhi saṃgati / tuṇavīṇasughoṣakādibhiḥ śabdo niścarate tadudbhavaḥ //* "For example, in reliance upon strings, wood, and manual effort, then by the conjunction of these three [factors], musical instruments such as *tuṇa* and *vīṇā* [lutes] issue a sound which arises due to these [factors]."

> On the Prāsaṅgika view, conventional truth is a set of brutely given practices which must be taken at face value. (Siderits 1989, 242)

For our purposes, however, we can take both Kamalaśīla's and Siderits's depictions of Prāsaṅgika together, as they both have as an essential feature that Prāsaṅgika thinkers supposedly had no use for any theorizing about philosophy or about our practices at all; they just "read off the surface" (Siderits 1989, 244) and reminded us of what we do and say, with (if we push matters) the relativism that could bring. As will become clearer later, not every serious interpretation of Prāsaṅgika-Madhyamaka *needs* to result in such an anti-intellectual and antitheoretical view, and fortunately there were some later interpreters who probably did not take conventional truth and even Candrakīrti's description of it in that way. That being said, a significant thing that needs to be granted in Kamalaśīla's and Siderits's favor is that their depiction—namely, that a Prāsaṅgika is voluntarily hamstrung to mere descriptive reminders of what people do, think, and say—does *grosso modo* come quite close to a prevalent Indo-Tibetan view of what it means to accept only what is acknowledged by the world and is a very natural reading of Candrakīrti's texts. Let me call this "typical Prāsaṅgika." *That* Prāsaṅgika is indeed what left Siderits unenthralled and is what Kamalaśīla detested.

Let's look at the broad lines of how the typical Prāsaṅgika proceeds. As Candrakīrti himself was only a curiously minor figure in Indian Buddhism, it's difficult to say much about how he was actually received in mainstream Indian Madhyamaka other than as the misguided duplicator and endorser of the world's errors that Kamalaśīla depicts him to be—we are thus obliged to flesh out our picture of Prāsaṅgika by turning largely to Tibet, where from the twelfth century on Candrakīrti assumed an extraordinarily exalted status. In any case, the crucial point is that most Tibetan interpreters of Candrakīrti, as well as the Indian commentator Jayānanda, will hold that the world's conventional truths are *wholly* erroneous (*'khrul ba = bhrānta*) from the perspective of "noble beings" (*ārya*), who see things properly; it is grasped as "really/truly so" in the eyes of the ignorant world but not in the eyes of a wiser being, like an *ārya* (see, e.g., Gorampa).[8] There is no division, à la Tsongkhapa, into a *part* (*cha*) of the world's understanding

8. This is how they generally take Mav VI.23 and other passages that show that ultimate truth is the domain of the āryas, who see rightly (*samyagdṛś*), and that *saṃvṛti* (lit. "covered truth") is the domain of the ignorant, who see wrongly/falsely (*mṛṣādṛś*). See VI.23: *samyagmṛṣādarśanalabdhabhāvaṃ rūpadvayaṃ bibhrati sarvabhāvāḥ / samyagdṛśāṃ yo viṣayaḥ sa tattvaṃ mṛṣādṛśāṃ saṃvṛtisatyam uktam //* Translated in chapter 1. Cf. Gorampa (*go rams pa bsod nams seng ge*), *dBu ma spyi don nges don rab gsal*, 384c: *bden pa gnyis yul can gyi blo rmongs ma rmongs sam brdzun pa mthong ba dang/ yang dag mthong ba'am/ 'khrul ma 'khrul gyi sgo nas 'jog dgos pas yul can gyi blo'i sgo nas 'jog pa ni rgya gar gyi thal rang thams cad mthun par snang la//* "The two truths must be brought about by the thoughts of subjects, thoughts that are [respectively] deluded or not deluded, see falsely or see rightly, are mistaken or not. Thus, they are brought about by [different] thoughts of subjects—all Indian Prāsaṅgika and Svātantrika would seem to agree on this." See chapter I in Thakchöe (2007).

that is also right—that is, established by epistemic instruments (*tshad ma* = *pramāṇa*)—for *āryas* themselves and a *part* that is wrong for them. The *wholesale* erroneousness of the conventional is sometimes formulated by saying that the conventional is "existent [only] from the point of view of mistaken thought" (*blo 'khrul ba'i ngor yod pa*) (cf., e.g., Jonangpa writers).[9] Its erroneousness is often (but not always) closely linked to the issue about whether Mādhyamikas can accept any epistemic instruments for states of affairs/things in the world. For many (cf., e.g., Jayānanda, Taktsang Lotsawa, Patsab Nyimadrak), the Candrakīrtian position is interpreted as being that there are no epistemic instruments (*pramāṇa*) and that conventional truth is itself just a series of erroneous inventions. Finally, what is also relevant to us here is the typical Prāsaṅgika take on the consequences of conventional existence being thoroughly erroneous and unreal in these ways. For espousing thoroughgoing antirealism and being constrained to accept as conventional only what is accepted by the world (*lokaprasiddha*) are clearly linked for many Indo-Tibetan exegetes. The fourteenth-century writer Üpalosel (*dbus pa blo gsal*), for example, explicitly makes that very move. Worldly things are taken by the Prāsaṅgika as completely unable to withstand analysis (= erroneous), and *therefore* the Prāsaṅgika just "reads off the surface" and adopts worldly descriptions. Üpalosel approvingly cites *Madhyamakāvatāra* VI.35 (and *Satyadvayavibhaṅga* k. 21 of Jñānagarbha!), verses that for him show that it is *because* a Prāsaṅgika does not accept that anything can be real or (what comes to the same) because nothing can withstand analysis that he will be a "Mādhyamika who proceeds in conformity with what is acknowledged by the world."[10]

III

Now, why might such Mādhyamikas think that a *blanket endorsement* of the world's beliefs or its practices *followed* from their thorough-going Mādhyamika antirealism? Why would they see themselves as in some sense constrained to a

9. See, for example, a modern Jonangpa textbook, the *rGyu 'bras theg pa mchog gi gnas lugs zab mo'i don rnam par nges pa rje Jo nang pa chen po'i ring lugs 'jigs med med gdong lnga'i nga ro* of Yon tan bzang po. In the section on the two truths (p. 116) we find statements like *de ltar gyi kun rdzob bden pa / chos can / khyod don dam bden pa ma yin te / khyod gshis kyi gnas lugs su ye shes dam pa'i spyod yul du mi bden pa'i phyir / der thal / khyod kyi rang bzhin na rnam shes 'khrul ngo tsam du zad pa gang zhig / 'phags pa mchog gi ye shes kyi gzigs ngor rnam yang ma grub pa'i phyir / kun brdzob bden pa yin na rnam shes 'khrul ngo tsam du zad pas khyab ste . . .* "Take such conventional truth as the topic: It is not ultimate truth because it is not true as an object of the highest wisdom about the absolute. This follows because in its nature it is nothing more than a mere perspective of mistaken consciousness and is never established from the perspective of the noble, supreme wisdom. If something is a conventional truth, this implies that it is nothing more than a mere perspective of mistaken consciousness."

10. Mimaki (1982, 170–173).

kind of "reading off the surface" because of holding that things are all empty (*śūnya*)? It's not obvious that one follows from the other. Indeed, it looks like the whys and wherefores of this typical Prāsaṅgika move are at most implicit in the actual Indo-Tibetan texts, at least as far as we can see; nor are its consequences explicitly drawn—we thus have to step gingerly outside the Indic and Tibetan literature to get a view of what may have happened and why.

Probably the key move and its consequences are due to Prāsaṅgika thinkers' stands on issues connected with what we now know as *fictionalism*. This is an approach that enables people to reject commitment to some or even all kinds of entities by adopting a type of *pretense* or *make-believe*. They might see talk of such entities as metaphorical or might even add to truth claims like "*p* is true" a disclaimer operator that *p* is true "in such and such a story" or "for such and such (mistaken) people," "in such and such a (false) version of history," and so forth.[11] To put things in a Buddhist context, while the world buys into its own wholesale errors, the typical Prāsaṅgikas will have none of it and know that they are false (*mṛṣā*); nonetheless, as fictionalists, they can, unduped by the world, still accept a kind of truth of the world's statements and beliefs; if need be, they will make that clear by prefixing the appropriate disclaimer, "conventionally . . . ," "in the world's account," "according to the world," and so on. More exactly, to use the terminology of current writing on fictionalism, the typical Prāsaṅgikas can be seen as *revolutionary* fictionalists who hold that adopting a pretense stance constitutes a type of progress. Instead of saying that the world itself already tacitly plays make-believe (what is known as "hermeneutical fictionalism"), they say that the world is completely mistaken about what it does and that it *ought to learn to say the things it says only in terms of pretend assertions.*[12]

The world thus proceeds according to what the typical Prāsaṅgika sees as an *error theory*;[13] the Mādhyamika, who knows better, nonetheless salvages the world's ideas as conventional truth by transposing the totality or at least a considerable number of the world's false statements into fictional truths, that is, conventional truths. Note that in contemporary fictionalism some such move

11. Cf. Stanley (2001, 37): "On a fictionalist view, engaging in discourse that involves apparent reference to a realm of problematic entities is best viewed as engaging in a pretense. Although in reality, the problematic entities do not exist, according to the pretense we engage in when using the discourse, they do exist." See Yablo (2001) for four philosophical varieties of fictionalism; adding the operator yields metafictionalism.

12. On revolutionary and hermeneutical fictionalisms, see Burgess and Rosen (1997); see also M. Eklund, "Fictionalism," *Stanford Encyclopedia of Philosophy*.

13. An oft-cited example of a modern error theorist is J. L. Mackie, who holds an irrealist position about moral properties: They don't exist, but people have sophisticated and structured beliefs that they do and act, think, and talk as if they do. Sensible people (= certain philosophers), however, know better. See Mackie (1986). See M. E. Kalderon's "standard formulation" of error theory: "The sentences in the target class express propositions that represent the putative subject matter but are systematically false" (Kalderon 2005, 105).

from an error theory to fictionalism is not infrequent, especially in ethical irrealist theories, which maintain that while people widely believe that there *are* properties like good and bad, in fact there are only ethical attitudes and standards for ethical reasoning. (Richard Joyce, for example, in *The Myth of Morality*, makes that move. It is argued that a philosopher should see the idea of there being actual moral properties as false but nonetheless conserve them as useful regulative fictions.[14]) The advantage of fictionalism, both for an ethical irrealist and for a Mādhyamika Buddhist, thus, is that a philosophical understanding that certain propositions are literally false will not lead one to simply eliminate all talk of the entities and properties in question.

For ethical fictionalists, reasoning can take place within the context of the fiction, that is, internal to the ethical "story," by invoking coherence and consistency, not significantly unlike the way one might speculate about what fictitious characters in a novel *would have done* or *should have done* if they had remained consistent with their fictitious personalities. Thus, while a considerable portion of a story needs to be taken as brutely given, there is room for extrapolation, correction, and reform. All this being said, the Prāsaṅgika seems to have perceived the *desirability* for reform to have been quite limited indeed and seems to have felt that *because* no account could ever be true, the world's story should be accepted largely intact *by default*. Sometimes these "by default" arguments are indeed on the mark. Candrakīrti deftly used such an argument against metaphysical theories like those of the Yogācāras, which sought to replace false ideas about there being external objects with a true idealist account. The argument here and in cases like it (e.g., against the logicians' ontology) is that the whole effort toward *reform motivated by ontology* is simply worthless, given that nothing more real or true is to be gained.[15] That much is sweetness and light. What is more troubling, however, is the nagging feeling that Candrakīrti and the typical Prāsaṅgika don't stop there. They seem to blur the distinction between on the one hand a metaphysical issue, something that might indeed best be left alone, and on the other hand a sophisticated scientific or technical issue (which may even proceed without many worries about

14. See also Joyce (2005, 298 et seq.).

15. Mav VI.48cd: *svapne 'pi me naiva hi cittam asti yadā tadā nāsti nidarśanaṃ te* // "Indeed, given that in a dream the mind does not [really] exist either for me, then you have no [valid] example [to show how the mind is real while external objects aren't]." Tsongkhapa, in his *rTsa ba'i she rab kyi bka' gnad brgyad*, p. 17, lucidly concludes: *des na tha snyad pa'i ngor don sems gnyis ka yod par mtshungs la / de kho na nyid sems pa'i ngor don sems gnyis ka med par mtshungs pas / don med la sems yod par mi rigs so* / "So, from the point of view of customary transactions (*tha snyad* = *vyavahāra*), [physical] objects and the mind are the same in existing. From the point of view of one contemplating the [ultimate] reality (*de kho na nyid* = *tattva*), both are the same in not existing. Therefore, [for the Mādhyamika] it is incoherent that the object be nonexistent and the mind existent." See Seyfort Ruegg (2002, 207).

ontology or anything more than minimalist accounts of truth). *Instead, it looks like all sophisticated explanation is lumped together and that sophistication is itself to be ruled out.* Saying, as does Candrakīrti repeatedly in debates with Sāṃkhya and his fellow Buddhists, that rice just leads to rice rather than barley, may well be a very good answer to the various metaphysicians who think either that the effect must really be present in the cause to ensure that causality is not haphazard or that cause and effect must be completely separate real entities. It is of course, however, a bad answer to a plant scientist inquiring about genetic features in rice that explain its growth, yield, color, form, resistance to disease, and so on. The problem is that Candrakīrti seems to have taken the type of answer appropriate to the metaphysical debate as also being the best answer to the second sort of inquiry. And you just cannot silence a biologist—especially, one supposes, a genetic engineer working for Monsanto—by saying that rice leads to rice.

So, although Candrakīrti *does* promote some substantial changes in people's ethical and political ideas and even in their ways of reasoning about ethics by pitting some of their attitudes against others,[16] and although he does allow for correction of obviously wrong beliefs and attitudes that depend upon gross misapplications of well-known epistemic standards,[17] nevertheless, in spite of these rudimentary mechanisms for reform, it looks like, for him, conventional

16. In the initial four chapters of the *Catuḥśataka* (CS) and Candrakīrti's *Catuḥśatakaṭīkā* thereupon, Āryadeva and Candrakīrti deal with a famous series of four illusions (*viparyāsa*) that are supposedly present in the confused minds of worldlings: thinking that transitory life is permanent, what is actually painful is pleasurable, what is dirty is clean, and what is selfless has a self. Translation in Lang (2003, 1986); Sanskrit fragments in Suzuki (1994). For the canonical schema of four *viparyāsa*, see *Abhidharmakośabhāṣya* ad V.8; French translation in L. de la Vallée Poussin (1923–1931, vol. 4, p. 21). To resume the critique in the CS and *ṭīkā* concerning the four illusions, ordinary people's confidence about the future is based on self-deception about their mortality (CS I.6–7); worldlings' attitudes to mourning are inconsistent (*'gal ba* = *viruddha*), so that they mourn what on reflection does not deserve it (CS I.13); pleasure and happiness are rare, contrary to widespread opinion; it is pain that is prevalent (CS II.4); people might think that work is a source of happiness, but it is a largely meaningless and slavish exertion to survive (CS II.18); attitudes about beauty and cleanliness are confused and would be seen to be wrong if we reflected upon them (CS III.3–5); possessiveness makes no sense (CS III.11); kings (and other so-called superior individuals) are more like social parasites, dependent upon others' work—they have no reason to feel justified of their status (CS IV.2); a king who is violent, corrupt, or cruel deserves to be denounced even though he claims to provide protection or to be the "father of the people" (CS IV.11–13), and so on and so on.

17. See Mav VI.25: *vinopaghātena yad indriyāṇāṃ ṣaṇṇām api grāhyam avaiti lokaḥ / satyaṃ hi tal lokata eva śeṣaṃ vikalpitaṃ lokata eva mithyā //* "The world understands what is apprehended by the six unimpaired faculties; indeed, that is what is real just according to the world. The rest is thought to be false simply following [the perspective of] the world." Skt. in *Bodhicaryāvatārapañjikā*, ed. P. L. Vaidya, p. 171. The examples in the *Catuḥśatakaṭīkā* of attitudinal changes are often somewhat weird and comical. Thus, for example, Candrakīrti's commentary to CS III.25: Discovering that one's wife is actually a flesh-eating demoness (*piśācī, sha za mo*) is said to produce profound changes in one's attitudes and desires toward her [*sic*]. Cf. also his commentary to CS III.23: When butter has been smeared on a cat's nose, the cat thinks his food is buttery and hence more attractive (*ghṛtaliptabiḍālanāsikasvādanavat*); the point is, of course, that the cat or, more generally, anyone whose senses are altered or impaired, can be said to have wrong beliefs and inappropriate attitudes about things because the cat's epistemic process is understood (even by ignorant worldlings) to be faulty.

truth is still very much a *dumbed-down truth.* Consistency with attitudes and mere diagnoses of obviously faulty sense organs do not take a typical Prāsaṅgika very far in allowing for sophisticated theoretical ideas. Indeed, looking at the bald simplicity of *Madhyamakāvatāra*'s and *Catuḥśatakaṭīkā*'s accounts of ordinary human actions and processes (as well as the seeds-sprouts causality), it seems that Prāsaṅgika requires that explanation of those nontechnical activities should largely reproduce the way the average person understands and describes them. This is extraordinarily crippling. In human sciences, for example, we would in effect be left with a version of what the philosopher and argumentation theorist John Woods has termed the "easy-easy principle," that is, the idea that not infrequently crops up in antitheoretical circles that "if a kind of human practice is competently performable without technical tutelage, then the theory of that practice must likewise be free of technical or theoretically abstruse content" (Woods 2006, 303–304).

IV

Easy-easy truth, or dumbed-down conventional truth, whatever be its possible attraction for a sixth-century Mādhyamika, is not attractive to most of us, nor should it be—technical subjects like logic, linguistics, and economics, not to mention physical science, would just plainly be impossible and would be eliminated in favor of oh-so-readily-understandable common sense. Nor was this easy-easy truth very attractive even to certain later self-styled Prāsaṅgikas in Tibet, that is, the followers of Tsongkhapa, who were avid theorists of logic, epistemology, philosophy of language, and other subjects that no doubt were abstruse to the ordinary cowherd. What went wrong, and what alternatives are there to keep conventional truth from being so dumbed down?

First of all, did the world picture *have* to be that pedestrian for a typical Prāsaṅgika fictionalist? Perhaps not. There may indeed be a non sequitur here (although historically speaking, many Prāsaṅgikas, including very likely Candrakīrti, did *think* a pedestrian world picture followed from their panfictionalist stance.) A modified parable from Stephen Yablo is interesting. Yablo (2000, 200) argues for the fictional nature of mathematics by a thought experiment that is known as the "oracle argument."[18] Let us suppose that we somehow learned from an oracle that there were no abstract objects; we would nonetheless be able to go on doing mathematics in much the sophisticated way we always have. Some philosophers suggest that we could just as well take

18. The idea initially figures in Burgess and Rosen (1997, 3).

Yablo one step further. We might also be able to go on as before, doing creative theoretical work in science, too, if the oracle taught us that there were no macroscopic objects but only real, extensionless particulars or some other substitute. Let's even suppose that the oracle taught us that there was nothing at all that existed externally and that Berkeleian idealism was the true account of things. Finally, the oracle takes a whiff of the Delphic vapors and tells us the last word: Even Berkeley doesn't cut it; it's all pure fiction, even though so many of us had thought otherwise for so long. Couldn't we still just go on as before, doing what we used to do and even coming up with sophisticated theories by following our epistemic procedures?[19] After all, *in any case* we have been keeping with the epistemic practices of the world, and those are actually very sophisticated and can even evolve, too, if need be.

So it may be that if a Yablo-style parable about fictionalism is right, the dumbing down in typical Prāsaṅgika is not actually a *consequence* of the all-encompassing error theory and fictionalism but more a result of Candrakīrti's and his followers' spectacular underestimation of the level of sophistication of the world's epistemic procedures. One Buddhist way out, then, would be to beef up significantly the Mādhyamika's account of how the world establishes the differences between what it accepts and rejects.

Still, if in order to get some such fictionalist account off the ground we needed to explain the ordinary person's cognition and discourse exclusively in terms of an unnuanced error theory, this is going to end up being a very hard sell. If the sales tactic is (as it often is) to put everything on the back of the supposed *usefulness* of the world's errors, this seems an unpromising approach, especially when those errors are all encompassing. Indeed, the problem is to imagine how human thinking and discourse, which according to the typical Prāsaṅgika scenario is thoroughly pervaded by falsity alone, could ever be of *use* to the degree needed to explain why an enormous number of false beliefs/statements about the ordinary world are and should be considered true in some nondismal way.[20] While we might (like an ethical irrealist) take as "true" *certain* shared errors, like beliefs in such and such actions as being good or bad because such mistaken beliefs make people more respectful, gentle, and so on, it would be hard to see how people's flat-out errors about *every* aspect of everything in the world could lead to significantly useful results.

19. See Eklund (2005, 559–561) for the extension of Yablo's oracle argument.

20. Cf. Stanley (2001, 46): "The problem facing a brute error theory of a discourse that is epistemically central . . . lies in explaining how a discourse laced through with falsity can nevertheless be useful. On the view we are considering, this problem amounts to explaining how a discourse that expresses mostly falsities may communicate true propositions."

Does one need to bite *that* bullet in order to be (some sort of) Mādhyamika? Now, philosophically speaking at least, such an error theory and fictionalism would be an extremely high price to pay for rejecting what Mādhyamikas say they reject, that is, metaphysical realism (*dngos po smra ba*), the view that things are what they are because of the properties they have intrinsically, independently of our conceptions (*kalpanā*) of them, our linguistic designations (*prajñapti*), and our actions upon (*pravṛtti*) them. There would seem to be an avoidable overkill in saying that *everything* must be thoroughly erroneous/fictional in order for one to simply reject that things are without intrinsic natures (*svabhāva*). Let us for the moment then put on a philosopher's hat rather than that of a philologist, historian, or close reader of texts: *atypical* approaches might be, philosophically at least, more promising. We leave Candrakīrtian exegesis and philology temporarily on hold.

If we do that, there are indeed a number of ways to avoid metaphysical realism, ways that somehow jettison the typical Prāsaṅgika idea that conventional truth is *wholly* erroneous (*'khrul ba = bhrānta*) for the profane and purely fictional for "noble beings" (*ārya*). The best way to go, instead of all-encompassing error theory and fictionalism about conventional truth, is to see Madhyamaka's two truths as a rung on a ladder that we climb to finally know better a unitary world (see chapter 10 in the present volume), one that was even there all along but veiled by conceptually created dichotomies and ignorance. Tibetan Nyingmapa (*rnying ma pa*) writers speak of this primordial unity in terms of the "two truths being inseparable" (*bden gnyis dbyer med*).[21] Arguably, this may not be far from the radical approach spoken about in the previous chapter by Priest, Siderits, and Tillemans, where mastery of the Madhyamaka critique of the world's inveterate realism leads one to a return to truths, unqualified as conventional or ultimate. And indeed, why not after all say that such simple truths are shared by *āryas* and the world alike (alas, confusedly, in the case of the world)?

There is a point then where the two truths and the Madhyamaka dialectic have done their job, so that truth just straightforwardly fulfills its normative role but without any metaphysical baggage of realism. To go back to the exposé of the previous chapter, there is a kind of enlightened deflationism (see

21. One radical Tibetan Buddhist way is what we find in the writings of the eleventh-century Nyingmapa thinker Rongzom (*rong zom chos kyi bzang po*). The idea seems to be that Madhyamaka talk of conventional truth as erroneous shows the inherent limitations of a dialectical system (*mtshan nyid kyi theg pa*) as it dissects and discriminates between right and wrong, rejection and acceptance, enlightenment and delusion, while the two truths are to be seen as inseparable (*bden gnyis dbyer med*). See chapter 3 and n. 235 et passim in Köppl (2008). Rongzom's key stance seems to be a kind of suddenism: A state of absence of error (i.e., purity and enlightenment) is not to be reached gradually by a process of dispelling error, but error is by its nature already pure and thus is itself enlightened (*de yang 'khrul ba bsal nas ma 'khrul ba zhig bsgrub tu med de / 'khrul ba ngo bo nyid kyis rnam par dag pas sangs rgyas pa yin te / de bas na chos thams cad ye nas mngon par rdzogs par sangs rgyas pa'o /*.)

chapter 8 on deflationism and other truth theories).[22] One considerable advantage of deflationism over typical Prāsaṅgika error theory/fictionalism is that it has no problems whatsoever accommodating far-reaching criticism and amendments to going worldviews. People can simply be dead wrong in believing some would-be truths. Or people can fail to understand and believe genuine truths that are too technical, theoretical, specialized, and so on for the unschooled layperson and that fact in no way detracts from their status as truths. In short, theories can remain sophisticated, and truths can remain elusive. Fortunately, they don't all have to be dumbed down to the level of easy-easy accessibility.

Now let's suppose we keep the two truths. What then? We could have an *atypical* Prāsaṅgika approach like that of Tsongkhapa: Conventional truths *simpliciter are* established as full-fledged truths for *both* the ordinary person and the *ārya* alike by full-fledged *pramāṇas* and are not just mere falsehoods that we widely believe in. Error comes in only where the ordinary person—and fortunately not the *ārya*, who knows better—adds a corrupting "superimposition" (*sgro 'dogs = samāropa*) of intrinsic natures (*svabhāva*) upon otherwise innocently existent things like *F*s and *G*s.[23] Here too, just as on the radical scenario, deflationism would seem to fit the bill better than fictionalism and brute error theory in that it would enable the truths about innocent *F*s and *G*s to be fully fledged (not just make-believe). Also, normativity is conserved without difficulty.[24] What exists then would be a series of deflationary facts, and the truth of the beliefs, propositions, and so on about them that are accepted by the world and the āryas alike would be explainable simply as deflationary truths. A "REALLY" operator could be introduced to account for Tsongkhapa's repeated admonitions that nothing is ultimately or REALLY (*don dam par*) the case. Thus, the Mādhyamika could cheerfully accept the truth of "*p*" and also "not REALLY *p*" (see chapter 8). Note, too, however, that both "*p*" and "not REALLY *p*" would be no more than deflationary truths—this might capture Tsongkhapa's idea that everything, even emptiness and the denials of intrinsic nature, is only conventionally established (*tha snyad du grub pa*).

We close, however, on an untraditional—indeed slightly heretical—note. These two very different sorts of Mādhyamikas, Nyingma and Geluk, were no

22. To our knowledge, the first attempt to interpret Buddhist ideas in terms of deflationism/minimalism was Perrett (2002).

23. On superimposition in Madhyamaka, see Tillemans (2004).

24. Note that if we still wished to go the fictionalist route to accommodate Tsongkhapa, it would be a hermeneutical fictionalism: We could say that ordinary people and āryas alike do themselves talk about *Fs* and *Gs* in a *fictionalist* way and that ordinary people somehow also add a corrupting superimposition to that. The usually cited difficulty in saying that ordinary people somehow talk in a make-believe fashion is that it is not at all clear what that means, for phenomenologically speaking they don't think they do or feel they do.

doubt extremely subtle thinkers, privileging philosophy; it should come as no great surprise that their stances are often in a significant and recurring tension with what the Indian texts say (on a natural reading of the Sanskrit). Compounding it all is that Candrakīrti himself goes frustratingly fuzzy and straddles the fence at certain critical points where one would have hoped for clearer direction.

So what is he? Typical or atypical Prāsaṅgika? Although there are important and tantalizing methodological passages at the beginning of *Prasannapadā* about the superimposition of intrinsic natures,[25] the *specific* arguments in Candrakīrti's works seem to invoke superimposition very little and rely instead on the idea that everything the world thinks is just plain wrong for an ārya. In short, philologically speaking, the typical Prāsaṅgika reading is indeed a straightforward account for most of what the text actually *says*. A writer like Tsongkhapa had to systematically add qualifiers to the specific Indian Madhyamaka arguments to interpret them as targeting the superimposed object to be negated, and he had to do considerable commentarial legerdemain with other Candrakīrtian textual passages, too, some of it quite unconvincing. It is, for example, incontestable that on a usual understanding of the Buddhist Sanskrit terms *worldling* (*loka*) and ārya, they will be taken as standing in sharp contrast, along the lines of a typical Prāsaṅgika interpretation like that of Gorampa. Tsongkhapa's contrary exegesis here is thus not convincing even if the philosophical gain may be considerable.[26] One can multiply these sorts of examples.

In the end, does it detract from an atypical Tibetan thinker that he had to read Indian writers like Candrakīrti in the strained way he did? No, not really, but it does often put him in a quite different light from the way the tradition depicts him. The positive point is that someone like Tsongkhapa emerges as a highly creative Mādhyamika with a steel-trap philosophical mind. The catch is that he may well have the (unavowable) merit of making Candrakīrti a significantly better philosopher than he actually was.

25. See Tillemans (2004).

26. On Tsongkhapa's exegesis of "the world" (*loka*) as including āryas (and not in contrast to them, as typical Prāsaṅgikas would have it), see the article by Sonam Thakchöe in chapter 3 of this volume.

10

Is Everything Connected to Everything Else? What the Gopīs Know

Mark Siderits

It will be claimed here that the Mādhyamika can embrace a view of conventional truth that leaves room for improvement in our epistemic practices—that avoids the dismal slough of pure conventionalism (see chapter 9). Of course, this will come at a price. Mādhyamikas must overcome their fear of intrinsic nature and learn to live with the view that real things have *svabhāva*. How can they do this without abandoning the core Madhyamaka claim that all things are devoid of intrinsic nature? We will get to that. But first some background is in order, beginning with an explanation of the title. Then we will consider a way of understanding that core claim of emptiness and how it can be justified.

One sometimes hears it said that the Madhyamaka claim about emptiness amounts to the view that everything is connected to everything else.[1] This is thought by some to offer a basis for a specifically Buddhist environmental ethic.[2] Others see it more generally as a welcome corrective to an excessively individualistic worldview. The normative consequences are dubious. More important though, it is far from clear that a Mādhyamika should say that

1. Instances of this claim abound in the literature. For a particularly careful and nuanced version, see Arnold (2005a, 170), who claims that, according to Nāgārjuna and Candrakīrti, "'dependently' or 'relatively' is the only way that anything could exist." He subsequently considers and seeks to answer the objection that this amounts to attributing to Madhyamaka an account of the ultimate nature of reality (see especially pp.171–173). Still, it is not clear that he succeeds in dispelling the suspicion that his Madhyamaka is close in spirit to Bradley or Whitehead.

2. See, for example, Cooper and James (2005).

everything is connected to everything else. This cannot be ultimately true, and it does not appear to be conventionally true, either. At least, it does not appear to reflect the epistemic practices whereby we come to a more useful understanding of the world. About this more later. For now, let us simply take it that there may be a connection between what we say about conventional truth and what we say about the nature of things. If we agree that there is only conventional truth, then in order to avoid the dismal slough, we may have to deny that our world is aptly characterized by the metaphor of Indra's net.[3]

To understand the claim that all things are empty, we must start with Abhidharma, where the notion of *svabhāva* has its origins. Ābhidharmikas held that only statements concerning things with intrinsic natures can be ultimately true. This is because ultimate truth is meant to conform to the rigorous standards of a realist conception of truth. On the realist conception, truth accrues to statements by virtue of correspondence to mind-independent reality, and Abhidharma takes aggregation to be strictly a mental activity. So no statement employing a concept of an aggregate can be ultimately true (or ultimately false, either). If it is the mind that does the aggregating, then partite entities do not exist apart from the mind's conceptualizing activity. Thus, there can be no objective facts concerning such entities that might make statements about them either true or false.

The stock example of an aggregate concept is that of a chariot. This means that chariots are seen as less than robustly real. One way of seeing why this should be is that the properties of the chariot are all "borrowed" from its parts. The weight of the chariot, for instance, is determined by the weight of its parts. Likewise for any other property that might be thought necessary to something's being a chariot or being this particular chariot. The nature of the chariot is not "its own" or intrinsic to the chariot.[4] That the nature of the chariot is not intrinsic but extrinsic (*parabhāva*) means that its contribution to the truth of assertions is always redundant. Any information we can glean from knowledge of its nature can be obtained elsewhere, from knowledge of the natures of the parts.

3. Indra's net is said to contain a jewel at each node. There are infinitely many such nodes, and each jewel at a node reflects the light from each other jewel in the net. The metaphor is used in Huayan to express its teaching that everything is in some sense interconnected.

4. That there are difficulties in characterizing the concept of an intrinsic property is pointed out in, for example, Lewis (1983). Suppose we define intrinsic properties as those an entity might have even if it were the only existing thing. The difficulty is that, if by "lonely" we mean the property of being the only thing in existence (the property of lacking worldmates), then while this property may be had by something lacking worldmates, yet it cannot be intrinsic since an intrinsic property should be one that an entity may have independently of whether it is accompanied by worldmates. (Something's being *lonely* is contingent on its having no worldmates.) One way around this difficulty would be to accept the restriction Nyāya places on absences: no absence without an existing counterpositive. In that case there is no such property as *lonely*, so the question of whether it is intrinsic does not arise.

The reverse is not true. We cannot come to know everything about the natures of the parts of the chariot just from knowing the nature of the chariot. This asymmetry shows why the parts but not the chariot are thought to belong in our final ontology, our list of things that "are there anyway." And this in turn should tell us why the Abhidharma conception of the ultimate truth might represent the last, best hope of the semantic realist, someone who thinks of truth as correspondence to how things are anyway. On the Abhidharma conception, only statements about *dharmas*, things with intrinsic nature, can be ultimately true. So they and their arrangements are the real truthmakers. Everything else is just a concession to human interests and cognitive limitations.

This conception of truth is not as distant from our ordinary conception as one might think. For we know that we do better when we try to filter out from our beliefs the contributions of our interests and cognitive limitations. This is why we today know more about the world than did ancient Indians—cowherds, women, and Candrakīrti himself.[5] We know more about the causes of and cures for diseases, for instance, because we have learned to think of the human organism as an aggregate composed of a huge number of molecules. And as we come to better understand the behavior of those molecules, we also come to see how our cognitive limitations—for example, the fact that our sense organs are macroscopes and not microscopes—would result in our thinking of those molecules all together as one big thing, an organism that is either healthy or sick. But it is the molecules that do all the work here. It is because of their behavior that exposure to various pathogens can lead to elevated temperature. It is by looking at the molecules as things with their own natures and seeing the organism as nothing but (nothing "over and above") those hugely many molecules that we overcome our former ignorance about disease. Ābhidharmikas held that it is facts about the *dharmas*—things with intrinsic natures—that explain why common-sense beliefs about things that lack intrinsic natures and so do not ultimately exist should nonetheless sometimes have utility. The success of the molecular-biological approach to medical science looks like vindication of the Abhidharma view.

Of course, we know that Mādhyamikas developed a whole arsenal of arguments designed to show that nothing could have intrinsic nature. If those arguments are any good, then the molecules that our bodies consist in cannot have intrinsic natures. Nor, for that matter, can the subatomic particles of which those molecules in turn consist. It also appears that at least some of those arguments

5. At PP 260.14 (ed. LVP), Candrakīrti notoriously speaks of "what is known to people like cowherds and women" (*gopālāṅganājanaprasiddha*) as a way of designating common knowledge. More is said about this problematic expression at the end of the chapter.

are good. But before looking at the consequences of this let us consider a possible Madhyamaka strategy that is not likely to work. There cannot be any one argument that will serve as a master argument for emptiness.[6] In particular, one cannot use the claim that everything originates in dependence on causes and conditions to prove that nothing has intrinsic nature. Ābhidharmikas held both that all *dharmas* originate in dependence on causes and conditions[7] and that *dharmas* have intrinsic natures. If there is an inconsistency here, it is not an obvious one. To say of something that its nature is intrinsic is to say nothing about how it came to exist bearing that nature. It is to say that its currently existing with that nature is compatible with nothing else now existing. Consequently, its coming into existence in dependence on causes and conditions is not by itself incompatible with its having an intrinsic nature. Further premises are needed for the inference of emptiness to go through.[8]

Moreover, it does not even follow from everything's being dependently originated that each entity is causally connected to every other. For it's relatively easy to imagine a case where all *dharmas* depend on causes and conditions and yet some are causally isolated from others. Just imagine two beginningless causal series of events, each event in the one series outside the light cone of any event in the other.[9] Since causal influence can be propagated no faster than the speed of light, no event in the first series can influence or be influenced by an event in the second series. Yet everything in this universe is dependently originated.

So the "Indra's net" strategy, which appeals to dependent origination, won't establish emptiness. Still, there are reasons to refrain from asserting that there are things with intrinsic natures. They stem not from any one argument but from the collective force of the plethora of Madhyamaka arguments against a wide variety of particular realist views. If there are such good reasons, they show that the very idea of ultimate truth is incoherent. The Mādhyamika, in other words, wants us to stop hankering after the one true theory about the nature of mind-independent reality. And this not because while there is such a nature, we are incapable of grasping it. The Mādhyamika does not disavow the claim of the Ābhidharmika that only things with intrinsic natures can be ultimately real.[10]

6. In this respect the situation of the Mādhyamika is much like that of the Pyrrhonian skeptic. For a discussion of the point that Sextus Empiricus has no "master argument" and its implications for Pyrrhonism, see Williams (1988).

7. Or at least almost all. The Vaibhāṣikas held that there are three unconditioned *dharmas*. See AK I.5.

8. There would be an inconsistency here only if cause and effect were held to exist simultaneously. Nyāya holds that what it calls the inherence cause exists simultaneously with the effect. Some Abhidharma schools may have held a similar view concerning the relation between the *mahābhūta* and the *bhautika* dharmas. However, Ābhidharmikas generally hold that cause precedes effect.

9. This is possible given the right distribution of sufficiently massive objects, such as black holes, in the universe.

10. See for example, *Buddhapālitavṛtti* ad MMK X.16; also PP ad MMK XIII.7–8.

Absent things with intrinsic natures, there can be nothing that is ultimately real, and the ultimate truth is supposed to state the nature of mind-independent reality. There being nothing that is ultimately real, the ultimate truth is without a subject matter. So the notion is incoherent. The teaching of emptiness gets called "ultimate truth" only because, according to Madhyamaka, it represents the final realization on the path to the cessation of suffering. But its semantic status is no different from that of "Milinda came in a chariot." Both are true in the only way that any statement could be true—conventionally.

What then is conventional truth, and how do we go about attaining it? Here is where things begin to get sticky. We have just seen why it could not be ultimately true that everything is connected to everything else. To take emptiness this way is to take the prefix *niḥ-* in *niḥsvabhāva* ("without intrinsic nature") to be an affirming negation or *paryudāsa* ("nonintrinsic natured"). Instead, the prefix must be taken as a nonaffirming, or verbally bound, negation (*prasajyapratiṣedha*), which functions like illocutionary negation. Still, one can see why the first reading is tempting. If nothing can have intrinsic nature, then since there surely are existing things, their natures must be extrinsic, and they exist in thoroughgoing interdependence. But now a new step suggests itself: Since it turns out that nothing can be ultimately real, then these things with extrinsic natures must be merely conventionally real. So is it conventionally true that everything is connected to everything else? Is the Mādhyamika simultaneously denying that there are ultimately real things with intrinsic natures and affirming that all conventionally real things get their nature through thoroughgoing interconnection with all the other conventionally real things?

If so, this would vindicate Candrakīrti, who criticized Bhāvaviveka for demanding that Mādhyamikas use well-formed negative inferences in debates with realist opponents. The criticism is that even if such inferences are understood to have force only at the conventional level, they still require that the Mādhyamika hold a position and defend it with evidence. And this, Candrakīrti seems to think, will inevitably entangle the Mādhyamika in commitment to things with intrinsic nature. Why? The suggestion now is that there can be epistemic instruments such as inference only if there are epistemic objects with intrinsic natures.[11] This, it could be argued, was established by Nāgārjuna in *Vigrahavyāvartanī*. If the Madhyamaka position is that there are no ultimately

11. Inference and perception are accepted by all as epistemic instruments. *Tarka* or *prasaṅga* is not generally considered to be an epistemic instrument. There is, however, some debate among Buddhists concerning (1) whether one who formulates a *prasaṅga* must accept the statement of pervasion that is used to derive the unwanted consequence, as well as (2) whether they have some obligation to provide evidence in its support. Candrakīrti denies both, while Dharmakīrti holds at least (1), and Prajñākaragupta and Dharmottara affirm (2). See Iwata (1993).

real entities of any sort and that the conventional reals have only extrinsic natures, then a Mādhyamika may not consistently employ any epistemic instruments. Only *prasaṅgas* (reductio ad absurdum) may be used.

This would explain much about Candrakīrti's stance. But there is one thing that might not fit into this picture. After subjecting Diṅnāga's epistemology to withering criticism, Candrakīrti endorses the Nyāya account of the epistemic instruments.[12] Now if the difficulty with Bhāvaviveka's stricture were that epistemic instruments require epistemic objects having intrinsic natures and the only kinds of existing things there are (conventional reals) have wholly extrinsic natures, then Candrakīrti is not entitled to affirm any account of the epistemic instruments. So if Candrakīrti really does think that, conventionally, everything is connected to everything else, then he must find something in the Nyāya account of the epistemic instruments that exempts it from the criticism of *svabhāva*-mongering he directs at Diṅnāga's account. In addition, there is some evidence that he does see the Nyāya enterprise as importantly different. Immediately after laying out the four epistemic instruments that he accepts, he adds that it is by means of these methods that worldly goals are attained and that since epistemic instruments and objects are established in mutual dependence, neither one may be seen as having its nature intrinsically.[13] So he seems to think that the Nyāya account of the epistemic instruments can be squared with the fact that nothing has intrinsic nature. Of course, the Naiyāyikas don't think so, but perhaps that is neither here nor there.

Toward the end of chapter 9 of this volume, Tom Tillemans suggests a possible strategy for Mādhyamikas wishing to escape the dismal slough: Take the difference between correct conventional truth and the way that the *āryas* see things as a matter of superimposition (*samāropa*) of intrinsic nature on things that are not in fact that way at all. If what makes correct conventional truth (the things that everyone, including ancient Indian cowherds, knows) nonetheless erroneous (*bhrānta*) is the adventitious superimposition of intrinsic nature,

12. See PP ad MMK I.1, 75 (ed. LVP), where he gives virtually the stock Nyāya definitions of the four epistemic instruments: perception, inference, testimony (which he calls *āgama* but Naiyāyikas call *śabda*), and introduction of new vocabulary through analogy (*upamāna*). It is worth noting that he claims that perception is ordinarily understood to take both the particular (*svalakṣaṇa*) and its universal characteristic (*sāmānyalakṣaṇa*) as objects whenever these are directly manifest through the senses. He thus endorses the Nyāya view that distinct epistemic instruments can ascertain the same object (the doctrine of *pramāṇasamplava*). Diṅnāga holds instead that each epistemic instrument has its own distinct object sphere. Garfield's claim that "Candrakīrti grafts Diṅnāga's *pramāṇas* onto Nāgārjuna's coherentism" (Garfield 2008, 519n14) appears to be a typo. As he makes clear elsewhere, it is the Nyāya account of the *pramāṇas* that Candrakīrti endorses, not Diṅnāga's. On the other hand, it is not at all clear that Nāgārjuna is a coherentist, but that is a dispute for another occasion.

13. PP 75.10–12 (ed. LVP): *tadevaṃ pramāṇacatuṣṭayāl lokasyārthādhigamo vyavasthāpyate // tāni ca parasparāpekṣayā sidhyanti, satsu pramāṇeṣu prameyārthāḥ, satsu prameyeṣv artheṣu pramāṇāni / no tu khalu svābhāvikī pramāṇaprameyayoḥ siddhir iti tasmāt laukikam evāstu yathādṛṣṭam.*

then perhaps there is some hope for reform in the methods whereby one seeks (conventional) truth. Tillemans expresses some reservations about interpreting Candrakīrti this way. (Garfield 2008 appears more sanguine.) This may have to do with the fact that such a strategy seems to go against Candrakīrti's statement that a Mādhyamika does not affirm any real subject of an inference and so cannot formulate a proper inference. But there may be a deeper reason to hesitate. To get at that reason we need to answer this question: Why does Candrakīrti endorse Nyāya epistemology and denounce Diṅnāga's? What is there in the former that he might find more congenial to Madhyamaka insights?

At one level, it would seem there is not that much that separates the two epistemological projects. Both Nyāya and Diṅnāga's school are semantic realist to the core. Both assume there is such a thing as how the world is anyway and that an epistemic instrument will be a procedure that gets things right about mind-independent reality. And the semantic realist, we have seen, should hold that the mind-independent reals that in the final analysis either compose or are the truthmakers are things with intrinsic natures. So what could lead Candrakīrti to think that the Nyāya account is more readily seen as simply superimposing intrinsic natures where they do not belong but as otherwise harmless? Perhaps the answer may have to do with the fact that Nyāya epistemology is less open to reductionist projects than is Yogācāra-Sautrāntika epistemology. This will require some explaining.

Reductionism is a metaphysical/semantic position. To be a reductionist about things of kind *K* is to hold that while the *K*s are not to be found in our final ontology, they are posits of a useful theory (a theory that helps us attain our ends) and so may be said to be conventionally real. Siderits (2003) addresses Buddhist reductionism, and there is no need to repeat any of that here. It is important, however, to recall here that the ontology and semantics of Diṅnāga's school represent the culmination of the reductionist tendency in Abhidharma thought. We must now explain why Nyāya may be thought to be less clearly reductionist. Nyāya does, after all, hold that all macrophysical objects are made of atoms, and this might look like at least the raw materials for a sort of reductionism. But while Nyāya says that where there is a pot, there is a very large number of atoms arranged potwise, it puts both the pot and the atoms in its final ontology. Atoms are, on its scheme, eternal substances, while pots are noneternal substances. Nevertheless, both are substances, real particulars in which inhere universals, quality particulars, actions, and the like. Nyāya accepts co-location of distinct substances: Any point in space in which a pot is located is also the location of some atom. This is very different from what the Buddhist reductionist of a Sautrāntika persuasion might say: that since co-location is impossible, strictly speaking only the atom exists at that point; the pot just consists in that and many other atoms, so that the pot is a mere conceptual fiction, a useful way for us to think about those hugely many atoms arranged potwise. For Nyāya the relation between pot and atoms is not the reductionist relation of *just consisting in;* it is instead the nonreductionist relation of inherence.

To many of us this claim of Nyāya's about the relation between pot and atoms looks rather odd. And certainly the Buddhist reductionist is able to bring out any number of difficulties with it.[14] What might have induced Nyāya to make the claim that both the pot and its constituent atoms are real when it brings in its train so many problems? The suggestion is that this is one manifestation of a deep commitment that underlies the Nyāya project: to develop a philosophical articulation of the common-sense worldview. Most likely no survey has ever asked whether people would say both pot and atoms are real in a univocal sense of "real." However, experience with beginning philosophy students suggests that this is a widely shared pretheoretical intuition. This would suggest that it is a philosophical elaboration of common sense to claim that pot and atoms are co-located and in some sort of real relation.[15] If so, then the Buddhist reductionist would say this is a part of common sense that cannot be accommodated in a single coherent scheme. Hence, the resort to the two truths. Naiyāyikas, by contrast, would insist that it is not the job of the philosopher to revise the ontological commitments of our going theories but merely to put them in philosophically regimented form. Where the Buddhist reductionist is a revisionary metaphysician, Naiyāyikas confine themselves to a more narrowly descriptive project.

What sorts of epistemological views are best suited to these two distinct approaches to ontology? When we look at the two systems, the differences may seem small. Of course, there are disagreements over things such as whether there are epistemic instruments beyond the commonly accepted perception and inference and how many members an inference must have, but these seem like relatively minor disputes. There is, though, one difference that may be of paramount importance here. This concerns whether or not there is "intermingling" (*samplava*) of the epistemic instruments. When Nyāya affirms such intermingling, it is claiming that a given object may be cognized using distinct epistemic instruments. Diṅnāga, of course, famously denies that perception and inference share a common object. To him it seems clear that the fire that is cognized through inference is a conceptual construction and so cannot be the

14. See, for example, Vasubandhu's *Abhidharmakośabhāṣya* ad AK III.100ab (Pradhan 189–90).

15. Perhaps ancient Indian cowherds did not believe that there are atoms. Still, they did know that pots are made from clay and that clay consists of particles of earth plus water. So cowherds at least believed that the particles of earth are co-located with the pot.

sort of efficacious particular that is the cause and hence the object of perception. Put another way, to his ears the Nyāya notion of determinate perception (*savikalpakapratyakṣa*) will sound like an oxymoron. If perception is to function as our direct means of access to the mind-independent reals (something he and the Naiyāyikas agree on), then the object of perception can only be *nirvikalpaka* or devoid of conceptualization, not *savikalpaka* or with conceptualization. Nyāya must affirm that perception is of an object as brought under some concept since it is only as a concept that an object may be cognized through inference. To a Buddhist, though, for whom all conceptualization represents some degree of falsification of the nature of mind-independent reals, this can only mean that the Nyāya epistemic instruments fail to give us cognition of the ultimate reals. Perhaps it is just this feature of Nyāya epistemology that recommended it to Candrakīrti.

Diṅnāga's claim that the two epistemic instruments, direct and indirect cognition (perception and inference), have distinct objects is tailor made for reductionism and its two-tier ontology. It allows us to see how the things affirmed by common sense might not be robustly real despite our beliefs about their having some degree of utility. For he can then say that the object of inferential cognition is conceptually constructed on the basis of input acquired through perception. So while, strictly speaking, that object is not real, its nature is determined by things that, being causally efficacious (insofar as they cause perceptual cognition), must be ultimately real. Hence, the object of inferential cognition (including perceptual judgment) is not wholly fictional; it borrows its nature from things that actually have natures to lend. It is just this feature of Diṅnāga's epistemology that makes it anathema to Candrakīrti. Indeed, in one of the most astute moves in his critique of Diṅnāga's account, Candrakīrti asks what epistemic instrument is used to ascertain that there are just these two objects of veridical cognition (ed. LVP 59). This and his other criticisms may or may not be justified. In any event it should be clear why Candrakīrti must prefer the Nyāya account of the epistemic instruments over Diṅnāga's account: The latter leads directly to commitment to things with intrinsic natures, while the former appears open to immunizing through the superimposition strategy.

We were wondering whether the superimposition strategy might help those sympathetic to Candrakīrti's Madhyamaka avoid the dismal slough. We have just seen why this would require something like Nyāya's account of the means of knowledge and not Diṅnāga's. But will it work even so? No. This is because Nyāya lacks the resources to account for epistemic improvement of the sort we are interested in. Take the case of medical science. For the Naiyāyika it must remain an utter mystery why going to the level of the molecule would yield useful knowledge about the organism. Not so for the Yogācāra-Sautrāntika. They can say that the utility of our beliefs about the organism reductively supervenes on facts about the molecules since the organism *just is* those molecules. This is why if we want to find a cure for fever (a property of the organism) we should move to the level of the molecule. Now, the Naiyāyaika is anything but a pure conventionalist. As a universal fallibilist, the Naiyāyika agrees that we might all be wrong about some matter. But for Nyāya, epistemic improvement must occur through a one-by-one replacement process. And the replacement belief must be located at the same level as that replaced: If the incorrect belief concerned a macrophysical substance, then so must its correcting replacement. There can be nothing here like a wholesale move from one level of description to another, more fine-grained level motivated by the realization that this corrects for errors induced by accommodations to human interests and cognitive limitations. Nyāya epistemology cannot account for the gains in objectivity that come with reductive analysis. Of course, Diṅnāga did not exactly have in mind the move from folk medicine to biochemistry when he formulated his account of the means of knowledge. He would probably be just as surprised at its success as Udayana. Still, his account is of the general type that is required if we are to make sense of our improved epistemic situation, and it is this feature that is behind Candrakīrti's rejection of his account.[16]

The importance of Diṅnāga's innovation has, however, been underappreciated. What he worked out is a way of accounting for our ability to form useful beliefs utilizing an instrument that takes a fiction as its object. We may fail to recognize the significance of this due to the difference in orientation between our epistemology and that of classical Indian philosophy. Since we usually start with the justified-true-belief analysis of knowledge, for us epistemology is generally a project of working out what constitutes justification. For Indian epistemologists, though, it is a matter of determining the reliable causes of cognitive episodes (which are not beliefs understood as dispositions but rather occurrent states). That focus makes quite palpable the question of how we can have cognitions that amount to knowledge concerning objects that are causally inert, either because they are abstract or because they are fictional—or both. (Buddhists would insist that all abstract objects are fictions.) Within an epistemology guided by the justified-true-belief approach, this question typically gets elided, and so the difference between Nyāya's *pramāṇasamplava* and Diṅnāga's *pramāṇavyavasthā* looks to us like a fairly minor matter. Indeed, the Nyāya approach seems the more reasonable. It is only when we begin to wonder just

16. The key assumptions here are that all explanation ultimately rests on causal explanation, and there is no top-down causation. These assumptions are controversial. For a defense, see Siderits (2003, 89–96). However, one point that is particularly important in the present context is that top-down explanations are typically teleofunctionalist explanations, and these we know how to discharge through selectionist accounts.

how the causal link might work when, strictly speaking, there is no object at one end, that we see the flaw in that approach, and we begin to see the point behind Diṅnāga's insistence that perception and inference take objects that are of ontologically distinct kinds. Had Locke taken a similar approach when he tried to work out the relation between primary and secondary qualities, the subsequent history of modern Western philosophy might have been quite different.[17]

Of course, this feature of Diṅnāga's system also leads to the assumption that there are things with intrinsic nature—and that in a way that does not seem open to mitigation through the "mere superimposition" strategy. So what is a Mādhyamika to do? It seems like bad faith to continue to enjoy the fruits of our enhanced knowledge of the world—such as modern medicine, air travel, and microelectronics—while retaining the ontology of the seventh-century CE cowherd. Good faith seems to require acknowledgment of things with intrinsic natures. But maybe not all is lost. To see why not, consider what it is that the Mādhyamika must say in the end concerning the doctrine of the two truths. To say that no entities have intrinsic nature is to say that there are no things about which ultimately true statements could be made. The result is that the very notion of the ultimate truth is undermined. Since there could be no ultimately real things, the idea that there is some one way that things ultimately are turns out to simply make no sense.[18] This in turn gives rise to the question in what sense it could be true that there is no such thing as the ultimate truth. The answer, it seems, is that it is conventionally true. But now notice that if there is only conventional truth, then "true" can mean only what is generally meant in the world by calling a statement true. And it is part of our conventional practice to take truth to be of the nature ascribed to it by the semantic realist. Semantic antirealism must be radically self-effacing, leading in the end to a sort of semantic nondualism that is importantly like what is nowadays called minimalism, or deflationism, about truth.[19] Mountains are once again mountains; rivers once again rivers.

17. For Locke both primary and secondary qualities are powers of an object to produce sensations. They differ only in that, in the former, the sensation typically resembles that in the object that produces it, whereas in the latter it does not. This way of making the distinction opened the door to Berkeley's idealist critique. The alternative would have been to make primary qualities natural kinds, with secondary properties then becoming constructions built up out of primary qualities. Color would then be merely conventionally real, while shape would be ultimately real.

18. This is the point at which Madhyamaka most clearly resembles Carnap. See Finnigan and Tanaka, this volume, chapter 11. Of course, there remains the important difference that Madhyamaka does not employ verificationism in its attempt to show the incoherence of the idea of ultimate truth.

19. Tillemans, in chapter 9, n. 21, also tells us that, according to certain Nyingmapa thinkers, the Madhyamaka distinction between the two truths must itself be overcome. Perhaps this is why. But if so, this may also be consistent with the Madhyamaka stance. Perhaps the *āryas* invoke the distinction between the two truths only as necessary, in dialectical contexts. Perhaps when left to themselves, they think in terms of just a single truth.

If we say there is only conventional truth, we end up saying there is just truth. The statement "There is only conventional truth" represents a moment in a dialectical progression. At the next stage of that progression, we arrive at a place that looks remarkably like where we began. There is a difference, though, and it is that difference that made Candrakīrti think he could safely endorse Nyāya's epistemology. The difference is that we shall no longer think, as we did at the outset of the journey, that true cognitions reflect the mind-independent natures of ultimately real entities. Because we no longer think this, we will no longer be tempted to take it as a test of an adequate epistemology that it show us how our cognitions come to correspond to the intrinsic natures of robustly real things. Nevertheless, we still require an epistemology, something that can explain how true and false cognitions differ in etiology. The Nyāya account of the epistemic instruments promises to do that. So it looks like it has the potential to take us around the dismal slough of pure conventionalism. What Candrakīrti failed to notice is that because it operates entirely within what from a Buddhist perspective can only be thought of as a realm of conceptual constructions, it can never account for the gains in utility that come with reductive analysis. It can account for the piecemeal improvement of "The shell is not yellow but white" but not for the wholesale improvement that comes from treating the white shell as no more than an array of molecules with such-and-such reflectance properties. And this is what in the end we need if we are to account for the improvement in practice that comes from rejecting "The shell is yellow" for "The shell is white." So it looks like Candrakīrti cannot get us out of the dismal slough after all. What looked like a mitigated conventionalism—Nyāya epistemology as the (minimalist) truth about our epistemic practices—turns out to be pure conventionalism in Brāhman robes.

Our dialectical progression is not over when we reach the minimalist stage of rivers being once again rivers. We must reinstate something like the distinction between the two truths as understood by Abhidharma. This is what I think Bhāvaviveka had in mind. And it is just what those who follow Candrakīrti fear will lead straight to the return of things with intrinsic nature, with all that implies. Can we avoid this dire consequence? Siderits (2003) argues that the Mādhyamika must deploy a kind of epistemological contextualism. By epistemological contextualism I mean roughly the view that a procedure counts as an epistemic instrument only relative to a context of inquiry, where contexts of inquiry are determined by factors such as the aims of the inquirer and the methods of inquiry available to the inquirer. So in one context of inquiry the statement "The shell is white" will count quite simply as true, while in another it will stand only as conventionally true, with some other statement concerning the reflectance properties of certain molecules being ultimately true. Relative to the latter context, reflectance properties count as intrinsic natures, and the molecules that have those properties will count as ultimately real. But this is so only relative to this context. And there will be some other epistemic context in which molecules turn out to be only conventionally real and reflectance properties thus count only as extrinsic properties. Now, in order for this to work and not amount to an "anything goes" relativism, these contexts must be seen as falling into a hierarchy, so that each is seen as an improvement on its predecessor. Otherwise, we cannot account for the sort of epistemic improvement we are concerned with. The trick is to not let this lead us to believe there is a final level at which the real *svabhāvas* stand revealed. We can avoid this if we follow Jñānaśrīmitra in taking there to be an unending series of sets of triples: false conventional, true conventional, true ultimate, where the true ultimate of one set is the true conventional of an adjacent set.[20] We might refuse to follow him in this on the grounds that there could not be such an unending series. But to say this is to commit the Platonist's fallacy of inferring the superlative from the comparative, of the best from the better. The Mādhyamika should diagnose this fallacy as a case of hypostatizing what is merely a regulative ideal. That there is a final, ultimate truth is just another bit of *upāya*, something it is useful for us to believe insofar as it makes us strive to resolve our disagreements.

So is everything connected to everything else? Not on this picture. For any given context of inquiry there will be some things with natures that are intrinsic. Nothing we have encountered to date turned out to have a nature that is intrinsic in every context; this is the truth of emptiness.[21] But here emptiness simply serves as a corrective to our seemingly inveterate tendency to take some context of inquiry or other as ultimate. It does not tell us how things really are. It just warns us not to take too seriously the question of how things truly are. Philosophers do take this question seriously. They are, after all, said to be in the wisdom business. And Buddhism encourages us to do philosophy as part of the path to overcoming suffering. Doing philosophy can lead to the sense that one has arrived at the final theory of everything, and this in turn can give one a sense of finally being at home in the world. The danger is that this brings with it a subtle form of the sense of "I" and "mine" that, on the Buddhist analysis, is a root cause of suffering. This can happen even to Mādhyamika philosophers. So it may be lucky that everything is not connected to everything else.

20. For more on Jñānaśrīmitra's contextualism see McCrea and Patil (2006).

21. Note that if there is no "master argument" for emptiness, this is all one can say—that the track record so far suggests that no candidate for the status of intrinsic nature will emerge from the Madhyamaka dialectic unscathed. My thanks to Graham Priest for pointing out the paradox that lurked behind the less cautiously worded original claim: that nothing has a nature that is intrinsic in every context.

Candrakīrti spoke of what is "known to people like cowherds (*gopālas* or *gopas*) and women." I'd like to close by saying a word about the gopīs, women who are cowherds. The gopīs always loved Kṛṣṇa, and they knew that from his early childhood Kṛṣṇa craved butterballs. This is why the gopīs sought ways to increase the butterfat content of the milk their cows produced. They soon learned that, when their cows ate grass from certain fields, their milk was richer. But the gopīs didn't stop there. They wondered why this should be, and their inquiries eventually led them to a detailed knowledge of biochemistry.[22] This helped them better control the butterfat content of their cows' milk. But it also revealed to them the source of the correlation between high butterfat consumption and heart disease, and it enabled them to understand why the human organism might crave the taste of butterfat. This in turn helped them develop methods for producing low-fat butterballs that still satisfy the craving. This made the gopīs happy, for they still love Kṛṣṇa. Their love has survived their knowledge of biochemistry, which showed them that he was wrong when he told Arjuna there is a self. Kṛṣṇa and Arjuna are nothing over and above assemblages of molecules. The gopīs are all bodhisattvas now, and their loving compassion encompasses all sentient beings as loci of suffering. Nonetheless, there is still a special fondness for Kṛṣṇa, and so they are glad that he can enjoy his butterballs without risking the suffering of heart disease. The gopīs now know more than they used to, and there is less overall suffering as a result.

22. On this point my fable may not be quite as far fetched as it seems. What often gets elided in discussions of knowledge is the role that material practices—and the practitioners of those practices—play in epistemic improvement. This erasure helps reinforce the classism that we can see behind Candrakīrti's remark about cowherds. Furthermore, to the extent that sexism is a product of a sexual division of labor, it also reinforces the sexism that is probably behind his mention of women.

11

Carnap's Pragmatism and the Two Truths

Bronwyn Finnigan and Koji Tanaka

Two Truths

In previous chapters, we saw how Mādhyamika philosophers, especially Candrakīrti, have elaborated on the notion of two truths. One puzzling feature of the notion of two truths concerns the notion of *truth*. The Mādhyamika, particularly the Prāsaṅgika, holds that everything is empty of intrinsic nature (*śūnya*). This has been thought to mean that, for the Prāsaṅgika, a conventional truth is an unreflective endorsement of what people already accept (*lokaprasiddha*), as supposed by Kamalaśīla. A consequence of this is that the normative role of truth is flattened, and thus the conventional authority of epistemic practices is undermined. (See the passage from the *Sarvadharmaniḥsvabhāvasiddhi* quoted on pp 153–154.) The problem Kamalaśīla points out is not just that the *truth* of conventional truths is unexplained but also that no sophisticated analysis of anything can be given. Thus, the Prāsaṅgika is trapped in the dismal slough of pure conventionalism.

In chapter 10 we saw epistemological contextualism as a (possible) solution to the dismal slough of pure conventionalism. The cost, if it is a cost, is that there may be a context where we take things as having intrinsic nature even though we must resist the temptation to believe in the real *svabhāvas*.

In this chapter we offer a line of thought that is not thematized by the Madhyamaka thinkers; nevertheless, it is a solution to the charge of the dismal slough that the Prāsaṅgika could offer. We thematize our solution in dialogue with the twentieth-century philosopher Rudolph Carnap, in light of his distinction between internal and external questions. It will emerge that the main issue for understanding the truth of conventional truths depends on understanding the relationship between the semantic issue of differentiating ultimate and conventional truths and practical matters such as action and ethics. A consideration of two truths in the context of Carnap brings this relationship to the surface. This chapter thus serves as a bridge between some of the previous chapters and the later chapters, which deal with practical issues such as action, ethics, and awakening.

Carnap on Internal and External Questions

In order to appreciate how a discussion of Carnap's distinction between internal and external questions can advance matters in the context of Madhyamaka philosophy, it is helpful to have before us the context in which he introduces this distinction. In his influential article "Empiricism, Semantics, and Ontology," Carnap argues that there is a fundamental confusion in the polemic over the question "Do numbers exist?" This confusion consists in an ambiguity between what he calls internal questions and external questions regarding existence. The distinction between these two kinds of questions is based on Carnap's presupposition of linguistic frameworks. Linguistic frameworks are systems of "forms of expression" and rules for their use (Carnap 1956, 213). For instance, the linguistic framework for the system of numbers consists of expressions such as "numerals like 'five'" and sentence forms like "there are five books on the table," as well as variables, quantifiers, and "the customary deductive rules" (p. 208). Moreover, we have a plurality of linguistic frameworks that are all "languages of science" (p. 208). Thus, just as there is a linguistic framework for numbers, Carnap also speaks of separate linguistic frameworks for "things," "propositions," "thing properties," and so on, each of which consists of different forms of expressions and rules for their use. According to Carnap, internal questions concern the existence of certain entities within a given linguistic framework, whereas external questions concern "the existence or reality of the *system of entities as a whole*" (p. 206).

For Carnap "the concept of reality occurring in these internal questions is an empirical, scientific, non-metaphysical concept" (p. 207). To recognize that a table in front of me is real is to succeed in incorporating particular observations into my linguistic framework of things in such a way that it coheres with other things that I recognize as real. In a similar way, to say that the number "three" exists is merely to say that it is part of the linguistic framework for numbers and can be recognized to be so by logical analysis. Fundamentally, "to be real in the scientific sense means to be an element of the system" (p. 207).

Given this, Carnap writes, "nobody who means the question 'Are there numbers?' in the internal sense would either assert or even seriously consider a negative answer" (p. 209). For Carnap, questions regarding numbers are answered analytically without any appeal to empirical matters of fact. Insofar as we speak of numbers, we have accepted the linguistic framework for numbers, including all of the logical implications of this framework. All we need in answering the question "Are there numbers?" is to consider whether we are using this particular linguistic framework. Moreover, in the very posing of the question we are exhibiting our acceptance of this linguistic framework, and, as a result, the answer to the question becomes trivial. Numbers exist insofar as we use the concept to pose the question and, in so doing, exhibit our acceptance of the very linguistic framework of numbers, which is the only mode in which they could be said to exist.

External questions, on the other hand, are considered by many philosophers to be "ontological questions" that must be raised and answered *before* new linguistic frameworks are accepted (p. 214). Thus, for example, the external question "Do numbers exist?" would be a case of asking whether numbers were "really real" in some way beyond our linguistic framework. However, Carnap argues, answers to questions regarding numbers can be found only within a particular linguistic framework. Hence, to ask whether they are real in some way beyond this would essentially be to ask whether the linguistic framework of numbers itself was real.

Carnap thinks that questions framed in this way are problematic and "without cognitive content" (p. 214). For Carnap, it is a linguistic framework that makes a question or statement meaningful. Without presupposing a linguistic framework within which the term "number" is understood and used, we could not be even aware of entities such as numbers, and hence the external question "Do numbers exist," for example, is meaningless.[1]

1. We, in fact, appeal to the thought of Wilfred Sellars in putting Carnap's point in this way. In his "Empiricism and the Philosophy of Mind," Sellars argues that awareness is conceptual. According to Sellars (1956), we cannot be aware of sense data or things without having prior concepts and a raft of background knowledge for the application of such concepts. We could not say "This is a computer," for instance, without having a raft of concepts that determines the ways in which we use the concept "computer." In order to say "This is a computer," we need to have "the knowledge or belief that the circumstances are of a certain kind without it merely being the fact that they are of this kind" (§33) in order to make this statement. Thus, for Sellars, "one couldn't have observational knowledge of any fact unless one knew many other things as well" (§36). Note, however, that there is a question of whether or not Sellars properly understood Carnap. See, for example, Carus (2004).

Carnap's Pragmatism

Presented in this way, Carnap's internal/external distinction relies on two things. First, it relies on the analytic and synthetic (or empirical) distinction. Quine's famous attack on Carnap's internal/external distinction in his "Two Dogmas of Empiricism" is based on this reliance (Quine 1951). Second, Carnap's distinction relies on the idea that "meaning" is given *internally* to a linguistic framework.

As Yablo (1998) has shown, it is not necessary for Carnap's internal/external distinction to rely on the analytic/synthetic distinction. More important, while Carnap's distinction may rely on an internalist semantics, it does capture something quite important about the nature of language. Consider the statement "Rice leads to rice" as presented in a conversation. We might think that the statement is *about* rice. Rice, the grains that we often mix with vinegar to make sushi (not to be confused with the name "rice"), is not a creation of our language. It exists "externally" to the language. The truth of the statement depends on what rice is "really" like.

The role of the "external" entity, that is, rice, does not stop there, however. Insofar as the truth status depends on rice itself, rice constitutes the meaning of the statement. But in order for rice to be so constituted, "rice," the name that we use to talk about rice, must be in accordance with the rule of the language. It is not because rice has certain properties, such as a certain chemical composition, that "rice" can intelligibly be used in the statement "Rice leads to rice," as opposed to "Leads to rice rice," for example, in our language. The name "rice" must respect the *syntax* of the language, which is internal to the language, in order for it to be part of the statement.

In considering the syntax of language, it is not that rice is treated as the basis in terms of which the statement can be said to be true or false. The issue here is not one of providing an ontological basis for the notion of truth. Rather, it has to do with the "internal" structure of language, and the "internal" standpoint looses the issue of *aboutness*. It is not because of what the statement is *about* that the sentence has the form it has but because of the syntax of the language.

But why does "rice" have to belong to a particular syntactic category? That is because, without a syntax that is shared by the language speakers, communication becomes difficult, if not impossible. Communication is a social phenomenon. In order for communication to be possible, it must obey social norms that are practiced in the language community. Thus, the important issue has moved from the question of what rice is "really" like to the question of what the methodology of communication is. Carnap's *principle of tolerance* in his *Die logische Syntax der Sprache* (*The Logical Syntax of Language*) (Carnap 1934) is a result of this line of thought:

> *Principle of Tolerance: It is not our business to set up prohibitions, but to arrive at conventions.* (§17)

Carnap elaborates on the principle thus:

> *In logic, there are no morals.* Everyone is at liberty to build his own logic, i.e., his own form of language, as he wishes. All that is required of him is that, if he wishes to discuss it, he must state his methods clearly and give syntactical rules instead of philosophical arguments. (§ 17)

As Gabriel (2003, 37) puts it nicely, "[t]he principle of tolerance is thus part of Carnap's endeavor to eliminate so-called metaphysical pseudoproblems from the sciences. It formulates a metatheoretical standpoint that amounts to replacing ontology with logical syntax."

Carnap's principle of tolerance, as is stated in the *Syntax*, is concerned with logic and the explication of syntactic rules that regulate scientific theories. What is important for our purpose, however, is Carnap's appeal to *practical* philosophy. For Carnap, it is syntax that allows effective communication in a language community. Thus, a syntax provides us with a *practical* realm for us to explore.

It is important to note that the question of the "admission" of syntax does not depend on "reality" outside of the language. It is not because of what rice is "really" like that "rice" can be put in a communicable statement such as "Rice leads to rice." The issue of the practical realm has not to do with the question of what the statement is *about* but the question of information encoded in the statement.[2] An internal question has to do with an explication of the structure of information that is communicated in a language.

However, we can ask how an effective syntax achieves its end. For Carnap, an external question is a question of this sort. An external question asks a pragmatic question regarding whether we should accept a certain linguistic framework on conventional grounds: for example, "efficiency, fruitfulness and simplicity" (Carnap 1956, 208). The decision to accept a linguistic framework is made on the basis of how efficient the framework would be in order to meet our purposes and interests. Thus, an external question is a question about our *practice*. Moreover, it has to do with the "planning and optimisation of the future of the species" (Carus 2004, 349). The question of aboutness,

2. One of the insights of fictionalists is that one can make a distinction between these two questions. Thanks go to Stephen Yablo, who put the point in this way in conversation.

the ultimate ontological question, in itself, does not contribute to this planning and thus should be discouraged. It is this practical philosophy that frames Carnap's philosophy.[3]

. . . and Two Truths

With this understanding of Carnap's internal and external questions, we are now in a position to reexamine the notion of two truths. In so doing, we will not address questions about how various philosophers in the tradition have understood this notion. Stepping outside of the tradition in this way allows us to shed a different light on the issues that have been debated within the tradition. In this way, we are able to excavate an insight that is contained in the notion of two truths that has not seen much daylight.

As we saw before, for the Prāsaṅgika, emptiness of all things is often thought to entail that a conventional truth is an unreflective endorsement of the world's beliefs. A consequence of this Prāsaṅgika view, as was pointed out by Kamalaśīla and others, is that *truth* in conventional truths has no normative role and that, as a result, conventional epistemic practices lack any authority. This means that the *truth* of conventional truths is unexplained, and so no sophisticated analysis of anything can be given.

We can agree with Kamalaśīla (and others) that this consequence of the Prāsaṅgika view is problematic. However, is it correct to infer this problematic consequence from the emptiness of all things?

The ultimate truth for Mādhyamika philosophers is that all things are empty of intrinsic nature. This means that nothing ultimately "grounds" the truth of any claim in the sense that there is ultimately nothing in terms of which the truth of a claim can be explained. So, ultimately, there are no truthmakers: There is ultimately nothing that makes any claim true. The nonexistence of the ultimate truthmakers is then taken as an indication that nothing is ultimately responsible for truth. This means that there is ultimately nothing about "reality" independent of language that can explain the truth of a claim.

Behind this line of thought is the idea that truth is normative in relation to truthmakers that exist independently of language. Without assuming the existence of truthmakers, we can't account for the truth status that conventional truths are said to enjoy. But truthmakers, on this conception, must do more than that. They are thought to function as the "standard" in terms of which we

3. See also Carnap (1959, §7), where the expression "Lebensgefühl" (attitude toward life) becomes a central theme.

can assess what we say. So if there are no truthmakers, then we cannot measure the "success" of what we say. Hence, so the argument goes, the lack of truthmakers suggests that no improvement of what we say, whether in science, politics, or economy, can be accounted for.

If this is indeed what underlies the inferences that led to our problematic consequence, then what's at issue seems to be the truth-making account of semantic realism. And, with Carnap, we might reject the truth-making account of semantic realism as an analysis of conventional truths and show that the inferences from the emptiness of all things to our problematic conclusion is not warranted.

We may be able to see how Carnap might make such a case. But how could the Prāsaṅgika do so? It is not clear that the Prāsaṅgika have ever made such a case (as far as we know). As we have seen in the previous chapters, the main concern of Prāsaṅgika, as well as Madhyamaka in general, seems to be with ontology. The epistemological contextualism that was offered as a possible solution to the dismal slough of pure conventionalism in chapter 10 also operates at the ontological level (albeit a conventional one).

Nonetheless, in dialogue with Carnap, we seem to be able to bring to the surface an aspect of two truths that has not been thematized within the tradition. For Candrakīrti, a conventional truth has to do with a truth established by our usual empirical activities based on our everyday experience:

> The world understands what is apprehended by the six unimpaired faculties; indeed that is what is real just according to the world.[4]

In other words, understanding based on apprehension by any of the six unimpaired faculties is true by the standard of everyday experience. There is nothing wrong in stating a commonsensical truth that rice leads to rice. "Rice leads to rice" is a report of our everyday experience, and thus it may be simply descriptive of what we experience and accept. But the utterance of that statement is a way of communicating our usual empirical activities. Most of our communication involves more sophistication than saying that rice leads to rice. Nonetheless, communicating that "rice leads to rice," just like reporting a debate we saw on TV last night, may be a meaningful *activity* that may achieve harmony in our community.

The problem arises only when we want to provide an explanation of this truth *based on* a "metaphysical" view of what rice is "really" like. The problem is really the assumption that such an explanation can be given only in a truth-making account of realist semantics. Such semantic realists appeal to truthmakers in terms of which *truth* is explained. Indeed, such an explanation is

4. Mav VI.25. See chapter 9, n. 17 for Skt.; Tib. in chapter 2, n. 18.

often beyond the reach of common sense. Here, however, we are addressing a different question. The communication of our everyday experience is one thing; a metaphysical study of what rice is "really" like is something else. A metaphysical study in itself does not achieve a *practical* end. It is only when the result of our metaphysical study is communicated to wider audiences that such a study becomes meaningful. But, as we all know, knowing what rice is "really" like is often not enough for a successful communication. (That is why it is so difficult to write a book like this.) We need to know a method (or syntax, to use Carnap's terminology) of communication that is shared by the language users.

The important question about the nature of such a method concerns the explication of "grammar" (what people accept and practice) so that the method of communication becomes explicit, and the question of which method is the "right" one is a conventional matter. The answer to such a question is not arrived at by adopting a metaphysical view based on a certain ontology. Rather, it is given on conventional grounds, for example, efficiency, fruitfulness, and simplicity. Some conventions may achieve a better practical end than others. For the community whose members aspire toward buddhahood or (perhaps) bodhisattvahood (*saṃgha*), the question maybe the efficacy of what people say and do toward the achievement of awakening. Thus, the important issue here has to do with the "planning and optimisation of the future" of *saṃgha*.

So a reform of conventional truths is a possibility. Indeed, which conventions best meet our interests and purposes is the "ultimate" question. Hence, we can see the dependent nature of conventional and ultimate truths as was claimed by Nāgārjuna in *Mūlamadhyamakakārikā* XXIV. But the possibility is not due to the status of "reality" existing independently of language or human activities. Both the question and the answer are, ultimately, conventional and practical ones.

Conclusion

In this chapter we have not given a sustained defense of the Prāsaṅgika view against someone like Kamalaśīla. Such a defense has to address not only how semantic considerations give rise to (or perhaps can give rise to) practical considerations but also what the accounts of action, ethics, and awakening are (or can be). Later chapters will deal with these issues. Nonetheless, our consideration of two truths has brought to surface the *practical* dimension that has framed Buddha's teaching and Buddhist traditions. This chapter functions as a bridge between some of the previous chapters, which focus on the semantic aspects of two truths, and the later chapters, which deal with issues that have to do with action, ethics, and awakening.

12

The Merely Conventional Existence of the World

Jan Westerhoff

It is the profession of philosophers to question platitudes others accept without thinking twice.

—David Lewis, *Convention*, 1969

A platitude questioned by many Buddhist thinkers in India and Tibet is the existence of the world. We might be tempted to insert some modifier here, such as "substantial," "self-existent," or "intrinsically existent," for, one might argue, these thinkers did not want to question the existence of the world *tout court* but only that of a substantial, self-existent, or otherwise suitably qualified world. But perhaps these modifiers are not as important as is generally thought, for the understanding of the world questioned is very much the understanding of the world everybody has. It is the understanding that there is a world out there—independent of our minds—and that when we speak and think about this world we mostly get it right.[1] But the Madhyamaka thinkers under discussion here deny that there is a world out there and claim that our opinions about it are to the greatest part fundamentally and dangerously wrong.[2] When we think that there is a world out there, we do not just claim that solipsism

1. Michael Devitt's definition of realism (1997, 41) puts this succinctly by defining it as the claim that "most current common-sense and scientific physical existence statements are objectively and mind-independently (deflationary) true."

2. They thus do not agree with David Lewis that "when a good philosopher challenges a platitude, it usually turns out that the platitude was essentially right" (1969, 1).

is wrong (as a matter of fact, the Mādhyamikas agree with this), but we take the world to consist of objects existing through their own power,[3] objectively, mind-independently, and established by their own nature.[4] Not only do the Madhyamaka thinkers deny the existence of any such objects, but they also do not share the epistemic optimism that characterizes the common-sense view of the world. Tsongkhapa observes that

> even though forms, sounds, and so forth appear to sensory consciousness as if they were established by their own nature they do not even possess this appearing nature conventionally. Therefore the teacher [Candrakīrti] regards them as mistaken even conventionally.[5]

For the Madhyamaka thinkers there is no possibility of regarding our usual picture of the world as even gradually approximating a true theory. Candrakīrti makes it very clear that the ordinary worldly conception of the reality fails entirely in presenting an accurate picture of how the world is.[6]

If our ordinary view of the world is rejected in this way, we will of course ask ourselves what it is to be replaced with. It is to be replaced with the view that the world and the objects in it are merely conventionally existent objects.[7] We are here concerned with the objectual dimension of the term *conventional truth*.[8] On this understanding it does not refer to a certain kind of truth-bearing intentional item (such as a statement), which is true only relative to a certain presupposed set of conventions but not otherwise, but rather picks out a kind of object that is regarded as a conventional truth. Even though it does not appear to us in this way *all* objects belong to this kind; they are all merely conventional truths. What this means is that what we ordinarily regard as a world of mind-independent objects is in fact only a collection of conceptual artifacts. The *Upālipariprcchā* v. 69–70a claims that:

> Variously coloured, beautiful, strung flowers bedeck the golden palace,[9] pleasing the mind. They also have no creator. They have been brought about by the power of conceptual construction (*kalpavaśa*,

3. *rang dbang du grub pa.*

4. *svalakṣaṇasiddhi, rang gi mtshan nyid kyis grub pa.*

5. Tsongkhapa (1985a, 623.13–15): *dbang po'i shes pa la gzugs sgra sogs rang gi mtshan nyid kyis grub par snang la snang ba ltar gyi rang gi mtshan nyid tha snyad du yang med pas na slob dpon 'di tha snyad du yang 'di dag 'khrul bar bzhed pa yin no.*

6. *de kho na nyid kyi skabs su 'jig rten rnam pa thams cad du tshad ma ma yin.* MavBh on Mav VI.31 (Candrakīrti 1970a, 112.20–113.1).

7. *saṃvṛtisat, kun rdzob tu yod pa.*

8. *saṃvṛtisatya, kun rdzob bden pa.*

9. Having just noted the thought-dependence of the hells the text here refers to the celestial realms. The point is to be understood as applying to all realms within cyclic existence, thus including the world we live in.

> *rtog pa'i dbang*). By the power of conceptual construction the world is made through imputation (*rnam brtags*).[10]

All conceptually created objects would completely disappear if the constructions that brought them into being were to stop. This is what Nāgārjuna has in mind when he says in the *Yuktiṣaṣṭikā* 37–38:

> Since the Buddhas said, "The world has ignorance as its condition," therefore, why is it not reasonable to say that the world is a conceptual construction? How could it not be clear that once ignorance is cleared away what will cease had been constructed by misknowledge?[11]

In his commentary on these verses Candrakīrti explains that:

> because it does not exist substantially the world is posited as a mere conceptual construction, in the same manner in which the construction of a man in the dark comes about.
>
> Similarly, having taught that while the wrong view exists, the world exists, in order to teach that if that wrong view does not exist [the world] does not exist [the following is said:] [. . .].[12]
>
> When there is illumination one does not perceive the appearance of the man in the dark. Once one gains knowledge one abides in the non-establishment of a conceptually constructed substantial nature since such mistakes are certainly due to misknowledge.

Viewing the world as a collection of conventionally existent objects or conceptual constructions is an interesting philosophical idea, even though it is quite

10. Skt. fragment and Tib. in Python (1973, 59–60): *citra manorama sajjita puṣpāḥ / svarṇavimāna jalanti manojñāḥ / teṣv api kāraku nāst'iha kaści / te 'pi ca sthāpita kalpavaśena // rtog pa'i dbang gis 'jig rten rnam brtags te . . .*

11. See Lindtner (1982, 117) for the Tibetan: *'jig rten ma rig rkyen can du // gang phyir sangs rgyas rnams gsungs pa // 'di yi phyir na 'jig rten 'di // rnam rtog yin zhes cis mi 'thad // ma rig 'gags par gyur pa na// gang zhig 'gog par 'gyur ba de // mi shes pa las kun brtags par // ji lta bu na gsal mi 'gyur //*. Loizzo (2007, 329–331) reads: *ma rig rkyen gyis 'jig rten zhes / 'di ltar rdzogs pa'i sangs rgyas gsung // de'i phyir 'jig rten 'di dag kyang / rnam par rtog par cis mi 'thad // ma rig 'gags par gyur na ni / gang rnams 'gag par 'gyur ba rnams // de dag mi shes kun brtags par / ci yi phyir na gsal mi 'gyur //*.

12. See Loizzo (2007, 330–331) for the Tibetan: *rang gi ngo bo grub pa med pas mun khung na mi'i tshul du yongs su rtog pa 'byung ba ltar 'jig rten yang rnam par rtog pa tsam du rnam par gzhag go / de ltar phyin ci log yod na 'jig rten yod par ci bstan nas / de ni phyin ci log med na med par bstan pa'i phyir* [. . .] *snang ba byung na mun khung na mi'i tshul du snang ba mi dmigs pa bzhin du rig pa byung na / gang log pa de nges par mi shes pas yongs su brtags pa'i phyir ngo bo nyid du grub pa med par gnas so*. I have adopted the reading *mun khung na mi'i tshul du* instead of *mun khung na me'i tshul du* even though the latter is the *lectio difficilior*. While mistaking an inanimate object (such as a pillar) for a man in the dark is a familiar Indian example of a perceptual illusion, I am not quite sure what could be meant by "imagined [apparitions] arising like flames in the darkness of a cave" (Loizzo 2007, 188).

difficult to spell out what this is supposed to mean in detail. It is relatively straightforward to understand what is meant by saying that a *piece of language* owes its existence to conventions. This is especially true against the background of theories that regard the connection between a term and its referent as a matter of natural necessity, independent of human intention or invention, such as those defended by the Mīmāṃsakas. Defending the conventional nature of language then just amounts to pointing out that the connection between a certain phoneme and a certain object does not stem from the nature of the two (as, for example, the connection between the molecular structure of a substance and its chemical properties) but is purely a result of a group of speakers deciding to associate a certain sound with a certain thing.

But what can be meant by saying that an *object* owes its existence to conventions? In some cases, such as the objects traded on the stock market, this might not be too difficult; indeed, it seems plausible that if the stock market disappeared, so would the objects traded there. Still, how are we supposed to extend this idea to a general ontological theory claiming that *all* objects have a similar, merely conventional or conceptually constructed existence? Surely the teacup in front of me, Mount Everest, and the stars in the Big Dipper are all there without my doing and do not require my participation in some system of conventions for their continued existence? How can we make sense of the idea that they would completely disappear if some system of conventions ceased to exist?

In this chapter we present a framework that allows us to make sense of the view that all objects are mere conventional existents. We will first discuss a contemporary account of the conventional nature of linguistic signs and suggest an expansion in such a way that it accounts not just for conventionally existent *names* but also for conventionally existent *objects*.

In the subsequent discussion we raise three important systematic points. The first is the notion of *truth*. We usually think that the truth of statements is constrained by the world, which is independent of our cognition of it. But if the objects in the world are the product of convention and thereby depend on us, does that not mean that we are left with a merely subjective account of truth, in which thinking that something is a certain way makes it so?

The second point concerns the idea of the *basis of construction.*[13] If we regard some object as a conceptual construction, we will have to specify what it is a construction from. But we then either end up in a regress, if this second thing is constructed from yet another one, or we reach a foundation at some point, coming across something that is not constructed. A regress is often problematic, and the assumption of an ontological foundation is not acceptable for

13. *gdags gzhi.*

a Mādhyamika. So is there a coherent way of maintaining a thoroughgoing constructivism without assuming that the basis of construction exists substantially?

The final notion is that of the *limitations of construction*. If there is no objective world constraining our constructions, can we establish conventions in any way we want? How can we explain the fact that we cannot just construct the states of affairs we desire? The thirsty man in the desert realizes that a glass of water conceptually constructed by him does not quench his thirst.

Names as Conventional

In this section we discuss the game-theoretic account of the conventional nature of linguistic signs first developed in Lewis (1969). In accounting for language as a convention-based link between word and world, Lewis faced the Quinean problem that in order to formulate a linguistic convention one must already have a language in which to formulate it (see Quine 1936). Languages therefore cannot be based on conventions all the way down.

Let us first consider an informal example of how a convention could be established without presupposing the existence of a language. Suppose Peter and Paul are trying to park a truck. Peter is behind the wheel and cannot see behind the truck, while Paul stands behind it but is not driving the truck. They need to cooperate in order to get the truck into the parking lot. For the sake of simplicity assume that there are only two actions Peter can do: go forward and reverse. Paul can do only two things to signal to Peter: stick up his hands, palms facing outward or make a waving motion. We also assume that there are only two situations relevant in this case, namely that there is space behind the truck or that there is not. Our goal is to connect the actions of Peter and Paul with the states of the world in such a way that they can park the truck. For example, the situation that there is space behind the truck could be associated with Paul's waving motion and with Peter's reversing. The situation that there is no space could be associated with Paul sticking up his arms and Peter going forward. But how do we get there if they cannot use language to agree on which signal means which?

The answer is of course to try it out. Peter just associates Paul's holding up his hands with reversing, while Paul connects this with the situation in which there is no space behind the truck. They crash it. At the next attempt, Peter realizes that he did not get it right and associates Paul's other gesture, the waving motion, with reversing. Unfortunately, Paul, having been disconcerted by the preceding lack of success has now switched tactics and connects the waving motion with the lack of space. They crash it again. If this process continues, however, and if there is a sufficiently large supply of fresh vehicles at hand, they will eventually manage to park the thing. They will then have come up with an association of the two states of the world (space or no space), Paul's actions (hands up or waving), and Peter's actions (go forward or reverse), which results in a successful conclusion of the parking endeavor. If they ever want to park a truck again, they will surely use the association again. Perhaps it even happens that other people observe the now very efficient truck parkers and do what they do, too. A system of conventions has been born, but nobody ever had to say that "doing a waving motion means that the driver should reverse." This association was brought about by the successful solution of the coordination problem, not by explicit stipulation.

This extremely rough-and-ready description of Lewis's idea is sufficient to keep the reader in the picture but leaves a lot of questions open. A particularly interesting one is whether there is only one feasible way of associating actions and messages. If there is more than one, how are we going to choose between the different ones? And what happens if different groups adopt different ways of associating them? Readers who are interested in this and also want to see some more details of Lewis's theory are invited to read the first part of the appendix to this chapter, "Lewis's Theory of Conventions." All others can continue with the next section.

Objects as Conventional

In the coordination problems described by Lewis the different participants will eventually settle on some signaling system or other. In such a system a conventional linkage between a state of the world, a message, and an action is established without the need for any prior linguistic agreement. Which de facto linkage is established is immaterial in the same way in which it does not matter whether we refer to a particular color by the word "red" or by the word "rouge"—both speakers of French and English can successfully speak about the color red.

Some readers may have observed that the situations Lewis deals with are described in wholly realist terms. Both participants in the coordination problem are placed in a ready-made world in which some situation (e.g., that there is space behind the truck) either obtains or fails to obtain. It is now interesting to investigate what happens if we drop the realist assumption that the states of the world are something given to the sender, who has only to look in order to know which one obtains, and select a message accordingly. An antirealist would want to assert that these states are in some way dependent on the mind of the sender or constructed by the sender. We can model this added complication in a fairly straightforward manner. Assume the states the sender reports consist of a set of natural numbers picked by the sender. The intuitive idea here is that the numbers corresponds to the sender's basic perceptual input or, to use the Carnapian phrase, to the sender's "elementary experiences." By putting some of them together into a set, the sender creates a complex of these elements to form a specific state of the world.

The game now proceeds as follows. The sender picks a set of numbers and selects a message to send to the receiver. Upon receipt of the message the receiver also picks his own set of numbers. In some cases both players will receive a reward, and in others neither will receive one. A sender strategy therefore correlates sets of natural numbers with messages, while a receiver strategy correlates messages with sets of natural numbers. The strategies to pick (and therefore the correlations to select) are those that are equilibria, that is, strategies that are mutually best replies. Given the strategy of one player, the other would not receive a greater reward by selecting a different strategy.

In a similar way, the sequence of successful interactions will lead to conventional linkages between two sets ("states of the world constructed by an observer") and a message ("a linguistic sign"). What it interesting to note is that in this case the emerging correlations do not only produce a conventional word-world linkage but also create conventionally established states of the world by singling out all those sets of numbers of the many possible ones that are linked to other sets via a message. Both the conventions of the languages the players use to refer to the world, *as well as the elements of the world themselves,* appear to emerge at the same time.

Let us illustrate this idea with a simple model. Assume we have a group of people, each of whom sits in a single room. Their only means of communication is via a telephone line. Each person also has a unique set of Lego blocks in front of them. One starts putting the blocks together into a structure. When he has finished, he calls one of the other participants and utters a phrase. The recipient then builds a Lego structure himself. In most cases nothing happens after that, and they dismantle the structures again. In some cases, however, after the recipient of the phone message has finished building a Lego structure, both he and the person who called him receive a doughnut from the psychologist who runs the experiment. Given that doughnuts rank high on the preference scales of all the participants, they want to maximize the chances of receiving more doughnuts. A good way of doing so is for the sender to use the same phrase when he builds that structure again and for the receiver to build the same structure he built when he first heard the phrase. In this way a collection of Lego structures and their linkages to phrases that function as their names come into existence at the same time. Each depends on the other: The names require the structures (for without them they would be mere phrases transmitted via the phone), but the structures also require the names because only the property of being linked to a name distinguishes an inert assembly of Lego blocks from a structure worth re-creating because doing so might yield further doughnuts.

Someone might object that this picture does not look very promising from an antirealist perspective. Given that the "constructions" the sender and the receiver carry out are selecting specific sets of numbers, the members of the set, that is, the basis on which the construction proceeds, are not constructed as well. People build structures from Lego blocks, but they do not make the blocks. It follows that a construction-independent world exists, and therefore our model fails to capture the antirealist assumption that there is no such thing.

There is a simple way of changing our model in order to accommodate this worry. We set up the system in such a way that natural numbers are no longer used in the constructions; instead, the system uses ordered pairs consisting of the player carrying out the construction and a natural number. Thus, the elements player *a* uses in the constructions are the pairs <*a*,1>, <*a*,2>, <*a*,3>, and so on, and those of player *b* are <*b*,1>, <*b*,2>, <*b*,3>, . . . and so on. This has the consequence that no element used in the constructions can be shared between the players (since every pair is "individualized" by its first member). Furthermore, since each pair depends for its existence on the player using it in constructions (since the set could not exist without all its members existing), it is impossible to conceive of the elements used in the constructions as some kind of "objective background" existing independently from the players involved in the game.

In the context of this example we would therefore assume that the Lego blocks are not accessible to other players. This does not commit us to asserting that they are not material; it could simply be the case that whenever we tried to remove a block from a room, it suddenly vanished, and that if somebody looked into someone else's room, that person could not see the Lego blocks in there. Arguing in this way that the bases of construction only ever have a subjective but no objective existence is one way of replying to the challenge that an appeal to constructions implies realism about the basis of construction.

Another possible reply, suggested by Nelson Goodman's theory of "world making" and its current defenders, claims that construction goes all the way down (see Goodman 1983; Schwartz 2000, 156.) In the same way in which there is no uniform foundation from which all physical making starts (the basis from which the baker starts is what the miller has made, while the miller starts from what the farmer has made), making the world similarly starts from what we find and not from an unmade basis: "[W]orldmaking is always *re*making" (Schwartz 2000, 158). The difficulty with this reply is that the making of worlds could never have been started. While it is clear that the notion of construction that constructivists are interested in, including the notion of world making, is not to be understood as the putting together of distinct physical objects, it does take place in time. Construction is, after all, what humans do, and everything humans do is a temporally stretched-out process. However, in this case the basis of a construction will be temporally prior to the construct, and if this basis is a construct, too, because all making is remaking, there will be another basis prior to it. If matters continue in this way, we have to face the problem that, while constructions may stretch back in time infinitely, human beings do not. Yet there are presumably no constructions without human beings. We will therefore not pursue this reply here any further. We may point out, however, that the Goodmanian problem would not have been a difficulty for the Indian Buddhist thinkers, who generally assumed the existence of beginningless ignorance (*anādyavidyā*) as the basis of cyclic existence. If the ignorance is beginningless, so is the existence of beings who have the property of being ignorant. The difficulty of how the entire convention-based process of cyclic existence could ever have started therefore does not arise.

Readers who would like to see how the modified account of conventional linkages just described can be set out in a table of strategies should look at the second section of the appendix to this chapter, "Conventions: An Anti-realist Formulation." All others may continue directly with a discussion of the philosophical implications of this account.

Representation and Objects Represented

The modified approach lets us formulate an answer to the representation problem frequently discussed in antirealist treatments of semantics. This is the problem that, in the same way in which the realist has to account for the linkage between language and a mind-independent reality, the antirealist will have to be able to tell some story how the link between linguistic items and the mind-dependent entities they refer to comes about. According to the picture sketched here, both relata of the reference relation (the linguistic, as well as the objectual side) are produced as part of the same process, based on the successful interaction between two players of a signaling game. There is no danger that the mind-dependent entities might somehow become detached from the linguistic ones since they are brought about together. This is particularly attractive as we do not have to make use of the correspondence-theoretic notion of linguistic and mind-dependent items sharing the same structure.

The world described in this system is quite minimalist. It consists of different collections of elementary experiences that cannot be shared but are unique to the collections to which they belong. These collections function as the subjects or persons in the system. Information can be exchanged between these subjects (in particular, they can send messages to each other). The subjects can form complexes of elementary experiences and associate the complexes with messages. In order to get the earlier game-theoretic model going, certain cases in which two subjects construct two distinct complexes of elementary experiences result in a payoff for these two subjects. In this way messages that mediated between such complexes can become associated with them by a correlation. An "object" in this system is then just a collection of the different complexes of elementary experiences constructed by the different subjects that have become associated with a single message. The fact that certain constructions can form the basis of a successful interaction by being linked to a single message establishes the division between the internal and the external or, to put it more precisely, between intersubjective objects and the merely subjective. A construction acquires intersubjective status by being able to enter into successful exchanges. If a construction does not achieve this (i.e., if a player associates it with a message but never reaps a payoff), it remains within the realm of the merely subjective. Even though we can draw a line between the subjective and the objective (or intersubjective) world, there is, nevertheless, no objective world in the sense of an objective background which is mind independent and exists equally for all subjects.

The realist might raise the worry that, according to his understanding, there is a very obvious answer to the question of why the correlation of a certain state of the world (such as the presence of a tiger) and a certain action (climbing up a tree) result in a positive utility. There are facts about the culinary habits of tigers, their limited climbing abilities, and the unpleasantness of being eaten alive that explain why matching this state with this action has a positive payoff. But there seems to be no way for the antirealist to explain why two subjects' constructing two distinct complexes of elementary experiences results in a positive utility. It is not as if there were any body of regularities associated with these subjective complexes that could explain the payoff. It rather has to be assumed as a brute fact. We cannot explain why we get the doughnuts. It certainly cannot be because two people in different rooms constructed Lego structures that are in some way similar. Remember that because other people looking into the rooms cannot see the Lego blocks, the psychologist dispensing the doughnuts could not tell when such similar structures have been made.

This, however, has much force as an objection only if the realist alternative is independent of such brute facts. Of course, this is not the case, which leaves the antirealist the possibility of replying with a *tu quoque*. As the existence of such positive utilities keeps the world going in the system just described, the realist's world is maintained by a collection of mind-independent objects that affect our senses in various ways. Why do these objects exist rather than fail to exist? There seems to be very little we can say apart from pointing out that it is a necessary assumption in any realist system that cannot be explained within the system. But this appears to be very much the same as saying that the existence of these mind-independent objects is a brute fact for the realist.

The realist might respond by arguing that the brute facts he is forced to accept explain the truth of his own view while the anti-realist's brute fact explain only the assertability of the anti-realist's view. After all the brute fact of the existence of mind-independent objects explains the truth of realism—the basis of realism is just the assertion of the existence of objects of this kind. But while the brute fact that certain interactions are successful explains why the antirealists are justified in making the claims they make about merely conventionally existent objects, it does not establish the falsity of the realist view (i.e., it does not establish the kind of mind-independent objects the realists presuppose do not exist).

However, it does not seem that we have made significant progress here. While mere assertability surely appears inferior from the realist's perspective, who can offer truth instead, the very existence of this alternative is doubted by the antirealists. He does not agree that there is anything more substantial than assertability to be had. As such, the fact that an account explains its own assertability is really all we can hope for.

Subjective and Conventional Truth

In the system described earlier, messages are a crucial constituent of the world since they link together different agent-relative constructions and thereby create objects. But how do we account for the truth of such messages? We obviously cannot appeal to familiar correspondence-theoretic notions since the correspondence between word and world in terms of some underlying similarity is informative only if the former is not constitutive of the latter.

In the present framework we have to distinguish two senses of truth. A message sent by a participant in a coordination problem is *subjectively true* if and only if the strategy "if you have constructed such-and-such a complex, send the message" is part of a selected correlation and if the participant has indeed constructed such-and-such a complex. In other words the subjective truth of a message consists of its linkage to a certain construction and the fact that it is sent after such a construction has been carried out.

This conception of truth is called "subjective" because the difference between appearance and reality does not arise. Since the constructions the agents carry out are not understood as representing, it could not be the case that a construction has been carried out but whatever it represents is not present. Drawing a distinction between something that appears elliptical to us and its actually being elliptical presupposes drawing a distinction between the apparently elliptical thing, the internal construction, which is the representation, and the thing it represents, which may be elliptical as well (or perhaps circular and seen from an oblique angle). However, given that our system conceives of the intersubjective objects in terms of constructions linked to a single message, this distinction is not available to us.

Nevertheless, this does not mean that we cannot distinguish at all between the merely apparent and the conventionally real. We can regard a message as *illusory* if it is subjectively true but does not lead to a successful interaction for both players.[14] In this case a participant in a coordination problem will carry out a certain construction which is linked to a message by a correlation. Another participant receives the message, carries out the construction linked to it but no payoff ensues. How could this happen? Imagine a situation in which I tell you that a disc is elliptical, while it only *looks* elliptical to me. You regard the disc as elliptical too, even though it is in fact round. We will therefore have difficulties coordinating our behavior involving the disc. In the anti-realist setup we are discussing here we could of course not say that our coordination fails because the disc is *really* elliptical, since there is no disc apart from various complexes linked to a common message. All we can say is that there are some cases where there is no successful interaction, even though everything looks as if there should be: Message and construct have been correlated by past successes, and both participants carry out the right constructions. In these irregular cases we speak of illusory messages, since they present the appearance that a successful interaction should ensue, even though it does not do so in fact. Most cases will not be like this, however, and a subjectively true message will be matched by a construction which generates a successful interaction. In these cases we call the message *conventionally true.*

It is therefore apparent that, even though the system just described does not ground truth in a mind-independent reality in which some facts obtain or

14. This is different from a subjectively false message, which is a message a player sends without having constructed the correlated state of affairs.

fail to obtain, this does not mean that all we can talk about is "truth for me," that is, how things appear to me. The notion of the conventionally true remains. As Tsongkhapa points out:

> When it is said that compounded phenomena are "merely conventional" from their perspective, the word "mere" excludes truth, but in no way excludes conventional truth. (*Ocean* 482)

Conventional truth spelled out in terms of the successful interaction in resolving coordination problems remains available us. It is this truth that allows us to move around in the world, change it, and be changed by it without requiring anything as substantial as an intrinsically existent world out there. Tsongkhapa's disciple Khädrupjay (*mkhas grub rje*), in his *sTong thun chen mo,* notes that emptiness:

> is not contradictory to the position that things function, but indeed that it is by virtue of the fact that things function that they are without intrinsic nature, and it is by virtue of the fact that they lack intrinsic nature that it is possible for things to function. (Cabezón 1992, 97)

We can agree with Candrakīrti, who, citing a passage from the *Ratnakūṭa,* argues that we should admit what the world admits to exist and deny the existence of what the world does not admit to exist.[15] There is no difficulty in accepting conventionally existent objects as conventionally existent objects. Difficulties arise only if we take these objects to be something that they are not.

It is apparent that language plays a central role in the creation of the world. Indeed, if we conceive as existent those things that are the subject of conventionally true statements, we can agree with the somewhat provocative claim made some time ago by Terry Winograd that "nothing exists except through language" (Winograd and Flores 1986, 11, 68). In his criticism of the then prevalent approach to artificial intelligence he notes that "the basic function of language is not the transmission of information or the description of an independent universe" but "the creation of a consensual domain of behaviour between linguistically interacting systems" (Winograd 1986, 50). In the model discussed earlier language fulfils the double purpose of transmitting information about the world between speakers while at the same time creating the contents of the world the speakers speak about.

15. PP ad MMK XVIII.8. See the initial section of chapter 9 for a translation and discussion of this sūtra passage.

The Basis of Construction

One of the primitive notions used in the account of conventionally existent objects presented are the individuals' elementary experiences, out of which such objects are constructed. They constitute the basis of construction (*gdags gzhi*). These experiences are existentially dependent on the mind in which they occur (they could not exist unperceived), but they do not depend on any other awareness in turn (the awareness of some object that turns out to be a construction from some elementary experiences depends on these, yet the elementary experiences do not in turn depend on other elementary experiences). They differ crucially from sense data to the extent that they do not have the properties that perceptually appear to us. In other words, from the fact that there is something that appears elliptical to us, we cannot infer that there is something that is elliptical, namely the sense datum of which we are aware.[16] In this way we can allow for the existence of indeterminate elementary experiences (e.g., when experiencing something as striped without experiencing it as having a specific number of stripes). If there really were the striped sense datum, we would have to assume that it had one number of stripes rather than another.

We also assume that elementary experiences—like the Gestalt-theoretically inspired Carnapian notion—are not broken up into experiential atoms, such as the color of a rose, its shape, its scent, and so on, which are later put together to form the experience of the rose. Rather, the identification of parts within the elementary experiences is already the result of a constructive process based on the similarity between these experiences.

There is no reason to question the reality of the elementary experiences. What is questioned, however, is the objective reality of the object created from the elementary experiences by means of convention (*btags chos*). This objective reality is not a property of the object but something mistakenly superimposed on it (*'khrul snang*). Śāntideva puts this well in saying that:

> How something is seen, heard, or cognized is not what is contested here, but it is refuted here that the projection is real, as that is the cause of suffering.[17]

We obviously do not make any assumptions about where the elementary experiences come from, and in particular we remain neutral on whether they are

16. Chisholm (1977) suggests that we should rather claim that in this case we are being appeared to elliptically.

17. BCA IX.26: *yathā dṛṣṭaṃ śrutaṃ jñātaṃ naiveha pratiṣidhyate / satyataḥ kalpanā tv atra duḥkhahetur nivāryate.*

caused by anything external. Nevertheless, our system does not collapse into solipsism since the existence of other minds is a necessary precondition for the game-theoretic account of convention that associates constructions with a message or label (*rtags*). We have to assume that there are minds that cannot share information directly but only by exchanging messages.

We have seen that the basis of construction constituted by the elementary experiences does not constitute an objective background from which the world is constructed because the existence of particular sets of such experiences depends on the particular minds in which they occur and is therefore not objective. Since a person's elementary experiences are accessible only to that person, there is no perspective from which the set of all elementary experiences could be surveyed.

A further argument for not regarding the basis of construction as a collection of substances that would provide a foundation for a chain of existential dependence relations can be based on the notion of successful interaction. If we assume that the successful interaction between different players (that is, the fact that they receive a positive payoff) is a necessary condition for the continued existence of these very players, and given that the constructed objects constitute an essential means of facilitating such successful interaction, then it follows that if there were no constructions, there would be no successful interaction and hence no players. Since the elementary experiences depend existentially on the player who depends existentially on the constructed objects, the elementary experiences themselves existentially depend on the constructed objects. We can therefore argue that the constructed objects and the elementary experiences mutually depend one each other.

Still, one might object that even though the elementary experiences do not constitute an objective background, the account described earlier still presupposes the existence of whatever determines whether or not some set of interactions yields a successful outcome. To this extent there is something "which is there anyway," something that exists independent of human interests and concerns. Such a realist assumption is, however, incompatible with Candrakīrti's claim that it is utterly incoherent to envisage the existence of something beyond our conceptual abilities, whether this is an inexpressible noumenon or a mysterious something that makes sure that some of our interactions are successful while others are not.

But perhaps we do not have to think that whatever it is that determines the payoff of an interaction is to be understood in realist terms. In a game of chess there is something that determines whether a certain position will lead to checkmate in four moves—this something is the rules of chess. Are the rules there anyway? No, even though they are an essential part of chess they should not be understood as something out there that determines whether a particular move will lead to victory or defeat. The rules are an integral part of the game and were created together with it. Similarly, we should not think that there is something out there that rewards or punishes our interactions and that this something would be there no matter what. It is rather that, based on interactions, we construct the merely conventionally existing objects that inhabit the world, and together with them we establish which kinds of actions on these objects will be successful and which will not be.

Is this approach circular? It certainly is, given that the very thing on which we base the coming about of conventional objects—the fact that certain interactions are successful—is in turn a result of the properties of these objects. But is it also *viciously* circular? It is not so clear that this is the case, as long as we do not use the same objects as being produced by and producing the success of interactions. And it is not apparent we have to do this. Remember the example of Peter and Paul parking the truck. Whether their interactions were successful was determined by objects in the world: by the truck and its size and by the space behind the truck and its size. However, there is no necessity to assume that it is their successful interaction that creates the truck and the space behind it. Assuming that these are merely conventionally existing objects, they could have been created by other, earlier, successful interactions. By reasoning in this way we can push back the explanation of the success of some interaction onto the objects and then push back the explanation of the existence of the objects to some earlier successful interaction.

Needless to say, we are never going to reach solid ground in this way. It is difficult to see how there could be successful interaction without objects which explain the success, and we do not want to assume the existence of objects which did not come about based on successful interactions in the way described. As indicated above this would be no problem for a Buddhist thinker who avails himself of the notion of beginningless ignorance. Furthermore it would be inadvisable for a Madhyamaka to make a demand for "something stolid underneath" as Goodman put it, as a first starting-point of the constructive process. Such a foundation would invariably be something "which is there anyway," existing independent of human interests and concerns, since it exists by definition prior to any constructive process.

Limitations of Construction

Even though the model described earlier does not provide us with a mind-independent world of objects but only with a collection of conventional constructions, it is evident that this does not entail unlimited license. We cannot just define objects into existence or make sentences true by fiat. That the truth of our sentences and the contents of our minds are not constrained by a world of objectively existent phenomena does not mean that they are not constrained at all. The constraints come from the fact that objects that make up the world are not just our constructions but constructions that are linked up with the constructions of others according to certain strategies. Moreover, a certain message is not made true by the fact that we carry out a construction correlated with such a message in our own mind, but this construction has to serve in addition as the basis of a successful interaction.

We live in a world of merely conventionally existent objects, but their conventional nature does not entail that we can unilaterally opt out or modify the world independently of the necessities the existence of the object entails. The reason that we cannot fill an empty cup with water just by imagining it to be filled is the same as the reason we cannot win a game of chess by picking up our opponent's king from the board and declaring ourselves the winner. As long as we play chess we can win or lose only by sticking to the rules. Similarly, while we are bound by the conventions of cyclic existence we can change the world around us only by paying heed to the necessities the objects in the world bring about: To fill the cup we have to go to the tap. This is the reason why Candrakīrti claims that the Mādhyamika does not argue with the world.[18] The Mādhyamikas do not deny that there is a tree outside of my window, that 7 + 5 = 12, or that water is H_2O. What they deny is the claim that there is anything to these true statements that we do not make ourselves, based on an ongoing and intricate process of conceptual construction. Their existence as merely conventionally existent objects is the only existence objects could have. Candrakīrti, in the *Madhyamakāvatārabhāṣya*, observes that:

> Even though [objects] do not exist [in a substantial sense], because they are taken for granted throughout the context of everyday experience, they are said to exist strictly with reference to worldly convention.[19]

That we cannot just construe things *ad libitum* is also stressed by Tsongkhapa in a passage from the *dBu ma dgongs pa rab gsal*, which comments on Candrakīrti's *Madhyamakāvatāra* VI.7:

> [F]rom the point of view of the way in which the pot and so forth are established by conceptual constructions (*rtog pa*), that may be

18. PP ad MMK XVIII.8.

19. Candrakīrti (1970a, 179): *yod pa ma yin yang 'jig rten kho na la grags par gyur pas yod do zhes 'jig rten gyi ngo bo kho nar brjod pa yin te.*

> considered to be sufficient [to regard it] as similar to a snake imputed onto a rope. However, the pair pot etc. and snake-rope are completely different when it comes to existence and non-existence, the power or the lack of power to perform a function and so forth.
>
> This is because the two are dissimilar in all respects with regard to the necessity or lack of necessity of their being ascertained conventionally (*tha snyad nges par bya*), with regard to whether their conventional designation (*tha snyad byed pa*) is undermined (*gnod pa* = *bādhā*) or not, and so on. It is reasonable to assume that each thing established by a conceptual construction has its ability to perform a function. According to those who have commented on the words and the meanings [of the Madhyamaka texts], Buddhapālita, Śāntideva, and the Master [Candrakīrti], for all three this is the extraordinary way in which they commented on [the works of] the two, the noble Father and Son [Nāgārjuna and Āryadeva]. That [which has just been explained] is the most subtle point of the highest Madhyamaka.[20]

If everything is a conceptual construction, it is of course correct to say that all constructions are on a par to the extent to which they are all constructions. But this does not mean that they are all on a par in all respects. Why is it that the construction of a pot from certain elementary experiences is okay but the construction of a snake from a rope is not? The reason is that a real thing, like a pot in front of us, and an unreal one, like a snake that is only a misapprehended rope, differ in a variety of ways *from within the framework of worldly conventions.* For starters, only one of the two exists since there is no snake in front of us. Second, the conceptually constructed pot can do what it claims to do, namely, hold conceptually constructed water. However, the conceptually constructed snake cannot kill an equally constructed mouse or do any of the other things usually associated with snakes. Finally, given that we aim for smooth interactions with people around us, we will be pushed in all sorts of ways to conceptualize a particular collection of elementary experiences as a pot, whereas the same is not true of a snake/rope. It is more advantageous if we do not construe

20. Tsongkhapa (1973, 139–140): *bum pa la sogs pa rnams rtog pas bzhag lugs kyi cha de tsam zhig / thag pa la sbrul du btags pa dang 'dra ba yin kyang / bum sogs rnams dang thag pa'i sbrul gnyis yod med dang bya ba byed par nus mi nus sogs ni gtan mi 'dra ste / de gnyis kyi tha snyad nges par bya dgos mi dgos dang / tha snyad byed pa la gnod pa yod med sogs rnam pa thams cad du mi mtshungs pa'i phyir ro // rtog pas bzhag pa de la rang rang gi bya byed 'thad pa ni / tshig dang don gyi 'grel mdzad rnams kyi nang nas / sangs rgyas bskyangs dang zhi ba lha dang slob dpon 'di gsum gyis 'phags pa yab sras gnyis kyi 'grel lugs thun mong ma yin pa'o // dbu ma'i lta ba mthar thug pa'i dka' sa yang 'di nyid do //*. Cf. ACIP ed. 76b–77a.

the rope as a snake and abstain, for example, from issuing unfounded snake warnings.

We therefore realize that it is the world itself that makes some of our constructions more successful and others unsuccessful. It is not a world that is to be construed in realist terms, however. That something can fulfill its functional role is a fact about its relation to other objects, as well as about its relation to the mind, which is, according to the Madhyamaka understanding, the constructor of all causal relations. However, given that the other objects, as well as the relations, are all conceptually constructed, too, we can never can come up with a notion of successful construction that is backed up by a world "that is there anyway" and would satisfy the realist's craving. That there is no such world does not mean, however, that in the world there is we can make up things any way we want to.

Conclusion

The reader will have noticed by now that in comparison to many of the other chapters in this book the present discussion was somewhat more removed from the Madhyamaka texts. So what have we been doing? The methodological background of this chapter can be clarified to some extent by comparing different approaches to ancient philosophical texts with different ways of studying ancient mechanics. If we were to investigate the automata described in the writings of ancient authors such as Hero of Alexandria or Al-Jazari, or the yantrāni mentioned in *Vātsyāyana's Kāmasūtra* we could do this in two different ways. On the one hand, we could produce a faithful account of how these devices are described in the original texts and in those of other ancient authors. On the other hand, we could adopt a systematic approach, asking ourselves how these automata were supposed to work, and whether they would in fact work in this way. If we were to realize that there are some problems in the ancient accounts, we could even suggest a way of improving the device in a way which would not go beyond the resources of ancient technology.

A philosophical argument can be understood as an automaton too, not as a physical but a conceptual automaton which has the purpose of producing a certain conclusion from certain premises. Conceptual automata can be studied either in a descriptive or in a systematic fashion as well: we can try to give a faithful account of what the argument says, and we can ask whether the argument works. If there is some aspect of the argument which is problematic, or if there is something which the ancient authors say it can do, but do not describe in great detail we can attempt to fill in this blank by coming up with an argument of our own which might repair the problem.

It is evident that the study of Madhyamaka presented in this chapter is primarily systematic, with a focus on a very specific issue (namely the status of conventional truths understood as conventionally existent objects). The aim is not to come up with a rational reconstruction of an argument in a particular passage or text (building a working model of an ancient device), but to address a problem which we do not find discussed in great detail in Madhyamaka texts (building a new piece of machinery to enhance an ancient device).

The problem is of course the question of what is meant in detail by the claim that all objects are conceptual constructions, and that the world as a whole is the product of conceptual imputation. Such a claim raises questions about what drives the constructive process, the materials from which the constructs are constructed, and what (if any) limitations are imposed on the constructive process, and whence they come. The preceding discussion presents a framework which at least provides partial answers to these questions. Even though no Madhyamaka source talks about game-theoretic semantics the above construal is something which the Madhyamaka writers might have found congenial, had it been presented to them. At the very least it does not appear to be in contradictions with any of the claims about conventionally existent object which we do find in their writings.

APPENDIX

Lewis's Theory of Conventions

Lewis develops his theory by considering the case of a simple signaling game. In this game there are two players, a sender (Paul) and a receiver (Peter). In the simplest case the sender observes which of two states of the world—▲ (no space behind the truck) or ▼ (space behind the truck)—obtains. He has a choice of two signals, △ (hands up) or ▽ (wave), which he can convey to the receiver. Having received the message, the receiver can chose between two actions, ⮝ (go forward) and ⮟ (reverse). If the receiver chooses ⮝ in case ▲ obtains and ⮟ in case ▲ obtains, both players receive a payoff (they manage to park the truck); otherwise the payoff for both players is zero (they dent it).

There are four possible pure strategies for each player:

S-Strategy	Sender	R-Strategy	Receiver
S1	if ▲ send △, if ▼ send ▽	**R1**	if △ do ▲, if ▽ do ▼
S2	if ▲ send ▽, if ▼ send △	**R2**	if △ do ▼, if ▽ do ▲
S3	always send △	**R3**	always do ▲
S4	always send ▽	**R4**	always do ▼

This kind of game is played repeatedly, and the roles of receiver and sender may be switched. Each player therefore has to choose one sender and one receiver strategy. This makes sixteen strategies altogether, which can be arranged in a table as follows:

	▲	▼	△	▽
S1	△	▽	▲	▼
S2	▽	△	▼	▲
S3	△	▽	▼	▲
S4	▽	△	▲	▼
S5	△	▽	▲	▲
S6	▽	△	▲	▲
S7	△	▽	▼	▼
S8	▽	△	▼	▼
S9	△	△	▲	▼
S10	△	△	▼	▲
S11	△	△	▲	▲
S12	△	△	▼	▼
S13	▽	▽	▲	▼
S14	▽	▽	▼	▲
S15	▽	▽	▲	▲
S16	▽	▽	▼	▼

Both strategies **S1** and **S2** are equilibria (i.e., strategies in which it would not be beneficial for the player to switch to another strategy, given the way the other player is going to act). Lewis refers to equilibria in games like the above as a *signaling system* (Lewis 1986, 132–133). Note however, that they are not the only ones. Another equilibrium is **S11**,[21] in which the sender always sends △ and the

21. Zollman (2005, 72) refers to these as "babbling equilibria."

receiver always does ▲. In this way they receive a payoff in half the cases, assuming that ▲ and ▼ are equally likely. Neither could do better by a unilateral choice of an alternative strategy.

The task is now to come up with a criterion that allows us to select one among the various equilibria. It is evident that **S11** is not a very attractive option since it does not lead consistently to the maximum payoff for either player. But even if we restrict ourselves to the equilibria that do so (**S1** and **S2** in our example), we still have a choice. Lewis introduces the notion of *salience* in order to resolve the tie in this and similar cases. A salient equilibrium is one "that stands out from the rest by its uniqueness in some conspicuous respect" (Lewis 1986, 35). The underlying idea is that some features of a pair of strategies are sufficiently striking to both players to cause them to adopt this pair independently of each other. In our example we can plausibly argue that **S1** is the salient equilibrium, as the symbols ▲ and △ are considerably more similar to △ and ▲ than they are to ▽ and ▼.

Nevertheless, it does not appear to be very attractive to rely on the notion of salience in the general case. States of the world and the messages they are connected with might not be in any way alike, and there may be no other property that singles out one particular assignment as conspicuous. An alternative approach has been described in Skyrms (1996, 88–94), based on the definition of an *evolutionary stable strategy* in Maynard Smith (1982). Let N, $M_1 \ldots M_n$ be alternative strategies and p(X,Y) the payoff of X played against Y. N is an evolutionary stable strategy if either

$$p(N, N) > p(M_i, N)$$

or

$$p(N, N) = p(M_i, N) \text{ and } p(N, M_i) > p(M_i, M_i)$$

The intuitive idea behind these conditions is that either natives (N) playing among themselves do better than mutants (M_i) playing against natives, or, if both do equally well, the natives do better playing against the mutants than the mutants do. Given certain boundary conditions, a population playing an evolutionary stable strategy cannot be invaded by a group of mutants playing an alternative. It is possible to demonstrate that the concepts of an evolutionary stable strategy and of a signaling system (i.e., an equilibrium in a signaling game) are equivalent (Skyrms 1996, 96). Not only are all signaling systems evolutionary stable, but they are also the only evolutionary stable ones: They cannot be invaded by a population of nonsignalers and will invade any other population (Zollman 2005, 73).

We still face the problem of how to distinguish between equilibria like **S1** and **S2**, though. Skyrms proposes to settle this by means of evolutionary dynamics. If we imagine a population such that exactly half plays **S1** and half plays **S2**, each member will get an average payoff of 0.5, assuming that there is an equal probability of meeting a player of either, and given that there is a payoff of 1 if one meets a player of the same strategy, and a payoff of 0 if one meets one of the alternative. As soon as the ratio of **S1** to **S2** is not one-half, however, players of the majority strategy have an advantage. Since they meet players of their own strategy more often than not, their average payoff is more than 0.5, so that they will eventually take over the population. The same will happen even in the case of an equal distribution of members playing **S1** and **S2** if there is random noise in the system. Assuming that this does not affect interactions following both strategies equally, the average payoff of the less affected strategy will increase, thereby conferring an evolutionary advantage on it. It is therefore a de facto certainty that a population playing two alternative signaling systems will eventually converge on one.

This, however, does not mean that the same will happen if we consider a population such that some members play each of the strategies **S1** to **S16**. This is due to the existence of *polymorphic traps*. A polymorphic trap is an evolutionary stable situation in which one portion of the population plays one strategy while another plays a different one.[22] It may be the case that a large proportion of the population ends up playing one strategy, while others pursue various alternatives. In this case we would end up with a variety of coexisting signaling systems without being able to resolve the tie between different equilibria. Skyrms tested this by means of a computer simulation of the preceding example. It turned out that in this case there were no polymorphic traps and that the population always converged on **S1** or **S2** with about equal probability (Skyrms 1996, 92). If this result generalizes, we will have found a way of dealing with the tie between different equivalent signaling systems in terms of evolutionary dynamics. Which system is selected in the end does not depend on the conspicuousness of any strategy but is purely a matter of chance.

Skyrms's model is built on the somewhat unrealistic assumption that any two members of a population have the same chance of interacting. Zollman (2005) has developed a spatial version in which members of the population are represented by squares on a grid; their interaction is limited to their eight directly adjacent neighbors. If one runs a similar simulation on this model, it turns out that even though almost all populations evolved to a state in which there are only signaling systems, they do not generally converge on one such

22. For an example of polymorphic traps in a simple bargaining game see Skyrms (1996, 11–16).

system, as in Skyrms's model. Rather, different areas of the spatially arranged population will adopt different strategies, and such arrangements will be stable (as opposed to Skyrms's precarious 50/50 split) (Zollman 2005, 73–74). In fact, this result should be regarded as an advantage for the model. After all, populations of human speakers inhabiting separate geographical regions have developed distinct signaling systems (i.e., languages), which generally prove to be stable (i.e., it is usually not the case that when these groups interact, one of the two languages quickly replaces the other).

Conventions: An Antirealist Formulation

Let us denote constructions from some pairs of numbers selected by a player *a* (that is, a state of the world constructed by *a*) by sa_1, sa_2, . . . Consider a game in which each player can construct two states and can send one of two messages, M_i or M_j. There are four possible pure strategies for each player:

S-Strategy	**Sender *a***	**R-Strategy**	**Receiver *b***
S1	if sa_1, M_i, if sa_2, M_j	**R1**	if M_i, sb_1, if M_j, sb_2
S2	if sa_1, M_j, if sa_2, M_i	**R2**	if M_i, sb_2, if M_j, sb_1
S3	always send M_i	**R3**	always construct sb_1
S4	always send M_j	**R4**	always construct sb_2

Since the roles can be switched, each player has to choose one sender and one receiver strategy; again there are sixteen such compound strategies:

	sx_1	sx_2	M_i	M_j
S1	M_i	M_j	sx_1	sx_2
S2	M_j	M_i	sx_2	sx_1
. . .	. . .	. . .	. . .	. . .
S16	M_i	M_i	sx_2	sx_2

It is immediately evident that there need not be any structural similarity between the constructed states of the worlds linked by a message like sa_1 and sb_1, as there is in the case of the objectively existent constituents of the worlds ▲ and ▲. All that is required is that what the sender has in mind when he says "M" and what arises in the mind of the receiver when he hears "M" can form the basis of a successful interaction (i.e. achieve a positive utility for both players). It is no problem if it happens that what looks red to me looks green to someone else as long as we both attach the same linguistic sign to the respective mental state.

13

Two Truths: Two Models

Graham Priest

The claim that there are two truths is a central philosophical plank of Mahāyāna Buddhism. Roughly, the conventional truth (Skt. *saṃvṛtisatya*, Chin. *sudi* 俗諦) is the way that things normally appear to us; the ultimate truth (Skt. *paramārthasatya*, Chin. *zhendi* 真諦) is the way that things appear to an awakened being. However, a precise understanding of what, exactly, these are and of the relationship between them is a thorny issue, especially in Madhyamaka and the Buddhist schools influenced by it.

It is this Madhyamaka tradition on which we focus here. Two ways in which one may think about the two truths and the relationship between them will be given—two models of the two truths. To focus on what is philosophically important and to avoid scholarly questions of who said what and what they meant by it, no claims will be made about any particular philosopher holding either of the views described. The models are to be thought of as something like ideal types, to which various actual accounts approximate. Not to be tendentious, let us call these two models simply "Model A" and "Model B."

One further preliminary matter: The Sanskrit word *satya* is ambiguous, at least when translated into English. It can mean "reality," what there is, and it can mean "truth," what we say about it.[1] This is an

1. See the discussion in chapter 1.

important distinction. So when *satya* is used in the context at hand, which of these does it mean? The answer, unfortunately, is both—sometimes at the same time. Arguably, this is sometimes the source of confusion in discussions of the matter. However, that is another topic. It seems to us that the most important issue in these debates is best thought of as reality, and we will use that word—though truth proper will make an appearance at the end.[2]

Setting up the Problem

Let us approach the models by looking at the background of the problem they address. The distinction between conventional and ultimate reality is central to Mahāyāna, but the distinction is implicit in earlier Buddhist discussions in the Abhidharma tradition[3]—in particular, in connection with the self. It would appear that a person has a self, something that identifies that person and persists through change. But on analysis, a person turns out to be a collection of parts (the aggregates) that come together, change and interact, and finally fall apart. How things appear to be is conventional reality; how they actually are under analysis is ultimate reality. Mahāyāna takes up this distinction, develops it, and applies it to all things.

The distinction is developed in a relatively straightforward fashion in Yogācāra Buddhism—or at least in one standard way of interpreting it—the other main school of Indian Mahāyāna. In Yogācāra, ultimate reality is the way that things actually are. Conventional reality is a mere appearance, an illusion that deceives. Thus, to use a standard example, ultimate reality is like a coil of rope; conventional reality is like the snake that a mistaken observer takes the coil to be.

Although there are echoes of this view in Madhyamaka,[4] matters there cannot be that simple. This is so for two reasons. The first is this. All Mahāyāna Buddhists agree that everything is empty. What this means in Madhyamaka is that all things are empty of intrinsic nature (Skt. *svabhāva*). Roughly, everything exists and is what it is only in relation to other things. How, exactly, to understand this thought is itself a tough question. However, we do not need to go into this. The important point for now is that in Madhyamaka, the *all* is to be taken very seriously. Everything is empty, including ultimate reality. This is the core doctrine of the emptiness of emptiness. Ultimate reality also exists and is

2. For a discussion of truth proper, see chapter 8. The word "truth" is used in the the title of this chapter because the usage is so standard.

3. See the discussions in chapters 8 and 10.

4. See the discussion in chapters 2 and 4.

what it is only in relation to other things—and in particular to conventional reality. Hence, in the end, its ontological status is no different from that of conventional reality. The appearance/reality model is not, therefore, appropriate. Indeed, an important Madhyamaka critique of Yogācāra is exactly that it reifies ultimate reality into something having intrinsic nature: You can't have a misleading appearance of something unless there is a something, but you can have the something without the misleading appearance.

The second reason that the Yogācāra model will not do—which is really a corollary of the first—is that, for all that the two realities are two, they are, in some sense, one. Ultimate reality is not something *over and above* conventional reality. The two are coordinate. To use another well-worn analogy, they are like the two sides of one coin. The idea has profound and apparently shocking soteriological consequences. Conventional reality is the realm of samsara, suffering; ultimate reality is the realm of nirvana, awakening. But the two are one. As Nāgārjuna puts it in the *Mūlamadhyamakakārikā* (XXV.19),[5] there is not the slightest difference between samsara and nirvana.

So now we have a problem. Metaphors about coins aside, how are we to understand this puzzling relationship between the two realities? How can they be both two and one? Modern developments in paraconsistent logic would allow us to understand these inconsistent claims quite literally.[6] If c and u are conventional and ultimate reality, then we can have both $c = u$ and $c \neq u$. But such a simple-minded understanding is not appropriate. If c is literally identical with u, then anything true of c is true of u, and vice versa. But then it cannot be the case that $c = u$: There are many things true of conventional reality that are not true of ultimate reality—for example, that the former cloaks the latter; the latter does not cloak itself. And conventional reality is a conceptual construction in a way that ultimate reality is not, so we must seek more subtle understandings. Such are indeed to be found in Madhyamaka and the schools it influenced. One can find, in fact, two rather different basic ways of understanding the situation. This brings us to our two models.

Model A

The first of these is historically the older model. Arguably, it is to be found in Candrakīrti, though, of course, interpretations of Candrakīrti vary, and, as already said, we take no stand in this chapter on whether this is the correct

5. See, for example, Garfield (1995).
6. For a brief and not too technical survey of paraconsistent logic, see Priest (1998).

interpretation. At any rate, in the *Madhyamakāvatāra* (VI.23),[7] Candrakīrti—one of the first Madhyamaka thinkers to clearly articulate the theory of two realities—tells us that every object has a dual nature. There is only one object, but it has two "aspects." There is, then, literally only one reality. The claim that the realities are one is to be understood in this way, as a direct denial of the dualism of the Yogācāra position. The sum total of reality is not of two kinds: All there is is the totality of all interdependent (co-arising) phenomena.

So how are we to understand the claim that the realities are two? As in the Abhidharma tradition, these are two ways of looking at the same reality: a misleading way and a more accurate way. It may be viewed in the more commonsense way, the way that we are accustomed to viewing it, as a realm of intrinsically existent entities. This is the conventional way and a misleading way of grasping reality—literally, since it is the grasping of things in this way that causes suffering. But it can also be looked at in an enlightened way as emptiness. (Though it is not possible to say what this is like since anything that can be described can be described only by using the categories of language, which help constitute the conventional.) It is not so much that conventional reality is an illusion. It is the way that we conceptualize it that is illusory.

Seen in this way, then, the difference between the two realities is one of perspective: The "distinct" realities are formed by different modes of apprehending one and the same thing. In this sense, it is subjective. One can hear it as ontological if one wishes: Reality has the properties of being such that it may be perceived in such and such ways. But these features are *dispositional*—the dispositions being to be apprehended in such and such ways. (In the same fashion, in Western philosophy, one may think of secondary properties as dispositions of objects to be perceived in certain ways.) The difference between the two realities is still, therefore, essentially subjectivity related.

Model B

Let us now turn to the second model. Historically, this arises later than Model A and spins off certain aspects of Yogācāra thought. In Yogācāra, conventional reality is a certain kind of manifestation of the most profound part of consciousness, the storehouse consciousness (Skt. *ālayavijñāna*). Specifically, karmic "seeds" are stored in the *ālaya*, and the *ālaya*, thus tainted, manifests itself in phenomenal consciousness (conventional reality). In Yogācāra, the *ālaya* is always the mind of some particular individual. In later thought this

7. See chapter 1, note 16, and the translation in Huntington and Wangchen (1989).

transforms into or assimilates the notion of the womb of Buddhahood (Skt. *tathāgatagarba*), the part of a person that is already enlightened, which in turn metamorphoses into something like the universal Mind, or buddha nature (Tib. *sems nyid*, Chin. *xinxing* 心性)—in some ways, like Hegel's *Geist*. In the process, it looses most of its mindlike qualities—the *ālaya* had few enough of these anyway. But the Yogācāra thought that it is the ground of the phenomenal world that is retained, as is the idea that this world is its manifestation. Buddha nature can therefore be taken to be ultimate reality, and conventional reality its manifestation.

This picture is reinforced when Buddhism moves into China and encounters the native philosophical traditions there. The most important of these for the present purposes is Daoism (or perhaps more accurately, a certain form of neo-Daoism that was then influential). According to this, there is a principle that underlies the phenomenal world, the Dao. In some sense, it is the cause of all we see in that world. The relationship between the Dao and the "myriad things" is not at all that between appearance and reality, however; the myriad things are the manifestations of the Dao, roughly in the same way that your actions are the manifestation of your personality. One cannot have a manifestation without the something of which it is a manifestation. Conversely, the form of being of the Dao is precisely in its activity (which is a nonactivity in the sense that it just happens—like normal breathing), so one cannot have the Dao without its manifestations. Because the Dao is not a thing but the cause of all things, one can say nothing about it. It is not a *this* or a *that*. It was therefore common for Daoists to describe it as nonbeing (Chin. *wu* 無), contrasted with the beings (Chin. *you* 有) of the phenomenal world.

When Buddhism entered China, it was natural for people to identify the Dao with emptiness, that is, ultimate reality. Both were, in some sense, the realm of nonbeing, and both were ineffable. Coordinately, the phenomenal world of the myriad things was conventional reality. So things came to be seen in the following way:

$$\frac{\text{Dao}}{\text{manifestations}} = \frac{\text{nonbeing/emptiness}}{\text{beings}} = \frac{\text{ultimate reality}}{\text{conventional reality}}$$

Of course, the identification of the Dao with Buddhist emptiness is distinctly misleading in many ways. However, by the time that Buddhism was sufficiently well understood in China for this to be appreciated, the analogy was too entrenched not to have a powerful effect on Chinese Buddhism. In particular, it provided a way of understanding the relationship between the two realities that resonated with the developments in *tathāgatagarbha* theory that we just have described: Conventional reality is a manifestation of ultimate reality.

This picture is to be found, arguably, in Fazang's *Treatise on the Golden Lion*.[8] (Again, we will not enter here into the question of whether this is the correct interpretation of Fazang.) Fazang uses the metaphor a golden statue of a lion to illustrate. Describing the ultimate/conventional distinction in terminology more familiar to Chinese thought, as between principle (Chin. *li* 理) and phenomena (Chin. *shi* 事), he likens *li* to the gold out of which the lion is made and *shi* to the lion. So we have the following analogy:

$$\frac{\text{gold}}{\text{lion}} = \frac{\text{ultimate reality } (li)}{\text{conventional reality } (shi)}$$

Again, on this model, there is only one reality: There is only one thing—the golden lion. The gold and the lion are nonetheless distinct. (The gold could be melted down and refashioned into the statue of the Buddha. The lion would then cease to exist, but the gold would not.) The relation between them is one of interpenetration (Chin. *ji* 即), as Fazang sometimes puts it. One cannot have the lion without the something of which it is made, the gold; conversely, the gold must manifest itself in some form or other, in this case, that of the lion. So neither has intrinsic existence.

Note, however, that the gold and the lion are not two different perspectives of the same thing. The relationship between a statue and its matter is an objective one. One simply could not *have* the one without the other. You can, of course, focus on one, and you can focus on the other, but they will always both be present since the one is the manifestation of the other.

Chinese Buddhists had not, of course, forgotten the mind, and it is related to the distinction between conventional and ultimate reality, but its relationship to the two realities is very different from that in Model A. As we have seen, the mind, or buddha nature, is ultimate reality itself. Mind is not something that provides different perspectives on the one reality. It is one aspect of that reality. Indeed, in some sense, it is all of it: Take away the gold, and there would be nothing left of the lion.

Awakening

We now have the two models before us. The distinction, in crude terms, is that in Model A, the difference between the two realities is one of a difference of perspective, while in Model B, it is a difference between manifestation and that of which it is the manifestation.

8. See, for example, Chan (1963, 409–414).

With the two models in place, the obvious thing to do next is to ask how each of them relates to other aspects of Buddhist thought—perhaps in order to determine which is preferable, perhaps to see how the models might profitably be combined. This is clearly far too big a task to take on here. However, let us look briefly at the relationship between the two models and the notion of awakening—surely one of the most important notions of Buddhist thought. Even this is a complex question, though; all we can hope to do here is initiate a discussion.

Model A allows a very simple and natural understanding of what it is to awaken. This is obtained by a perspective shift (obtained by the appropriate conceptual [textual] and perceptual [meditative] practices.) The unenlightened person has only the conventional perspective of reality. At awakening, this shifts. With regard to how it shifts, there is room for dispute, but perhaps the most common view is that, at enlightenment, both perspectives become available at once, as does, consequently, the misleading nature of the conventional-only perspective.

This account of awakening does not jibe easily with Model B, just because all talk of subjective perspective has disappeared in that model (though, of course, it can be tacked on to it). The model of enlightenment that fits best with model B is in terms of action. Since awakening is always and already present in the form of buddha nature, enlightenment is not *being* anything different; it is *doing* something different—or perhaps, more precisely, doing things in a different way. Just as in Daoism, the sage acts by spontaneously manifesting the Dao, so in Buddhism, the awakened person's acts spontaneously manifest Buddha nature. (A particular example of this is Dōgen's doctrine that awakening is not something that happens as a result of meditative activity; this activity *is* awakening.[9]) The account does not jibe well with Model A, precisely because action is not part of that story at all (though, of course, it can be tacked on to it).

It is worth noting that there is a part of the story that is common to all accounts of awakening. All agree that awakening involves the disappearance of intentional thought and the dualism between subject and object involved in this. However, this disappearance plays out in different ways in the two accounts of awakening. In the first, the distinction between subject and object is absent in the ultimate perspective. (And even if the conventional perspective, in which there is such a dualism, is still available, its illusory nature is simultaneously perceived.) In the second, spontaneous action is action not mediated by the conceptual thought which generates dualities: It is conception-free.[10]

9. See Kasulis (1981, ch. 6).

10. For a discussion of action in the context of enlightenment, see Finnigan (200+).

A final note: Both Model A and Model B need to talk about ultimate reality (buddha nature, etc.), both in explaining what awakening is and in other ways. This itself poses an apparent problem. As all agree, whatever it is, ultimate reality is indescribable. So how, without contradiction, can one say anything taken to be true about it? One can't. This is a feature of Mahāyāna Buddhism, and one has to learn to live with it. So paraconsistency will get in on the act, at least at this point.[11] This feature is shared by any theory—such as Advaita Vedānta, Kantianism, and Heideggerianism—that claims that there is something ineffable and then goes on to talk about it (for example, by explaining why it is ineffable).[12] Mahāyāna gives a very distinctive account of why the ultimate is ineffable, however; roughly, it is because language (concepts) effectively constructs the *conventional.* The ultimate truth—the truth about ultimate reality—is therefore contradictory, and this is so on both of the models described.[13]

Conclusion

In this chapter two models of the relationship between conventional and ultimate reality have been sketched. Buddhist scholars may be discomforted by the fact that no attention has been paid to the detailed exegesis and analysis of particular texts—though, of course, the discussion of matters is informed by an understanding of many texts. Naturally, the concrete interpretation of texts is essential to serious Buddhist scholarship. But interpretation is always interpretation *from* somewhere. Here, we have taken a step back from texts themselves to provide a point of perspective from which to see them. It is, we hope, a fruitful one.

11. There are Mādhyamika thinkers who were, arguably, skeptics and who thus maintained nothing at all. (See chapter 6.) For reasons that it would be out of place to discuss here, this is, arguably, a very implausible interpretation of both Nāgārjuna and Candrakīrti. It is not even clear that such skepticism is coherent. See Priest (2002, ch. 3) for a discussion of the closely related Pyrrhonian skepticism.

12. See Priest (2005).

13. See Deguchi, Garfield, and Priest (2008).

14

Ethics for Mādhyamikas

Bronwyn Finnigan and Koji Tanaka

Our primary concern in this book is to ascertain the sense in which conventional truth is a truth for Mādhyamikas and to investigate its philosophical implications. The earlier chapters address epistemological issues. This is the primary philosophical context in which debates on the nature of conventional truth are conducted in the historical Indo-Tibetan context, and that historical context frames our contemporary inquiry. We have also discussed the metaphysical and semantic aspects of conventional truth. As our joint inquiry has proceeded, however, issues concerning the *practical* implications of this notion have increasingly come to the fore. This reflects, in part, a collective recognition that epistemology, metaphysics, and semantics are intimately bound to the practical, ethical, and soteriological project of Buddhism. In the last chapter, we investigated some of these implications for the possibilities of awakening. In this chapter we shall focus our investigation on implications for ethics. How might we think of ethics for Mādhyamikas?

All Mādhyamika philosophers avow and endorse the bodhisattva precepts and the Mahāyāna account of the virtues. However, no prominent Mādhyamika philosophers articulate systematic ethical theories aimed at justifying the status of these precepts or virtues. Mādhyamikas do not address the question of whether they are justified in holding these precepts or virtues given their epistemological and semantic commitments.

In the first half of this chapter we investigate whether it is possible for Mādhyamikas to justify the bodhisattva precepts consistently with adherence to the doctrine of two truths. We appeal to arguments provided in earlier chapters to suggest ways Mādhyamikas might be able to justify the status of the bodhisattva precepts as conventions.

In the second half of this chapter we argue that whether or not Mādhyamikas have the resources to justify the bodhisattva precepts systematically in ethical theory, a Madhyamaka ethic is concerned more with the instantiation of bodhisattva precepts and virtues in practice. The absence of ethical theorization does not constitute an abandonment of ethics. Rather, it reflects implicit recognition of the limitations of justification and suggests an expansion of the scope of ethics. We conclude by arguing that the very possibility of fulfilling bodhisattva precepts in conduct depends upon an intimate and mutual relationship between value and epistemology that, in turn, requires taking conventional truth seriously.

I

Indian Mādhyamika philosophers saw themselves as engaged in a soteriological project with ethical dimensions. In particular, they accepted distinctions between good and bad conduct. The Mādhyamika thinker most famous for his explicitly ethical concern is Śāntideva. In his *Bodhicaryāvatāra* (BCA), Śāntideva explicitly and repeatedly disavows certain actions as wrong (BCA II.63), cruel (I.33), and evil (II.28) and prescribes certain other behaviors as good (I.31), meritorious (IV.9), and skillful (IV.18) with respect to certain ethical codes (V.42) or precepts (III.23). Nāgārjuna endorses the Mahāyāna bodhisattva path and specifies that it involves practicing the virtues of generosity, ethics, patience, effort, concentration, wisdom, and compassion (*Ratnāvalī* v. 435–439), many of which presuppose evaluative distinctions between kinds of conduct. According to Tsongkhapa, all Mādhyamikas agree on the structure of the path (see *Compassion* 129).

A crucial aspect of the bodhisattva path is propriety (*śīla*). According to Candrakīrti's *Madhyamakāvatāra* II.1ab, as a bodhisattva progresses along the bodhisattva path, she achieves a state where she "possesses the quality of perfect morality, and therefore has extirpated the stain of immorality even in her dreams."[1] Tsongkhapa explicates this verse as claiming that as one progresses along the bodhisattva path, one reaches a stage where one no longer possesses

1. *de tshul phun tshogs yon tan dag ldan phyir/rmi lam du yang 'chal khrims dri ma spangs//* (ed. LVP, p. 32).

the afflictions that give rise to lapses from propriety or to the performance of vicious actions (see *Compassion* 192).

Maintaining propriety is not simply a matter of not transgressing these codes or precepts, however. It is not simply a matter of refraining from actions such as killing, stealing, sexual misconduct, lying, divisive talk, harsh speech, and senseless chatter. It also involves having forsaken the motivations that give rise to immoral conduct (*Compassion* 193). This entire discussion is conducted against the background assumptions that ethical precepts, in fact, distinguish good and bad conduct and that progression along the path involves eliminating those elements that obstruct one from fulfilling these precepts in practice, not merely in waking life but also in one's dreams (see *Compassion* 193).

Despite such clear examples of ethical commitment, at no point do Candrakīrti, Śāntideva, or Tsongkhapa explain why they are warranted in holding these precepts or virtues given their epistemological and semantic commitments to the notion of two truths.[2] Do they have enough resources to justify the bodhisattva precepts in a way that is consistent with adherence to the doctrine of two truths?

2

In chapters 1, 2, 4, 11, and 12 we addressed the challenge posed by the Mādhyamikas' assertions that conventional truth is illusory, wholly erroneous, and rooted in ignorance. If we were to take these claims at face value, there would end up being only one truth for the Mādhyamikas: that is, ultimate truth, the view that nothing has intrinsic nature. If Mādhyamikas held the ultimate truth as the only truth, then certain strategies would be unavailable for justifying ethical precepts. For instance, they would not be able to appeal to actual properties or states of affairs in the world to function as truthmakers. From the standpoint of the ultimate truth, there are no actual properties or states of affairs in the world that could function in this way.

Even if ethical precepts cannot ultimately be justified, might they be justified conventionally or as conventions? In answering this question, we must be careful to avoid the "dismal view" described in chapter 9—the view that to be conventionally true is simply to be held as true by somebody somewhere. This flattens out the possibility for distinction between true and false. It also flattens out the distinction between good and bad conduct. If a precept counts as

2. Of course, all three do provide justifications of the precepts in various contexts, but none of these address the thorny problem with which we are concerned here: How are those justifications consistent with Prāsaṅgika Madhyamaka metaphysical and epistemological commitments?

morally sound just in case somebody somewhere adopts it, then *any* practice could turn out to be virtuous. In such a case, there would be no moral distinction between different practices and types of actions (they are *all* good), and the bodhisattva path would have no point.

We fall into the dismal slough if we respond to the worry that ethical precepts are not ultimately virtuous by *simply* claiming that they are conventionally virtuous. To avoid this we need some way of distinguishing between conventionally acceptable conduct and conventionally unacceptable conduct. One way a Mādhyamika might justify such a distinction is to deploy a kind of *ethical* contextualism on the model of the epistemic contextualism introduced in chapter 10 and suggested by the moral fictionalism discussed in chapter 9. That is, ethical precepts might be justified as conventions appropriate to some context. But then, we must ask, what would be the relevant context? For Mādhyamikas, it would be the soteriological project of the bodhisattva path, as it is with respect to this context that ethical precepts are taken by Mādhyamika thinkers. Thus, one might say, while there are no real, ultimately existing properties that can *ultimately* justify the bodhisattva precepts, these precepts are nonetheless *conventionally* justified in the context of the bodhisattva path. Nonetheless, we must still ask why *certain* precepts are conventionally acceptable and others are not. Why does "giving" count as an ethical precept or virtue on the bodhisattva path, whereas "stealing" and "killing" and "sexual misconduct" do not?

Mādhyamikas could take, as Siderits (2003) has argued, the relations between the action and the ends that obtain as a consequence of following a precept to be criteria for justification. That is, we take "giving" as a justified precept and generosity as a virtue because adopting this precept and cultivating this virtue is generally a skillful means (*upāya*) of eliminating suffering.[3] The goal of eliminated suffering (*nirodha*) is, on this view, an intrinsically valuable state of affairs. A bodhisattva precept, thus, is justified because that end generally obtains as a consequence of acting in accordance with the precept. A particular action is justified because it constitutes following the relevant precept and, thereby, producing the anticipated consequence.

If Mādhyamikas took this approach, however, it might seem that they would need to invoke some real effects resulting from behavior, such as a tangible reduction in suffering. But this cannot be to invoke real properties with intrinsic natures. Hence, not only must precepts be conventionally established for a Mādhyamika, but so too must the reduction of suffering, the

3. Williams (1998), Velez de Cea (2004), Clayton (2006), and Goodman (2008) also defend versions of this position. Velez de Cea and Clayton particularly emphasize the utility of virtues.

general means-end relation between actions and their consequences, the status of this relation as a general criterion for justification, and the actual instantiation of this relation in terms of particular actions generating particular outcomes.

There is no doubt that prominent Mādhyamika philosophers hold that suffering is a bad state of affairs, that certain actions result in its reduction, and that those that undertake these actions are worthy and good (see *Bodhicaryāvatāra* I–IX). It might be possible to demonstrate that these claims can all be conventionally established by appealing to the arguments presented in chapter 12. One implication of the ethical contextualist approach to justification, however, is that Mādhyamikas no longer have the resources to persuade non-Buddhists to opt into the context of the bodhisattva path even if they happen to believe that the reduction of suffering is a valuable state of affairs (and, hence, are apt to be persuaded). Once the relations of behavior to effects, as well as the effects themselves, are conventionally established *within* the bodhisattva path, they have no justificatory status outside this context in order to persuade someone outside to opt into this context.[4]

Of course, this is not to say that the causal relations and behavioral patterns tracked by Mādhyamikas are unavailable to non-Buddhists; there is no reason to think that practitioners and non-Buddhists alike would not share some common conventional contexts. Nor is it to say that a non-Buddhist cannot value certain precepts or relations that are also valued by Mādhyamikas. A non-Buddhist can independently value the elimination of suffering and believe that certain types of conduct generally achieve this end. The point is that, if we opt for ethical contextualism, the reasons Mādhyamika thinkers can provide for the value of the precepts on the bodhisattva path will not have justificatory status outside of this context. That is, there is a crucial distinction between (a) establishing criteria for justifying precepts that are identifiable independently of context and, as such, provide universal motivation and suasive force, and (b) precepts being conventionally acceptable within a context. Ethical contextualism might establish the latter, but it cannot establish the former. Moreover, any attempt to establish the former by widening the context to include non-Buddhists threatens a return to the dismal slough that ethical contextualism was introduced to avoid. This distinction becomes salient when we consider Patsab's account of Prāsaṅgika Madhyamaka, discussed in chapter 6.

4. There may of course be many possible explanations for why agents opt into the bodhisattva path (some of which will relate to the agent's upbringing and temperament). The point, here, is merely that the reasons Mādhyamika thinkers can provide for opting onto the path will not have any justificatory status outside of the context.

3

According to Patsab, Nāgārjuna demonstrates that no epistemic instruments (*pramāṇa*) can justify any claims without begging the question or generating an infinite regress. Patsab takes this to mean that Prāsaṅgika Mādhyamikas cannot engage in any constructive theorizing or attempt to establish a particular view at all. According to Patsab, Prāsaṅgikas must limit themselves to *reductio*, merely pointing out the inconsistencies in their opponents' assumptions.

If Patsab is right, it follows that Prāsaṅgika Mādhyamikas cannot justify any ethical precept. But if they cannot even adopt precepts as *conventionally* acceptable, then it is impossible to endorse Mahāyāna ethics and be a *consistent* Prāsaṅgika. Patsab might accept that ethical precepts can be somehow justified within or in terms of a context such as the bodhisattva path, but even this is unclear. Prima facie, Patsab's position simply commits him to the idea that a Prāsaṅgika cannot *himself* offer positive argumentation to justify the conventions to which he adheres.

Patsab's Prāsaṅgika Madhyamaka seems more radical than this, however. It is not only that a Prāsaṅgika "cannot . . . argue that her decision is right and should have any *binding force* on others" (chapter 6, p. 111) but also that a Prāsaṅgika cannot "hold that what appears to her as true has any *normative force*, even conventionally" (chapter 6, p. 111). That is, on the analysis defended in chapter 6, ethical precepts justified in the context of the bodhisattva path have neither suasive force for non-Buddhists nor any *normative force* for Buddhists *on* the bodhisattva path. For Patsab, a Prāsaṅgika is committed to a complete "suspension of normativity" (chapter 6, p. 111). This is not to abandon all ethical precepts, however. Rather, precepts function as "pragmatic guidelines on how to go on living one's life" (chapter 6, p. 104).

What is the distinction between pragmatic guidelines for living, which do not have normative force, and precepts with normative force? Normativity is grounded in justification, which in turn depends upon argumentation. Patsab denies the possibility of argumentation to justify ethical precepts on the bodhisattva path. On his view, ethical precepts are neither justifiable *by* a Prāsaṅgika in theory nor justifiable *by the agent* in ordinary practical reasoning. The *activity of justifying ethical precepts* is not a practice on the bodhisattva path.

This discussion shifts our focus from a concern with the justification of ethical precepts toward the role (or lack thereof) of such precepts in motivating the activity of agents engaged in the "actual practice of Buddhism" (chapter 4, p. 60). Mādhyamikas might agree that it is not necessary for an agent self-consciously to represent ethical precepts in reasoning prior to and in order to act in ways those precepts enjoin. They might agree with Śāntideva that the virtuous actions of a bodhisattva, for instance, "come effortlessly" (I.35) and without recourse to deliberation. Mādhyamikas could also agree that to follow a precept or instantiate a virtue in conduct is not to be compelled or motivated by the relevant precept itself as a motivation. Depending on what kind of Mādhyamika they are, they might disagree about whether ethical precepts can be justified conventionally in the context of the bodhisattva path, and, hence, they might also disagree about whether ethical precepts need to be justified for a novice practitioner on the path to be motivated to attempt to follow them.[5]

The crucial point for a Madhyamaka approach to ethics, however, is that whether or not it is possible for a Mādhyamika to justify the bodhisattva precepts, neither the fact that these ethical precepts are justified nor the act of justifying them will be *sufficient* for a practitioner to fulfill these precepts in conduct. Instead, a connection is required between the precepts that agents accept, on the one hand, and their behavioral dispositions, motivations, and phenomenology, on the other.

Madhyamaka ethics is distinctive in its explicit focus on the fulfillment of ethical precepts in conduct rather than their justification. Indeed, the fact that there is little systematic ethical theorizing in Madhyamaka suggests an implicit recognition of the limitations of justification in ethics. This is compatible with the general skepticism toward constructive theorizing held by some Mādhyamikas, as discussed in chapters 6 and 7. Moreover, in focusing on practice rather than justification, Mādhyamikas might be thought to expand the domain of ethics to incorporate a concern with the role of an agent's attitudes, dispositions, motivations, and phenomenology for the very possibility of ethical practice and the perfection of virtue.[6]

If Madhyamaka ethics is concerned with practice rather than justification, one might wonder whether there remains any substantive relationship between ethics and the doctrine of the two truths. What bearing can the notions of ultimate and conventional truth have on ethics if there is no place for systematic justification of bodhisattva precepts? The answer to this question becomes apparent when we realize that following the Mahāyāna precepts requires the conventional existence of objects and that interaction with these conventionally existent objects is informed by the agent's attitudes, dispositions, and motivations. In what remains, we shall modify an example introduced in the beginning of this book to offer a

5. For instance, it is arguable whether Svātantrika Mādhyamikas may be able to consistently accommodate the possibility of providing justifications for ethical precepts and, hence, have grounds for defending the view of justification functioning as a possible motivational capacity.

6. For a detailed discussion of the role of phenomenology in attaining bodhisattvahood in the context of the Bodhicaryāvatāra, see Garfield (forthcoming).

preliminary sketch of some of these complex aspects of practice with an aim to highlight the intimate relation that holds between ethics and epistemology.

4

Recall the mirage example introduced in chapter 2. Bill sees a mirage as water and responds by warning his companions. Alice sees a mirage as a mirage and responds by reassuring Bill. Charlie sees nothing because he is wearing polarized glasses and wonders what the others are talking about. Now, consider the same trio of agents, but this time in a more classical, ethical scenario; each agent is walking down a street where a child is begging for money. Each of these agents accepts the bodhisattva precepts. In particular, they all accept the precept of "giving" and have made a vow to exercise generosity.

Charlie does not see the child and walks directly past. He does not see the child and ignore her; he literally does not *see* her. Perhaps the child is blocked from view; perhaps the sights and colors on the opposite side of the street distract him; or, perhaps his attention is elsewhere, and the details of the street scene are forced to the periphery of his awareness. In any case, Charlie does not *experience* or register the child as being there.

The begging child *does* stand out to Alice and to Bill as an object calling for response. This distinction is not simply a matter of value-neutral perceptual skills and gets to the meaning and importance of *upāya*. We might say in such a case that Alice and Bill, unlike Charlie, observe the passing scene in a way animated by *actively held* values. Alice and Bill not only *adopt* generosity as a precept but also actively *seek* ways to embody this virtue; they are *alert* to situations that may call for generosity in order that they might *respond* to them generously. One who actively holds a value is not only committed to acting on it but is also perceptually sensitive to aspects of situations that are relevant to this value and may call for its expression. Charlie, Alice, and Bill equally judge that generosity is a valuable aspect of the bodhisattva path. However, Charlie does not *actively* value generosity in this sense, as he is not actively looking for possibilities or opportunities to express this virtue. As a consequence, he does not register the existence of the begging child. *Upāya* is central, not incidental, to the exercise of a bodhisattva's virtues, and *upāya* involves the cultivation of ways of *seeing*, not just ways of *acting* once one has seen.

Of course, the fact that a begging child stands out to Alice and Bill as an object calling for response is not *sufficient* for expressing a bodhisattva's generosity. Generosity, patience, propriety, and mindfulness are virtues cultivated on the bodhisattva path, and virtues are excellences in conduct.[7] According to Candrakīrti, *compassion* is the root of all the bodhisattva virtues. *Madhyamakāvatāra* I.1cd states:

> A compassionate mind, nondualistic awareness and
> The aspiration for enlightenment are the causes of the bodhisattvas.[8]

Candrakīrti's *Madhyamakāvatārabhāṣya* then elaborates on these three causes and introduces I.2 as follows:

> However, because compassion is the root of both the aspiration for enlightenment and nondualistic wisdom, we wish to proclaim that compassion is what is primary.[9]

Generosity is not merely a behavioral type that consists in doing some good to another who is in need. It also involves instantiating compassion (*karuṇā*). In particular, it involves instantiating compassion in one's response to the needs of others, as emphasized by Śāntideva in the *Bodhicaryāvatāra*. Compassion in this sense is not an emotional response or a kind of sympathy but a genuine commitment to benefit others and to alleviate their suffering (Dalai Lama 1999, chapters 8–10; Garfield forthcoming).

In Mahāyāna ethics, a bodhisattva is one who is actively altruistic or has fully activated *bodhicitta*. At the heart of *bodhicitta* is a type of compassion (*mahākaruṇā*, or *great compassion*) grounded in an apprehension of emptiness. That is, in realizing the interdependence of all sentient beings (and, hence, in one of the senses identified by Candrakīrti, their conventional reality; see chapter 1, p. 13), bodhisattvas extend their compassion equally to all sentient beings. Śāntideva (BCA I. 9–10) distinguishes aspirational from engaged *bodhicitta*. The first is a sincere aspiration grounded in compassion and an inferential understanding of emptiness and dependent origination to attain awakening for the sake of sentient beings. The second is a spontaneous virtuous engagement mediated by a direct apprehension of emptiness and dependent origination. The second emerges only at the end of the bodhisattva path inspired by the first. While Śāntideva recognizes the value of the aspiration to

7. Here, we resist Keown's (2001) interpretation of virtues as mental motivators (i.e., dharmas) that have intrinsic powers to influence the choice of certain kinds of behavior. Keown's interpretation presupposes an Ābhidharmika ontology, which Mādhyamikas reject. For explicit challenges to Keown's interpretation of Buddhist ethics, see Finnigan "Buddhist Meta-Ethics" and Goodman (2008).

8. *snying rje'i sems dang gnyis su med blo dang / byang chub sems ni rgyal sa'i rnams kyi rgyu //* (ed. LVP, p. 1).

9. *byang chub kyi sems dang gnyis su med pa'i ye shes gnyis kyi rtsa ba yang snying rje yin pa'i phyir na snying rje gtso bo nyid du bstan par 'dod pas* (ed. LVP, p. 7).

great compassion and a unified set of bodhisattva virtues grounded in apprehension of the two truths for the cultivation of virtue, he nevertheless recognizes a great difference between aspiring to this great compassion and its actualization. The possibility of the latter requires proficient perceptual skills and dispositions that are free from attachment, ignorance, and confusion (BCA I, IX; Garfield forthcoming)

Generosity informed by compassion will be distinctive in the manner, timing, and motivations of the action. While Alice and Bill may both experience the begging child as calling for generosity, they respond in different ways and, thereby, in part, express various degrees of compassion. Bill responds *affectively*. He *feels* bad for the child and *feels* guilty for having access to more wealth; he is thereby subtly *attached* to the child, *averse* to the child's suffering, and *averse* to his own feelings of guilt, which suggest a subtle *attachment* to self and a perception of other things in terms of their relationship to that self. Motivated by his sympathy and guilt, Bill gives some coins directly to the child (who passes the money on to the pimp who manages him and a few hundred other beggars). Bill immediately feels much better but has unknowingly demonstrated a deficiency in *upāya* and fails to fully actualize engaged *bodhicitta*.

Alice, with more *upāya* and less attachment, sees a social problem. After some kind words to the child, she gets involved with a charitable organization that helps to eliminate the industry of child begging. Her actions have a much more positive effect and occupy much more of her time and attention. She never feels satisfied with the results but continues to strive. This marks the difference between aspirational *bodhicitta* and engaged *bodhicitta*, as well as the difference between acting from sympathy and acting from *karuṇā*. All three of these actors are on the bodhisattva path, but they are at very different stages, and each stage requires apprehension of conventional truth and engagement with conventional reality. It is the difference in the mode and depth of the engagement that makes the moral difference. While giving the coins to the child may fit the act-type "giving" (if understood merely as the act of doing something good for one in need), it falls far short of instantiating the Mahāyāna virtue of generosity understood as rooted in great compassion. Of course, variety in situations will often call for variety of response; placing bread in a child's hand may be appropriate in some circumstances but not others.

The mere acceptance of a precept does not enable fully virtuous response. The cultivation of Mahāyāna compassion and the perceptual skills, conative attitudes, and skills in action it enables is required for the fulfillment of these precepts and full actualization of bodhisattva virtues in complex moral situations. The engaged *bodhicitta* of a bodhisattva involves an apprehension of interdependence (which, as we noted in chapter 1, is one of Candrakīrti's definitions of conventional truth) and hence of the two truths, as well as a rich engagement with conventional reality.

5

In previous chapters we have seen that Mādhyamikas can consistently maintain that objects of experience may have *conventional* existence and lack ultimate existence. While it is not ultimately true that there is a begging child in the street, conventionally there is one, and it is the conventional engagement of a conventionally real agent with this conventionally real object that morality demands and that the bodhisattva path enjoins. The bodhisattva precepts and their role as active values require a robust engagement with the conventional world.

It has sometimes been argued that ethical inquiry in the various Buddhist traditions should be pursued independently of epistemology, metaphysics, or semantics (Keown 2001, 19). The concern is that Buddhist metaphysics and epistemology may undermine, rather than ground, ethics. This threat may appear to loom particularly large when we consider ethics in relation to the doctrine of the two truths because it seems that the justificatory basis of ethics is undermined.

But this concern is unwarranted. The fact that Mādhyamika philosophers such as Candrakīrti and Śāntideva explicitly connect Madhyamaka metaphysics with Mahāyāna ethics should reassure us. And as we have seen, the doctrine of two truths is essential to bodhisattva ethics because it provides the epistemic basis for the objects of experience to which moral agents respond and the basis of the cultivation of the form of response distinctive of the Mahāyāna. Not only can one consistently integrate the epistemic and ethical components of the Mādhyamika, but an acceptance of the doctrine of the two truths also requires that one do so.

References and Abbreviations

Note: The authors used numerous older and modern editions of Buddhist texts; included here are all of the relevant bibliographical details. The authors' principal abbreviations are also included.

ACIP = Asian Classics Input Project. http://www.asianclassics.org.

Agrawal, M. M. 2001. *Six Systems of Indian Philosophy: The Sūtras of Six Systems of Indian Philosophy*. Delhi: Chaukhambha Sanskrit Pratishthan.

AK = Abhidharmakośa of Vasubandhu. For Skt. text of *Abhidharmakośa* and *Abhidharmakośabhāṣya*, see Vasubandhu (1967). French translation in La Vallée Poussin (1923–1931).

Aṅguttaranikāya. Pali text: *The Aṅguttara-nikāya*. Part 1, *Ekanipāta. Dukanipāta. And Tikanipāta*, ed. Richard Morris. Text series, Pali Text Society. London: Routledge, 1976. English translation: *The Book of the Gradual Sayings, Aṅguttara-Nikāya, or More-numbered Suttas*, trans. F. L. Woodward and E. M. Hare, with an introduction by C. A. F. Rhys Davids. Translation Series, Pali Text Society. London: Luzac, 1965–1973.

Aṅguttaranikāya Aṭṭhakathā Manorathapūraṇī, attributed to Buddhaghosa, ed. M. Walleser. Text Series, Pali Text Society. London: Routledge, 1966–1979.

Armstrong, David M. 2004. *Truth and Truthmakers*. New York: Cambridge University Press.

Arnold, Dan. 2005a. *Buddhists, Brahmins, and Belief: Epistemology in South Asian Philosophy of Religion*. New York: Columbia University Press.

———. 2005b. "Madhyamaka Buddhism." In the *Internet Encyclopedia of Philosophy*, http://www.iep.utm.edu/b/b-madhya.htm#H5.

———. 2005c. "Materials for a Mādhyamika Critique of Foundationalism: An Annotated Translation of *Prasannapadā* 55.11 to 75.13." *Journal of the International Association of Buddhist Studies* 28(2): 411–467.

Aṣṭasāhasrikāprajñāpāramitāsūtra. 1960. Skt. in *Aṣṭasāhasrikā Prajñāpāramitā*, ed. P. L. Vaidya. Darbhanga: Mithila Institute.

Ayer, A. J. 1936. *Language, Truth, and Logic*. London: Gollancz.

BCA = *Bodhicaryāvatāra* of Śāntideva. Skt. text in Prajñākaramati (1960). English translation in Crosby and Skilton (1998).

Bhattacharya, Kamaleswar. 1986. *The Dialectical Method of Nāgārjuna: Vigrahavyāvartanī*, 2d ed. Delhi: Motilal Banarsidass.

bKa' gdams gsung 'bum = *bKa' gdams gsung 'bum phyogs bsgrigs*, vol. 11. 2006. Lhasa: Peltsek Institute for Ancient Tibetan Manuscripts.

Blanshard, Brand. 1939. *The Nature of Thought*. London: Allen and Unwin.

Buescher, John B. 2005. *Echoes from an Empty Sky: The Origins of the Buddhist Doctrine of the Two Truths*. Ithaca, N.Y.: Snow Lion.

Burgess, J., and G. Rosen. 1997. *A Subject with No Object*. Oxford: Clarendon.

Burnyeat, Myles. 1983a. "Can the Skeptic Live His Skepticism?" In M. Burnyeat, *The Skeptical Tradition*, 117–148. Berkeley: University of California.

———. 1983b. *The Skeptical Tradition*. Berkeley: University of California.

Burton, David. 1999. *Emptiness Appraised: A Critical Study of Nāgārjuna's Philosophy*. London: Curzon.

Cabezón, José I. 1992. *A Dose of Emptiness: An Annotated Translation of the sTong thun chen mo of mKhas grub dGe legs dpal bzang*. SUNY Series in Buddhist Studies. Albany: State University of New York Press.

———, and Geshe L. Dargyay. 2007. *Freedom from Extremes: Gorampa's "Distinguishing the Views" and the Polemics of Emptiness*. Studies in Indian and Tibetan Buddhism. Boston: Wisdom.

Candrakīrti. 1970a. *Madhyamakāvatāra* (Tibetan text), ed. Louis de la Vallée Poussin (LVP) in *Madhyamakāvatāra par Candrakīrti, traduction tibétaine*. Bibliotheca Buddhica IX. St. Petersburg: Imprimerie de l'Académie impériale des sciences, 1912. Reprint, Osnabrück: Biblio, 1970. Includes Tibetan of *Madhyamakāvatāra* (P. 5261, 5262) and *Madhyamakāvatārabhāṣya* (P. 5263) of Candrakīrti (pdf file of LVP's edition downloadable at the University of Toronto scanning center, http://www.archive.org/details/madhyamakavataraoocanduoft).

———. 1970b. *Prasannapadā Madhyamakavṛtti*, ed. Louis de la Vallée Poussin. *Mūlamadhyamakakārikās (Mādhyamikasūtras) de Nāgārjuna, avec la Prasannapadā commentaire de Candrakīrti*. St. Petersburg: Bibliotheca Buddhica IV, 1903–1913. Reprint, Osnabrück: Biblio, 1970.

———. 1993. *dBu ma la 'jug pa'i bshad pa*. Sarnath: Kagyu Relief and Protection Committee.

———. 1994. *Madhyamakāvatārabhāṣya*. Varanasi: Sakya Student Union.

———. 1996a. *Catuḥśatakaṭīkā*. Varanasi: Kargyud Students' Welfare Committee.

———. 1996b. *Madhyamakāvatāra*. In the *Rtsa ba phyogs bsdus*. Varanasi: Sakya Student Union.

———. 2003. *Mūlamadhyamakavṛtti Prasannapadā* (Tibetan text). Sarnath: Gelukpa Students' Welfare Committee.

———, and Ju Mipham. 2002. *Introduction to the Middle Way: Chandrakirti's Madhyamakāvatāra with Commentary by Ju Mipham*, trans. Padmakara Translation Group. Boston: Shambhala.

Carnap, Rudolf. 1934. *Logische Syntax der Sprache*. Vienna: Springer. Translated by A. Smeaton as *The Logical Syntax of Language*. London: Kegan Paul, 1937.

———. 1956. *Meaning and Necessity: A Study in Semantics and Modal Logic*. Chicago: University of Chicago Press.

———.1956. "Empiricism, Semantics, and Ontology." In *Meaning and Necessity: A Study in Semantics and Modal Logic*, 2d ed., 205–221. Chicago: University of Chicago Press.

———. 1959. "The Elimination of Metaphysics Through Logical Analysis of Language." In A. J. Ayer (ed.), *Logical Positivism*, 60–81. New York: Free Press.

Carus, A.W. 2004. "Sellars, Carnap, and the Logical Space of Reasons." In Steve Awodey and Carsten Klein (eds.), Carnap Brought Home: The View from Jena, 317–355. Chicago and La Salle: Open Court.

Chan, Wing-Tsit. 1963. *A Sourcebook in Chinese Philosophy*. Princeton, N.J.: Princeton University Press.

Chin. = Chinese.

Chisholm, Roderick. 1977. *Theory of Knowledge*, 2d ed. Englewood Cliffs, N.J.: Prentice-Hall.

Clayton, Barbra. 2006. *Moral Theory in Śāntideva's Śikṣasamuccaya: Cultivating the Fruits of Virtue*. London: Routledge.

Compassion = Tsongkhapa (1980).

Cooper, David E., and Simon P. James. 2005. *Buddhism, Virtue, and Environment*. Burlington, Vt.: Ashgate.

Crane, Tim. 2001. "Intentional Objects." *Ratio* 14: 336–349.

Crosby, Kate, and Andrew Skilton. 1998. *Bodhisattvacaryāvatāra*. New York: Oxford University Press.

CS = *Catuḥśataka* of Āryadeva with *Catuḥśatakaṭīkā* of Candrakīrti. Sanskrit fragments in Suzuki (1994); chapters 1–4 translated in Lang (2003); chapters 12–13 translated in Tillemans (1990); translation of CS alone in Lang (1986).

Cutler, Joshua W. C., and Guy Newland, eds. 2000, 2002, 2004. *The Great Treatise on the Stages of the Path of Enlightenment: Lam Rim Chen Mo of Tsong-kha-pa*. Ithaca, N.Y.: Snow Lion. Vol. 1, 2000; vol. 2, 2004; vol. 3, 2002.

D = *sDe dge Tibetan Tripiṭaka, Bstan Ḫgyur*, preserved at the Faculty of Letters, University of Tokyo, 1977

Dalai Lama Tenzin Gyatso, H. H. 1999. *Ethics for a New Millenium*. New York: Penguin.

D'Amato, M., J. Garfield, and T. Tillemans, eds. 2009. *Pointing at the Moon: Buddhism, Logic, Analytic Philosophy*. New York: Oxford University Press.

Deguchi, Y., J. Garfield, and G. Priest. 2008. "The Way of the Dialetheist: Contradictions in Buddhism." *Philosophy East and West* 58: 395–402.

Devitt, Michael. 1997. *Realism and Truth*, 2d ed. Princeton, N.J.: Princeton University Press.

Diamond, Cora. 1991. *The Realistic Spirit: Wittgenstein, Philosophy, and the Mind*. Cambridge, Mass.: MIT Press.

Dīghanikāya. 1975–1982. Ed. T. W. Rhys Davids and J. E. Carpenter. Text Series, Pali Text Society. London: Routledge.

Dreyfus, Georges. 2009. "Patsab and the Origin of Prāsaṅgika." *Journal of the International Association of Buddhist Studies* (in press).

———, and Sara McClintock, eds. 2003. *The Svātantrika-Prāsaṅgika Distinction: What Difference Does a Difference Make?* Boston: Wisdom.

Dummett, Michael. 1976. "What Is a Theory of Meaning? (II)." In G. Evans and J. McDowell, eds., *Truth and Meaning: Essays in Semantics*. New York: Oxford University Press, pp 67–137.

Edgerton, Franklin. 1977. *Buddhist Hybrid Sanskrit Grammar and Dictionary*. Delhi: Motilal Banarsidass. Originally printed in 1953.

Eklund, Matti. 2005. "Fiction, Indifference, and Ontology." *Philosophy and Phenomenological Research* 71(3): 557–579.

Eltschinger, Vincent. 2000. *"Caste" et philosophie bouddhique. Continuité de quelques arguments bouddhiques contre le traitement réaliste des dénominations sociales.* WSTB 47. Vienna: Arbeitskreis für Tibetische und Buddhistische Studien Universität Wien.

Fine, Kit. 2002. "The Question of Realism." *Philosopher's Imprint* 1. Reprinted in A. Bottani, M. Carrara, and P. Giaretta, eds., *Individuals, Essence, and Identity: Themes of Analytic Metaphysics*, 3–41. Boston: Kluwer.

Finnigan, Bronwyn. Forthcoming. "Buddhist Meta-Ethics." *Journal of the International Association of Buddhist Studies.*

———. Forthcoming. "How Can a Buddha Come to Act? The Possibility of a Buddhist Account of Ethical Agency." *Philosophy East and West.*

French, Peter A., and Howard K. Wettstein, eds. 2001. *Midwestern Studies in Philosophy*. Vol. 25, *Figurative Language*. Oxford: Blackwell.

Gabriel, Gottfried. 2003. "Carnap's 'Elimination of Metaphysics through Logical Analysis of Language.'" In P. Parrini, W. C. Salmon, and M. H. Salmon (eds.), *Logical Empiricism*, 30–42. Pittsburgh: University of Pittsburgh Press.

Garfield, Jay L. 1990. "*Epoché* and *Śūnyatā*: Scepticism East and West." *Philosophy East and West* 40(3): 285–307. Reprinted in Garfield (2002, 3–23).

———. 1995. *The Fundamental Wisdom of the Middle Way*. New York: Oxford University Press.

———. 2002. *Empty Words: Buddhist Philosophy and Cross-cultural Interpretation*. New York: Oxford University Press.

———. 2006. "Reductionism and Fictionalism: Comments on Siderits." *American Philosophical Association Newsletter on Asian and Comparative Philosophy* 6(1): 1–8.

———. 2008. "Turning a Madhyamaka Trick: Reply to Huntington." *Journal of Indian Philosophy* 36: 507–527.

———. Forthcoming. "What Is It Like to Be a Bodhisattva? Moral Phenomenology in Śāntideva's *Bodhicaryāvatāra*." *Journal of the International Association of Buddhist Studies.*

———, and G. Priest. 2003. "Nāgārjuna and the Limits of Thought." *Philosophy East and West* 53: 1–21.

Gedün Chöphel (*dGe 'dun chos 'phel*). 1990. *dBu ma'i zab gnad snying por dril ba'i legs bshad klu sgrub dgongs rgyan*. Lhasa: Bod ljongs bod yid dpe rnying khang.

Goodman, Charles. 2008. "Consequentialism, Agent-neutrality, and Mahāyāna Ethics." *Philosophy East and West* 58(1): 17–35.

Goodman, Nelson. 1983. "Notes on a Well-made World." *Erkenntnis* 19: 99–107.

Gorampa Sönam Senge (*Go rams pa bsod nams seng ge*). 1969a. *dBu ma spyi don nges don rab gsal*. In *The Complete Works of the Sakya Scholars*, vol. 12. Tokyo: Toyo Bunko.

———. 1969b. *lTa ba ngan sel*. In *The Complete Works of the Sakya Scholars*, vol. 13. Tokyo: Toyo Bunko.

———. 1969c. *Yang dag lta ba'i 'od zer*. In *The Complete Works of the Sakya Scholars*, vol. 12. Tokyo: Toyo Bunko.

———. 1994. *lTa ba'i shan 'byed theg mchog gnad gyi zla zer*. Sarnath: Sakya Student's Union.

———. 2001. *lTa ba ngan sel*. Sarnath: Sakya Students' Union.

———. 2002. *dBu ma spyi don nges don rab gsal*. Sarnath: Sakya Students' Union.

GRS = Tsongkhapa's *dBu ma la 'jug pa'i bshad pa dgongs pa rab gsal*. Dharamsala: Shes rig par khang edition, n.d.

Hallie, Phillip, ed. 1964. "Introduction," in *Scepticism, Man, & God: Selections from the Major Writings of Sextus Empiricus*. Trans. Sanford G. Etheridge. Middletown, Conn.: Wesleyan University Press, pp 3–28.

Hopkins, Jeffrey. 1983. *Meditation on Emptiness*. London: Wisdom.

———, ed. and trans. 2007. *Nāgārjuna's Precious Garland: Buddhist Advice for Living and Liberation*. Ithaca, N.Y.: Snow Lion.

———. 2008. *Tsong-kha-pa's Final Exposition of Wisdom*. Ithaca, N.Y.: Snow Lion.

Horwich, Paul. 1998. *Truth*, 2d ed. Oxford: Blackwell.

———. 2006. "A World without Isms: Life after Realism, Fictionalism, Non-cognitivism, Relativism, Reductionism, Revisionism, and so on." In P. Greenough and M. Lynch, eds., *Realism and Truth: New Debates*, 188–202. New York: Oxford University Press.

Huntington, C. W., Jr. 2007. "The Nature of the Madhyamaka Trick." *Journal of Indian Philosophy* 35: 103–131.

———, and N. Wangchen. 1989. *The Emptiness of Emptiness: An Introduction to Early Indian Mādhyamika*. Honolulu: University of Hawaii Press.

Iwata, Takashi. 1993. Prasaṅga *und* Prasaṅgaviparyaya *bei Dharmakīrti und seinen Kommentatoren*. WSTB 31. Vienna: Arbeitskreis für Tibetische und Buddhistische Studien Universität Wien.

James, William. 1909. *The Meaning of Truth: A Sequel to "Pragmatism."* New York: Green.

Joyce, Richard. 2001. *The Myth of Morality*. New York: Cambridge University Press.

———. 2005. "Moral Fictionalism." In Mark Eli Kalderon, ed., *Fictionalism in Metaphysics*, 287–313. Oxford: Clarendon.

Kalderon, Mark Eli, ed. 2005. *Moral Fictionalism*. New York: Oxford University Press.

Kamalaśīla. *Sarvadharmaniḥsvabhāvasiddhi*. P. 5289.

Karunadasa, Y. 1996. *The Dhamma Theory: Philosophical Cornerstone of the Abhidhamma*. Wheel Publication 412/413. Kandy, Sri Lanka: Buddhist Publication Society.

———. 2006. "Theravāda Version of the Two Truths." Presentation to Korean Conference of Buddhist Studies, http://www.skb.or.kr/2006/down/papers/094.pdf.

Kasulis, T. P. 1981. *Zen Action, Zen Person*. Honolulu: University of Hawaii Press.

Kathāvatthuppakaraṇaṭṭhakathā, attributed to Buddhaghosa. 1979. Pali text, ed. N. Jayawickrama. Text Series, Pali Text Society. London: Routledge (distributed).

Keown, Damien. 2001. *The Nature of Buddhist Ethics*, 2d ed. New York: Palgrave Macmillan.

Kirkham, Richard L. 1995. *Theories of Truth: A Critical Introduction*. Cambridge, Mass.: MIT Press.

Klein, Anne. 1994. *Path to the Middle*. Albany: State University of New York Press.

Köppl, Heidrun I. 2008. *Establishing Appearances as Divine: Rongzom Chözang on Reasoning, Madhyamaka, and Purity*. Ithaca, N.Y.: Snow Lion.

Kripke, Saul A. 1982. *Wittgenstein on Rules and Private Language*. Oxford: Clarendon.

La Vallée Poussin, Louis de. 1923–1931. *L'Abhidharmakośa de Vasubandhu: Traduction et annotations*. Six vols. Paris: Geuthner. New edition prepared by E. Lamotte, Mélanges chinois et bouddhiques, vol. 16. Brussels: Institut Belge des Hautes Études Chinoises.

Lang, Karen C. 1986. *Āryadeva's Catuḥśataka*. Indiske Studier VII. Copenhagen: Akademisk Forlag.

———. 2003. *Four Illusions: Candrakīrti's Advice to Travelers on the Bodhisattva Path*. New York: Oxford University Press.

Lewis, David. 1969. *Convention: A Philosophical Study*. Cambridge, Mass.: Harvard University Press.

———. 1983. "Extrinsic Properties." *Philosophical Studies* 44: 197–200.

Lindtner, Christian. 1981. "Buddhapālita on Emptiness." *Indo-Iranian Journal* 23: 187–217.

———. 1982. *Nagarjuniana: Studies in the Writings and Philosophy of Nāgārjuna*. Indiske Studier 4. Copenhagen: Akademisk Forlag.

———. 1986. *Master of Wisdom: Writings of the Buddhist Master Nāgārjuna*. Berkeley: Dharma.

Loizzo, Joseph. 2007. *Nāgārjuna's Reason Sixty (Yuktiṣaṣṭikā) with Candrakīrti's Commentary (Yuktiṣaṣṭikāvṛtti)*. New York: Columbia University Press.

LRC = Tsongkhapa's *Byang chub lam rim che ba*. 1985. Xining: mTsho sngon People's Press.

LVP = Louis de la Vallée Poussin; editions of Mav, MavBh, MMK, and PP. See Candrakīrti (1970a, 1970b).

Mackie, John L. 1986. *Ethics: Inventing Right and Wrong*. New York: Penguin.

Mates, Benson. 1996. "Introduction," in *The Skeptic Way*. New York: Oxford University Press.

Matilal, Bimal K. 1970. "Reference and Existence in Nyāya and Buddhist Logic." *Journal of Indian Philosophy* 1: 83–110.

———. 1971. *Epistemology, Logic, and Grammar in Indian Philosophical Analysis*. The Hague: Mouton.

———. 1985. *Logic, Language, and Reality*. Delhi: Motilal Banarsidass.

———. 1986. *Perception*. Oxford: Clarendon.

Mav = *Madhyamakāvatāra* of Candrakīrti; see Candrakīrti (1970a, 1993).

MavBh = *Madhyamavatārabhāṣya* of Candrakīrti; see Candrakīrti (1970a, 1994).

May, Jacques. 1959. *Candrakīrti Prasannapadā Madhyamakavṛtti*. Paris: Adrien Maisonneuve.

———. 1979. "Chūgan, Hōbōgirin V," 470–493. Paris: Librairie d'Amérique et d'Orient.

Maynard Smith, John. 1982. *Evolution and the Theory of Games*. New York: Cambridge University Press.

McClintock, Sara. 2000. "Knowing All through Knowing One." *Journal of the Association of Buddhist Studies* 23(2): 225–244.

McCrea, Lawrence J., and Parimal Patil. 2006. "Traditionalism and Innovation: Philosophy, Exegesis, and Intellectual History in Jñānaśrīmitra's *Apohaprakaraṇa*." *Journal of Indian Philosophy* 34: 303–366.

Mimaki, Katsumi. 1982. *Blo gsal grub mtha.'* Kyoto: Zinbun Kagaku Kenkyusyo (Institute for Research in Humanities, Kyoto University).

MMK = *Mūlamadhyamakakārikā* of Nāgārjuna. For Skt. edition see Candrakīrti (1970b).

Nāgārjuna. *Mūlamadhyamakakārikā*. For Skt. text see Candrakīrti (1970b).

———. *Ratnāvalī*. Skt. and Tib. ed. Michael Hahn. *Nāgārjuna's Ratnāvalī*. Vol. 1, *The Basic Texts (Sanskrit, Tibetan, Chinese)*. 1982. Bonn: Indica et Tibetica 1. Translated from the Tibetan in Hopkins (2007).

Neurath, Otto. 1983. *Philosophical Papers 1913–46*, ed. R. S. Cohen and M. Neurath. Dordrecht: Reidel.

Newland, Guy M. 1992. *The Two Truths in the Mādhyamika Philosophy of the Ge-luk-ba Order of Tibetan Buddhism*. Ithaca, N.Y.: Snow Lion.

NS = *Nyāyasūtras* of Gautama.

Ocean = Tsongkhapa (2006).

Owens, David. 1989. "Levels of Explanation." *Mind* 98(389): 59–79.

P = Peking edition of Tibetan canon.

Patsab Nyimadrak (*pa tshab nyi ma grags*). 2006. *rTsa ba shes rab kyi ti ga bstan bcos sgrom ma gsal byed pa*. In bKa' gdams gsung 'bum, vol. 11. Lhasa: Peltsek Institute for Ancient Tibetan Manuscripts.

Peirce, Charles S. 1905. "What Pragmatism Is." *Monist* 15: 161–181.

Penelhum, Terence. 1983. "Skepticism and Fideism." In Burnyeat (1983b, 287–318).

Perrett, Roy W. 2002. "Personal Identity, Minimalism, and Madhyamaka." *Philosophy East and West* 52(3): 373–385.

PP = *Prasannapadā;* Tib. in Candrakīrti (2003), Skt. in Candrakīrti (1970b). Unless otherwise indicated, references are to the Tibetan.

Prajñākaramati. 1960. *Bodhicaryāvatārapañjikā*, ed. P. L. Vaidya. Buddhist Sanskrit Texts Series 12. Darbhanga: Mithila Institute, 1960.

Priest, Graham. 1998. "Paraconsistent Logic." In vol. 7 of E. Craig, ed., *Routledge Encyclopedia of Philosophy*, 208–211. London: Routledge.

———. 2002. *Beyond the Limits of Thought*, 2d ed. New York: Oxford University Press.

———. 2005. "The Limits of Language." In vol. 7, 2d ed., of K. Brown, ed., *Encyclopedia of Language and Linguistics*, 156–159. Amsterdam: Elsevier.

PTS = Pali Text Society.

Python, Pierre. 1973. *Vinaya-Viniścaya-Upāli-Paripṛcchā: Enquête d'Upāli pour une exégèse de la discipline*. Paris: Adrien Maissoneuve.

Quine, Willard Van Orman. 1936. "Truth by Convention." In O. H. Lee, ed., *Philosophical Essays for Alfred North Whitehead*, 90–124. New York: Longmans, Green.

Quine, W. V. O. 1951. 'Two Dogmas of Empiricism." *Philosophical Review* 60: 20–43.

Radhakrishnan, Sarvepalli. 1998. *Indian Philosophy*, vol. 1. New Delhi: Oxford University Press.

Ramsey, Frank P. 1927. "Facts and Propositions." *Proceedings of the Aristotelian Society, Supplemental Vol. 7*: 153–170.

Ratnāvalī. See Nāgārjuna, *Ratnāvalī*.

Russell, Bertrand. 1907. "On the Nature of Truth." *Proceedings of the Aristotelian Society* 7: 228–249.

Śāntideva. *Bodhicaryāvatāra*. Skt. text in Prajñākaramati (1960), *Bodhicaryāvatārapañjikā*. Translation of Śāntideva's *Bodhicaryāvatāra* in Crosby and Skilton (1998).

Scherrer-Schaub, Cristina. 1991. *Yuktiṣaṣṭikavṛtti*. Brussels: Institut Belge des Hautes Etudes Chinoises.

Schwartz, R. 2000. "Starting from Scratch: Making Worlds." *Erkenntnis* 52: 151–159.

Sedley, David. 1983. "The Motivation of Greek Skepticism." In M. Burnyeat (1983b, 9–30).

Sellars, Wilfrid. 1956. "Empiricism and the Philosophy of Mind." In vol. 1 of H. Feigl and M. Scriven (eds.), *Minnesota Studies in the Philosophy of Science*, 253–329. Minneapolis: University of Minnesota Press.

Seyfort Ruegg, David. 1977. "The Uses of the Four Points of the *Catuṣkoṭi* and the Problem of the Description of Reality in Mahāyāna Buddhism." *Journal of Indian Philosophy* 5: 1–71.

———. 1981. *The Literature of the Madhyamaka School of Philosophy in India*, vol. 7 of *History of Indian Literature*, ed. J. Gonda, fascicule 1. Wiesbaden: Harrasowitz.

———. 1983. "On the Thesis and Assertion in the Madhyamaka / dBu ma." In E. Steinkellner and H. Tauscher, eds., *Contributions on Tibetan and Buddhist Religion and Philosophy*, 205–241. WSTB 11. Vienna: Arbeitskreis für Tibetische und Buddhistische Studien Universität Wien.

———. 1989. "Does the Mādhyamika Have a Thesis and Philosophical Position?" In B. K. Matilal and R. D. Evans, eds., *Buddhist Logic and Epistemology*, 229–237. Dordrecht: Reidel.

———. 2000. *Three Studies in the History of Indian and Tibetan Madhyamaka Philosophy*. WSTB 50. Vienna: Arbeitkreis für Tibetische und Buddhistische Studien Universität Wien.

———. 2002. *Two Prolegomena to Madhyamaka Philosophy*. Candrakīrti's *Prasannapadā* Madhyamakavṛttiḥ on Madhyamakakārikā 1.1 and Tsoṅ kha pa blo bzaṅ grags pa / rGyal tshab dar ma rin chen's dKa' gnad/gnas brgyad kyi zin bris. Annotated translations. Studies in Indian and Tibetan Madhyamaka Thought, Part 2. WSTB 54. Vienna: Arbeitskreis für Tibetische und Buddhistiche Studien Universität Wien.

———. 2006. "The Svātantrika-Prāsaṅgika Distinction in the History of Madhyamaka Thought." *Indo-Iranian Journal* 49(3–4): 319–346.

Siderits, Mark. 1980. "The Madhyamaka Critique of Epistemology I." *Journal of Indian Philosophy* 9: 307–335.

———. 1981. "The Madhyamaka Critique of Epistemology II." *Journal of Indian Philosophy* 9: 121–160.

———. 1989. "Thinking on Empty: Madhyamaka Anti-realism and Canons of Rationality." In Shlomo Biderman and Ben-Ami Scharfstein, eds., *Rationality in Question: On Eastern and Western Views of Rationality*, 231–249. Leiden: Brill.

———. 2003. *Personal Identity and Buddhist Philosophy: Empty Persons*. Burlington, Vt.: Ashgate.

———. 2008. "Contradiction in Buddhist Argumentation." *Argumentation* 22(1): 125–133.

Skt. = Sanskrit.

Skyrms, Brian. 1996. *Evolution of the Social Contract*. New York: Cambridge University Press.

Stanley, Jason. 2001. "Hermeneutic Fictionalism." In French and Wettstein (2001).

Stoltz, Jonathan. 2006. "Concepts, Intension, and Identity in Tibetan Philosophy of Language." *Journal of the International Association of Buddhist Studies* 29(2): 383–400.

Striker, Gisela. 1983. "The Ten Tropes of Aenesidemus." In Burnyeat (1983b, 95–116).

Suzuki, Koshin, ed. 1994. *Sanskrit Fragments and Tibetan Translation of Candrakīrti's Bodhisattvayogācāracatuḥśatakaṭīkā*. Tokyo: Sankibo.

s.v. = sub voce.

Taktsang Lotsāwa (*Stag tshang lo tsā ba*). 2001. *Grub mtha' kun shes nas mtha' bral sgrub pa zhes bya ba'i bstan bcos* and *Grub mtha' kun shes nas mtha' bral sgrub pa zhes bya ba'i bstan bcos rnam par bshad pa legs bshad rgya mtsho*. In the *Grub mtha' kun shes kyi rtsa ba dang de'i 'grel ba*. Sarnath: Sakya Students' Union.

Tarksi, Alfred. 1936. "*Der Wahrheitsbegriff in den formalisierten Sprachen*." *Studia Philosophia* 1: 261–405. Reprinted in English in *Logic, Semantics, Metamathematics*. Oxford: Oxford University Press, 1956.

Tauscher, Helmut. 1995. *Die Lehre von den zwei Wirklichkeiten in Tsoṅ kha pas Madhyamaka-Werken*. WSTB 36. Vienna: Arbeitskreis für Tibetische und Buddhistische Studien Universität Wien.

Thakchöe, Sonam. 2007. *The Two Truths Debate: Tsongkhapa and Gorampa on the Middle Way*. Boston: Wisdom.

———. (2009). "Prāsaṅgika Epistemology: Debate between Tsongkhapa and His Critics on the Use of *Pramāṇa* in Nāgārjuna's and Candrakīrti's Madhyamaka." School of Philosophy, University of Tasmania.

Tib. = Tibetan.

Tillemans, Tom J. F. 1986. "Identity and Referential Opacity in Tibetan Buddhist Apoha Theory." In B. K. Matilal and R. D. Evans, eds., *Buddhist Logic and Epistemology*, 207–227. Dordrecht: Reidel.

———. 1990. *Materials for the Study of Āryadeva, Dharmapāla, and Candrakīrti*. WSTB 24.1 and 24.2. Vienna: Arbeitskreis für Tibetische und Buddhistische Studien Universität Wien. Reprint, Delhi: Motilal Banarsidass, 2008.

———. 1999. *Scripture, Logic, Language: Essays on Dharmakīrti and His Tibetan Successors*. Studies in Indian and Tibetan Buddhism. Boston: Wisdom.

———. 2000. *Dharmakīrti's Pramāṇavārttika: An Annotated Translation of the Fourth Chapter (Parārthānumāna)*, vol. 1 (k. 1–148). Österreichische Akademie der Wissenschaften Philosophisch-historische Klasse Sitzungsberichte, 675. Band. Vienna: Verlag der Österreichischen Akademie der Wissenschaften.

———. 2003. "Metaphysics for Mādhyamikas." In Dreyfus and McClintock (2003, 93–123).

———. 2004. "What Are Mādhyamikas Refuting? Śāntarakṣita, Kamalaśīla *et alii* on Superimpositions (*Samāropa*)." In S. Hino and T. Wada, eds., *Three Mountains and*

Seven Rivers: Prof. Musashi Tachikawa's Felicitation Volume, 225–237. Delhi: Motilal Banarsidass.

———. 2009. "How Do Mādhyamikas Think? Notes on Jay Garfield, Graham Priest, and Paraconsistency." In D'Amato, Garfield, and Tillemans (2009, 83–100).

Tsongkhapa Lozang drakpa (*Tsong kha pa blo bzang grags pa*). 1970. *rTsa ba shes rab kyi dka' gnas chen po brgyad kyi bshad pa*. Sarnath: Pleasure of Elegant Sayings Press.

———.1973. *dBu ma dgongs pa rab gsal*. Sarnath: Gelugpa Students' Welfare Committee. Reprinted 1984, 2004.

———. 1980. *Compassion in Tibetan Buddhism:* Tsongkhapa's *dBu ma dgongs pa rab gsal*, ed. and trans. Jeffrey Hopkins. London: Rider.

———. 1985a. *Lam gtso rnam gsum gyi rtsa ba*. In the *dBu ma'i lta khrid phyogs bsdebs*. Sarnath: Gelugpa Students' Welfare Committee.

———. 1985b. *Lam rim chen mo*. Xining: mTsho sngon (Qinghai) People's Press.

———. 1992. *rTsa shes ṭik chen rigs pa'i rgya mtsho*. Sarnath: Gelukpa Students' Welfare Committee.

———. 1993. *Byang chub lam gyi rim pa chen mo*. Sarnath: Gelugpa Students' Welfare Committee.

———. 1994. *rTen 'brel stod pa legs bshad snying po*. In G. Namdol and N. Samten, trans. and eds., *Pratītyasamutpādastutisubhāṣitahṛdayam of Ācārya Tsongkhapa*. Dalai Lama's Tibeto-Indological Series, vol. 3. Sarnath: Central Institute for Higher Tibetan Studies.

———. 2006. *Ocean of Reasoning: A Great Commentary on Nāgārjuna's Mūlamadhyamakakārikā*, trans. N. Samten and J. Garfield. New York: Oxford University Press.

v. = verse.

van Heijenoort, Jan. 1967. *From Frege to Gödel: A Source Book in Mathematical Logic, 1879–1931*. Cambridge, Mass.: Harvard University Press.

Vasubandhu. 1967. *Abhidharmakośakārikā* and *Abhidharmakośabhāṣya*. Skt. text ed. P. Pradhān. Patna: Jayaswal Research Institute.

Velez de Cea, Abraham. 2004. "The Criteria of Goodness in the Pāli Nikāyas and the Nature of Buddhist Ethics." *Journal of Buddhist Ethics* 11: 123–142.

Vose, Kevin. 2008. *Resurrecting Candrakīrti*. Studies in Indian and Tibetan Buddhism. Boston: Wisdom.

VV = *Vigrahvyāvartanī* of Nāgārjuna. Sanskrit and Tibetan texts in Yonezawa (2008).

Williams, Michael. 1988. "Scepticism without Theory." *Review of Metaphysics* 41: 547–588.

Williams, Paul. 1998. *Altruism and Reality: Studies in the Philosophy of the Bodhicaryāvatāra*. London: Curzon.

Winograd, Terry, and Fernando Flores. 1986. *Understanding Computers and Cognition: A New Foundation for Design*. Norwood, N.J.: Ablex.

Wittgenstein, Ludwig. 1922. *Tractatus Logico-philosophicus*. London: Routledge and Kegan Paul.

Woods, John. 2006. "Pragma-dialectics: A Retrospective." In Peter Houtlosser and Agnès van Rees, eds., *Considering Pragma-dialectics*, 285–296. Mahwah, N.J.: Erlbaum.

Woodward, F. L., and E. M. Hare (1965–1973). See *Aṅguttaranikāya*.

WSTB = Wiener Studien zur Tibetologie und Buddhismuskunde.

Yablo, Stephen. 1998. "Does Ontology Rest on a Mistake?" *Proceedings of the Aristotelian Society*, supplemental vol. 72, 229–262.

———. 2000. "Apriority and Existence." In Paul Boghossian and Christopher Peacocke, eds., *New Essays on the A Priori*, 197–229. New York: Oxford University Press.

———. 2001. "Go Figure: A Path through Fictionalism." In French and Wettstein (2001).

Yonezawa, Yoshiyasu. 2008. "*Vigrahavyāvartanī*, Sanskrit Transliteration, and Tibetan Translation." *Journal of the Naritasan Institute for Buddhist Studies* 31: 209–333.

Zollman, Kevin. 2005. "Talking to Neighbors: The Emergence of Regional Meaning." *Philosophy of Science* 72: 69–85.

Index

Abhidhāna, 13
Ābhidharmika, 8
Abhidharma, 8, 18, 136–148, 168–188
Abhidharmakośabhāṣya, 8
Analogies, 53
Aṅguttaranikāya, 6n7
Antifoundationalism, 51
Anumāna, 41n6, 44
Aristotle, 132
Armstrong, D., 133
Arnold, D., 3n1, 51n26, 167n1
Arthakriyā (practical efficacy), 145
Āryadeva, 8
Aṣṭasāhasrikāprajñāpāramitāsūtra, 150
Aṭṭhakathā, 17–18
Avataṃsaka schools, 21
Ayer, A., 135

Baier, A., 127n7
Barnes , J., 122
Bhattacharya, K., 27n10, 28n13, 53n30, 91n1, 116n2, 150n25
Bhā(va)viveka, 4, 73, 125, 171
Blanshard, B., 134
Bodhicaryāvatāra, 202, 222, 225–229
Bodhicaryāvatārapanjikā, 5n4, 9, 16
Bodhicitta, 229–230
Bodhicittavivaraṇa, 10, 11n20
Bodhisattva, 221–223
dBu ma dgongs pa rab gsal, 49
Buddha's conventional cognition, 49–51
Buddhaghosa, 5
Buddhapālita, 7, 73, 125–126
Burgess, J., 158n12, 161n18
Burnyeat, M., 102n15, 103, 122
Burton, D., 95
sbyor ba = *prayoga* (probative argument), 97

Cabezón, J., 140n11, 201
Candrakīrti,
- on agreement with the world, 151, 154–157, 160–161, 187
- on convention as obscuration or as deceptive, 23–24, 31–32, 39–40, 47–51, 191–192
- on conventional truth as truth, 34–35, 47–51, 69–70
- on cowherds, v–vi

Candrakīrti (*continued*)
on epistemic authority, 35–36, 41–46, 69–70, 187
on epistemic instruments, 29, 39–40, 41–46, 54–55, 172–173, 175, 178
on ethics, 221–223, 229, 231
on intrinsic nature, 61, 78
on mundane knowledge, 41–46
and Patsan Nyimadrak, 95, 105
on rational insight, 46–47
on Sāṃkhya, 160
on *samvṛti*, 12–14
as a skeptic, 105, 124–130
on Svātantrika, 171–172
on two natures, 9, 24–25, 32–33, 58–59, 74
on Yogācāra, 159
Carnap, R., 20, 177–182, 186n3
On internal and external questions, 182–183
Pragmatism, 184–186
Carus, P., 185
Catuḥśatakaṭīkā, 10n18, 41–42, 44, 45, 48, 78, 160n16, 161
Chan, W., 218
Chisholm, R., 202n16
Chökyisangpo (rong zom chos kyi bzang po), 147
Chöpel, Gendün, 40
Clayton, B., 224n3
Conceptual Designation, 64–67, 190–194
Construction, 202–207
and convention, 202–204
limits of, 204–207
Tsongkhapa on, 205–207
Cooper, D., 167n2
Coordination, 194–197, 199–202
Coventry, A., 127
Crane, T., 10n19
Cutler, J., 76n1

gdags gzhi (basis of construction), 192
dam bcas pa tsam gyis grub pa = pratijñāmātreṇa, 152
Daoism, 21, 216–219
Dargyay, L., 140n11
Deceptiveness of conventional cognition, 29–31, 47–51, 67–71
Candrakīrti on, 29–31, 47–51
Tsongkhapa on, 29–31, 67–71
Deflationism, 18, 132–134, 143–147, 162
Deguchi, Y., 149, 150n25, 220n13
Dependent arising, 53, 62–67, 81
and Abhidharma, 170–172
and emptiness, 172–174
Tsongkhapa on, 62–67
Devitt, M., 189
Dhammapada, 5n4
Dharmakīrti, 10, 12n21, 16, 19, 67, 135, 152–153
Dharmapāla, 15n26
Diamond, C., 94n3
Dīghanikāya, 8n14
Dignāga, 10, 16, 19, 53n32, 125, 172–176
Diogenes, 21n32
Dōgen, 219
Dreyfus, G., 3n1, 17, 18n30, 95n6
Dummett, M., 135
Dzogchen (*rdzogs chen*), 147, 219

Eckel, D., 60n5, 117, 119
Edgerton, F., 12n22
Eklund, M., 158n12, 162n19
Eltschinger, V., 12n21
Emptiness, 58–59
and conventional existence, 58–59
as a negation, 73–75
Epistemic authority, 26–30, 35–36, 47–51, 54, 66, 82–83, 118
and truth, 26–30, 35–36
Epistemic instruments, 41–47
and mundane convention, 41–44
and non-deceptiveness, 47–51
Nyāya on, 172–176
and rational insight, 46–47
and ultimate reality, 45–46
and warrant, 44–47
Epistemic objects, 28, 36, 39, 41, 43, 45, 47, 53–54, 83, 171–172
Ethics, 221–231

and *bodhicitta*, 229–230
and justification, 222–223
and practice, 227–230
and skepticism, 225–227
and *Upāya*, 224–225, 229–230

Fazang, 218
Fictionalism, 19, 58n2, 144–150, 157–164
Fine, K., 147
Finnigan, B., 19, 21, 145, 219n10, 229n7
Flores, F., 201
Foundationalism, 27, 27n8, 51
Candrakīrti, 51–55
Nāgārjuna, 27

Gabriel, G., 185
dgag bya (object of negation), 17
Garfield, J., 9n16, 16–18, 37, 55n35, 64, 92–94, 150n25, 172n12, 173, 215n5, 220n13
on emptiness, 96n7
on fictionalism, 144n15
on skepticism, 93–94, 104n16, 106, 115, 124n5
Gedun Chöpel, 40n5
Generosity, 229–230
Goodman, C., 196, 204, 224, 229n7
Gorampa, 4, 17, 39, 40n3, 44n11, 49, 82–87, 101
on negation, 73, 82–87
on reality of existent objects, 84
grags pa = *prasiddha, pratīta* (simply acknowledged), 153

Hallie, B., 102n15
Hegel, G., 217
Heidegger, M., 220
Hopkins, J., 3n1, 11n20
Horwich, P., 132, 141, 143, 147–148
Hume, D., 93, 127
Huntington, C.W., 55n35, 126, 216n7

Ineffability, 220
Inferential cognition, 41
Intrinsic characteristics, 39
Intrinsic establishment, 54
Intrinsic natures, 13, 15, 29, 39, 41, 43, 51, 54, 68, 75, 116, 120, 139–143, 146, 163–165, 167–177, 179, 224
Iwata, T., 171n11

James, W., 135, 167n2
Jayānanda, 156
rJes thob = *pṛṣṭhalabdha* (subsequent attainment), 49
Jonangpa school, 14, 157
Joyce, R., 159

bKa' gdams gsung 'bum, 95
Kalderon, M., 158n13
Kamalaśīla, 4, 18, 152–153, 157, 186–188
Karunadasa, Y., 5n4, 12n21
Kasulis, T., 219n9
Kathāvatthu, 5–6
Keown, D., 229n7, 231
Khädrupjay (mKhas grub rje), 201
khas len kun bral (thesislessness), 100
khyab ba = *vyāpti* (pervasion), 97
Kirkham, R., 131, 132, 135
Klein, A., 64
Köppl, H., 163n21
Kripke, S., 93–94, 106, 127n7
Kṛṣṇa, 180

Lam gtso rnam gsum (*Three Principal Aspects of the Path*), 82
lam gyi dgag bya (soteriological object of negation), 76
Lam rim chen mo (*Extensive Exposition of the Stages of the Path*), 60–62, 76–82
Lang, K., 160n16
Lewis, D., 20, 145, 189, 189n2, 193–197, 208–212
on coordination, 194–197
theory of conventions, 208–212
Lindtner, C., 7n9, 11n20, 15n26
Loizzo, J., 191n12

loka, 41–42
lokaprasiddha (accepted by the world), 43
lokasaṃvṛti (mundane convention), 42
lokasaṃvṛtisatya (mundane conventional truth), 24, 42
lokavyavahāra (transactions), 13
lung dang rigs pa'i dgag bya (object of negation by scripture and reasoning), 83

Mackie, J., 158n13
Madhyamaka philosophies, 16
  ethics, 221–231
  interpretation of, 16–17
Madhyamakāvatāra, 9, 15–16, 24, 31, 39, 41, 44, 45, 48, 58, 154, 157, 161, 202, 216, 222, 229
Madhyamakāvatārabhāṣya, 23, 31, 41, 125, 205, 229
Mahāsumati, 95
Mahāvibhāṣa, 15
Mahāyāna, 5n4, 8
Maheśvara, 7
Mates, B., 102n15, 124n5
Matilal, B.K., 90, 91–93, 99, 102n14, 115, 144
May, J., 3n1, 4
McClintock, S., 3n1, 18n30, 105n19
McCrea, L., 179n20
McEvilly, T., 115
Meditative equipoise, 49n19
Middle way, 3, 89, 103, 112, 120, 126
Mimaki, K., 154n6, 157n10
Mīmāṃsā, 11, 192
Mipham, 119n4
Mirages, 9, 29–34, 36–38, 58, 68, 81, 146, 228
Mūlamadhyamakākarikā, 5, 7, 30, 86, 116, 188, 215
Mundane convention, 43

Nāgārjuna, 3, 6, 10, 25, 27–29, 30, 61, 86, 191, 222
  on ethics, 222
  on foundationalism, 27
  Mūlamadhyamakākarikā, 5, 7, 30, 86, 116, 188, 215
  Prāsaṅgika epistemology, 52
  Ratnāvalī, 222
  and skepticism, 91–103, 115–116
  Vigrahavyāvartanī, 26, 27, 36, 37, 53, 91, 116, 171
  Yuktiṣaṣṭikā, 191
rnal 'byor mngon sum = *yogipratyakṣa* (yogic perception), 99
Nālandā monastery, 3
rnam grangs pa'i don dam (represented ultimate), 119
Narāyāna, 7
Negation, 73–82
  and conventional truth, 75–76
  emptiness as, 73–75
  external vs internal, 73–75
  Gorampa on, 82–87
  object of, 76–87
  Tsongkhapa on, 76–82
Neurath, O., 134
Newland, G., 3n1, 9n16, 11n20, 14n25, 16, 70, 76n1, 108n23, 149n23
Neyārtha, 4
Nges don rab gsal (*Illumination of the Object of Ascertainment*), 83
Nihilism, 51n26, 82, 93
Nītārtha, 4
Nyāya, 26, 27, 29, 53, 91, 97, 168–178

Object of negation, 76–87
Ocean of Reasoning, 30–32
Owens, D., 59n4

dPal ldan grags pa (Geshe Palden Drakpa), 66
parabhāva (other nature), 138
Paraconsistent logic, 215
paramārthasat (ultimate existents), 8
paramārthasatya (ultimate truth), 43
parasparasaṃbhavana (mutual dependence), 13
parikalpitasvabhāva (imagined nature), 142n13

Patil, P., 179n20
Patsab Nyimadrak (Pa tshab nyi ma grags), 4, 17, 89–113, 118–121
on Prāsaṅgika, 96–107
as a skeptic, 107–109, 112–113, 118–121
Peirce, C., 135
Penelhum, T., 109
Perceptual cognition, 41
Perrett, R., 164n22
Person, conventional status of, 5–6
Pitṛputrasamāgamasūtra, 9n57
Poussin, L., 7n11, 8n12, 9n16
Pradhan, P., 174n14
Pragmatism, 134–136, 184–186
pramāṇa (epistemic instruments), 16, 26–30, 39
and Candrakīrti, 29, 152–157
and epistemic authority, 26–30
and Nāgārjuna, 27–29
and *svabhāva*, 39
and truth, 26–30, 152–157
prameya (epistemic objects), 28, 39
Prāsaṅgika, 16–19, 41, 44, 48, 58, 67
epistemology, 39–40, 52, 55
Patsab's defense of, 90, 226
vs Svātantrika, 18, 61n6
Prasannapadā, 12, 24, 29, 31, 41–43, 52, 54, 125–127, 165
pratijnā = *phyogs* (theses), 17
pratijñāmātreṇa = *dam bcas pa tsam gyis grub pa*, 152
pratītyasamutpāda (dependent arising), 13
pratyakṣa (perceptual cognition), 41, 44
prayoga = *sbyor ba* (probative argument), 97
Priest, G., 9n16, 18, 20, 128, 149, 162, 179n21, 220n13
spros pa (fabrication), 85

Quine, W.V.O., 184, 193

Rabjampa, L., 14
Radhakrishnan, S., 53n32
Ramsey, F., 132
rang gi mtshan nyid kyis grub pa (established through their own characteristics), 83
rang rgyud kyi rjes dpag = *svātantrānumāna* (autonomous inference), 97
rang bzhin = *svabhāva* (intrinsic nature), 58
rational insight, 46–47
Ratnakūṭa-sūtra, 12n22, 115–116, 151, 201
Ratnāvalī, 222
Reductionism, 173–174
Representation, 197–199
rigs pa'i dgag bya (epistemological object of negation), 76
rigs pas dpyad mi bzod pa (inability to withstand rational analysis), 41n6, 77
rigs shes, (rational insight) 46–47
Robinson, G., 116
Rosen, G., 158n12, 161n18
Ruegg, S., 3n1, 18, 94n4, 98n9, 100n11, 102n14, 116n2n159
Russell, B., 134

Saitō, A., 4n2
Samādhirājasūtra, 40
sāmānyalakṣaṇa (universals), 142n13
saṃmati (consensus, agreement), 12
sammutināna (linguistic conventions), 8
saṃvṛti, three senses of, 11–15, 23–24
and concealment, 12–13
and consensus, 12, 13
and convention, 11–12
and ignorance, 14
and language, 12
Tsongkhapa on, 13–14
and *vyavahāra* 11
saṃvṛtisatya, *vyavahārasatya* (conventional truth), vi
Saṃyuttanikāya, 6–7
Saṅgītisutta, 8
Śāntarakṣita, 15n26, 105n19, 128, 155
Śāntideva, 9, 15, 21, 202, 225–229, 231
Bodhicaryāvatāra, 202, 222, 225–229
Śikṣasamuccaya, 9n15

Sarvadharmaniḥsvabhāvasiddhi, v, 153–157, 181
Satya and *Truth*, 4–5
Satyadvayavibhaṅgapanjikā, 15n26
Sautrāntika, 173
savikalpakapratyakṣa (determinate perception), 175
Scherrer-Schaub, C., 95, 100n11, 116n2
Schwartz, R., 196, 197
Sedley, D., 103, 108n22
Sellars, W., 183n1
Sextus Empiricus, 17, 92–128, 170n6
Siderits, M., 18–19, 53n32n55, 89, 107n21, 125, 146, 147n20, 149n23, 155–156, 176n16, 178
  on Candrakīrti's epistemology, 53n32, 107n21, 125, 55–156
  on causation, 176n16
  on contextualism, 178
  on Prāsaṅgika use of reason, 55
  on truth, 147n20
  on ultimate truth, 149n23
Śikṣasamuccaya, 9n15
śīla, 222–223
Skepticism, 89–104, 108–113, 115–130
  Academic v Pyrrhonian, 17, 92–94, 108–110, 115–116, 121–124
  Buddhist Madhyamaka, 17
  and Candrakīrti, 124–129
  and ethics, 225–227
  and Madhyamaka, 89–90, 91–95, 106–109, 124–129
  and Nāgārjuna, 94–95, 115–116
  and Patsab, 107–109, 118–121
  Pyrrhonian, 17, 93–130
  Stoic opponents, 108
Skyrms, B., 210–212
Sprung, M., 14
Stanley, J., 158n11, 162n20
Stcherbatsky, T., 14
Stoltz, J., 10n19
Striker, G., 101, 102n15
Subsequent attainment, 49
śūnyatā, 7
svabhāva = *rang bzhin* (intrinsic nature), 39, 58, 167–168
  and *pramāṇa*, 39
svābhāvikī siddhi (intrinsic establishment), 54
svalakṣaṇa (intrinsic characteristics), 39
svalakṣaṇa (ineffable particulars), 142n13
Svātantrikas, 15, 18–19
  Candrakīrti's debate with, 15, 15n7
  debate with Prāsaṅgika, 18

T-schema, 132–141
lTa ba ngan sel (*Elimination of Erroneous Views*), 82
Taktsang Lotsawa, 40n4
Tanaka, K. 19, 21, 146
Tarski, A., 132
Tauscher, H., 3n1, 7n10
rTen 'brel stod pa (*Praise of Dependent Arising*), 81
tha snyad = *vyavahāra* (customary transactions), 2, 3
Thakchöe, S., 16–17, 49n17, 67, 86, 126, 156n8
Tillemans, T., 10n18n19, 12n21, 51n26, 135n6n139, 150, 153n9, 165n25
  on Buddhist philosophy of language, 10n19, 12n21
  on Candrakīrti, 165n25
  on contradiction, 153n9
  on Dharmakīrti, 135n6
  on foundationalism, 51n26
Trisvabhāvanirdeśa, 142n13
Truth, *Reality*, and *satya*, 4–5, 213–214
Truth, theories of, 132–138
  Abidharma accounts, 136–138, 142
  deflationism, 132–134, 143–147
  fictionalism, 144–150, 157–164
  Madhyamaka, 142–150
  pragmatism, 134–136, 184–186
  and the T-schema, 132–141
  what is acknowledged by the world, 152–156
tshad ma, 16, 26, 66n7

Tsongkhapa, 4, 9n16, 13–14, 20, 23–25, 30–34, 57–71, 76–82, 190, 205–207
on conceptual designation, 64–67
on conventional truth as truth, 25–26, 30–33, 57–58
and deceptiveness, 67–71, 190
on dependent origination, 62–67
on ethics, 222
on limits of construction, 205–207
on meaning of *saṃvṛti*, 13–14, 23–24, 57
on object of negation, 76–82
on two truths, 32–34, 58–61
Two truths, 5–11, 42, 44–45, 213–220
Candrakīrti on, 42, 44–45
Chinese theories, 216–218
as classes of entities, 8–9
identity and difference, 37–38, 215–216
and levels of explanation, 58–60
and Madhyamaka, 142–150
and modes of existence, 9–11
and person, 5–6
And pragmatism, 186–188
and skillful means, 6–8
and the T-schema, 138–142
Tsongkhapa on, 32–34, 58–62
as two natures, 32–34, 44–45, 58–59
as two realities, 131
and Yogācāra, 214–215, 216–218

Upālipariprcchā-sūtra, 190–191
Üpalosel (dbus pa blo gsal), 157
Upāyakauśalya (skillful means), 7–8

Vaidya, P., 4n2, 5n4, 7n10, 150n25
Vaiśeṣikas, 98
van Heijenoort, J., 135n7
Vasubandhu, 8n13
Vedānta, 220
Velez de Cea, A., 224n3
Vigrahavyāvartanī, 27–28
vikalpa (conceptual thought), 142n13
Vose, K., 95n6, 128n8
vṛṇoti, 12
vyāpti = *khyab ba* (pervasion), 97
vyavahāra, 11
vyavahārasatya (conventional truth), vi

Walshe, M., 6n6
Wangchen, N., 216
Westerhoff, J., 20, 145
Williams, P., 70n6, 224n3
Winograd, T., 201
Wittgenstein, L., 93, 94, 127, 133, 149n24
Wright, C., 127

Yablo, S., 58n2, 144–145, 158n11, 162, 184
yadṛcchāśabda / yādṛcchikaśabda, 12n21
yang dag lta ba'i 'od zer (*The Bright Light of the True View*), 85
Ye shes thub bstan (Kensur Yeshe Thupten), 66
Yogācāra, 15, 142, 159, 214–215, 216–218
Yogācāra-Sautrāntika, 154, 173, 175
Yuktiṣaṣṭilkā, 191
Yuktiṣaṣṭikāvṛtti, 191
Yonezawa, Y., 23n2, 27n9, 28n12n13, 53n31, 116n2

Zollman, K., 209n21, 210–212

CPSIA information can be obtained
at www.ICGtesting.com
Printed in the USA
BVHW031205270320
576174BV00001B/23

9 780199 751433